Italy and the Grand Tour

Italy and the Grand Tour

Jeremy Black

Yale University Press
New Haven and London

For Marian and Nigel Ramsay

For information about this and other Yale University Press publications, please contact:
U.S. Office: sales.press@yale.edu   yalebooks.com
Europe Office: sales@yaleup.co.uk   www.yaleup.co.uk

Set in Minion by Northern Phototypesetting Co. Ltd.
Printed in China through Worldprint

Library of Congress Cataloging-in-Publication Data

Black, Jeremy.
   Italy and the grand tour/by Jeremy Black
      p. cm
Includes bibliographical references and index.
   ISBN 0-300-09977-0 (cloth: alk. paper)
   1. Italy—Description and travel. 2. Travelers—Italy—History—18th century. ¾. Title
   DG424.B63 2003   914.504'7—dc21   2003005828

A catalogue record for this book is available from the British Library.

10 9 8 7 6 5 4 3 2 1

Published with assistance from the Annie Burr Lewis Fund.

Endpaper: *Gavin Hamilton Leading a Party of Grand Tourists to the Archaeological Site at Gabii*, by Giuseppe Cades, 1793. © The National Gallery of Scotland

Contents

Illustrations

Notes on Dates and Currency

Dates

In the eighteenth century, until the 1752 reform of the calendar, Britain conformed to Old Style, which was eleven days behind New Style, the Gregorian calendar used in Italy and most of the rest of Europe. In this work, all Old Style dates are marked (os). The New Year is taken as starting on 1 January, not 25 March.

Currency

Prices are given in eighteenth-century (i.e. pre-decimalisation) British units of currency: £1.00 = 20 shillings (s) = 240 pennies (d). Therefore one shilling = 5 new pence. A guinea was 21 shillings. In Italy, the sequin (*zecchino*) was worth 10 shillings, i.e. two were worth £1.00.

Preface

On our way to Milan we stopped at a pretty large town called Novara the last in the King of Sardinia's dominions, here we had a true Italian breakfast consisting of the large Italian pigeons and tripe dressed with oil and Parmesan cheese, grapes, figs, and an excellent polenta which is a kind of pudding made of the flower of Indian wheat mixed with oil and cheese.

Margaret, Viscountess Spencer, 1763[1]

No place in the world can afford so unexhaustible a fund of amusement or so much variety.

Henry, 2nd Viscount Palmerston, Rome, 1764[2]

The search for Italy helped define pleasure and interest in the eighteenth century. This book sets out to recreate and to understand this search. It is designed to attract those who travel today, as well as armchair tourists, and others interested in the Grand Tour of the eighteenth century. The characteristic feature of my work on the Grand Tour, which provides a distinctive voice, is that I rely heavily on archival sources in order to provide the real tourist experience rather than an account that is essentially based on travel literature, like most work on the subject. By focusing on the mechanics of the Grand Tour, I try to bring the whole thing to life.

Concentrating on manuscript accounts is not without its problems. Many tourist letters are poorly catalogued and scattered in general political or family correspondence and, in consequence, difficult to find. Some of the surviving material is anonymous or provides only isolated items of information concerning tourists about whom little else is known. As with the printed material, so with the unprinted: much is repetitive.

Yet, there is also much of value, not least because of its spontaneity. Letters written on the spot and at the time by travellers who were not writers by profession are a more accurate guide to experience than the published prose of calm recollection, however quotable or literary the latter might be. New material from the archives gives a fresh 'warts-and-all' feel to what otherwise can seem rather formal accounts of a stately and familiar mode of edifying travel. What George, Viscount Villiers termed 'the difficulties of travelling, that is completely bad and dirty inns',[3] need to be borne in mind alongside the splendid canvases that frame our current remembrance of the Tour. Indeed Villiers referred to these problems several years after coming home. He had clearly remembered them. Furthermore, there was obviously a gap between ideal and reality: what people were meant to do and what they actually did; what was talked up in the guidebooks as splendid and how people actually responded to it. This book moves beyond the conventional expectations of the Grand Tour.

While sensitive to the wider cultural dimensions, I am also very interested in the experience of the tourists, particularly the circumstances they encountered. These ranged from fleas to the heightened sensitivity. Mary, Lady Palmerston noted at Ancona on the shores of the Adriatic in 1793: 'the Adriatic which looks as blue as in Guercino's *Aurora* . . . The sea was the finest blue such as I have often seen described in painting but never till I saw the Mediterranean had I any idea [of] its existing but in the imagination of the painter'.[4] The fresco of *Aurora* in Rome was Guercino's masterpiece and a major work of Baroque art. There is a heavy emphasis on quotations from manuscript sources in this book because they best capture the flavour of the tourist experience.

Since writing *The British Abroad. The Grand Tour in the Eighteenth Century* (Stroud, 1992), I have undertaken fresh work in a number of archives and collections I had until then not fully probed, or unwisely neglected, including the Palmerston papers in the Broadlands Archive in Southampton University Library, the Drake papers in Magdalen College Oxford, the Villiers papers in the Greater London Record Office, and the Hawkins and Pendarves papers in Cornwall Record Office. I would like to thank all those who provided hospitality and encouragement during this period. They have been more helpful than they probably appreciate.

I have also benefited from the opportunity to present papers at a number of gatherings, including the 1994 conference of the Datini Institute in Prato, a conference on *L'Europe des politesses et le caractère des nations* held in Paris at the Sénat in 1995, the 1997 University of London, Centre for Extra-Mural Studies study day on the Grand Tour, the conference on 'Travel, Travellers and the Book Trade' held at the Royal Geographical Society, the annual conference of the Newport Preservation Society, and the conference on *El Grand Tour en el Siglo XVIII: viajar por Europa* held at San Lorenzo de El Escorial in 2002, and also to give lectures at the Tate Gallery, the National Portrait Gallery, the Victoria and Albert Museum, the DeWitt Wallace Decorative Arts Museum, Vanderbilt University, and for the History Today tour to the Gulf of Naples and Vanderbilt University's London programme. The stimulating comments and company of other participants has helped me to sharpen up my ideas, as have a number of exhibitions, not least Kenwood's 'Pompeo Batoni and his British Patrons' (1982), the Tate Gallery's 'Richard Wilson' (1982), Norwich Castle Museum's 'Norfolk and the Grand Tour' (1985), the British Museum's 'Vases and Volcanoes: Sir William Hamilton and his Collection' (1996), the Tate's 'Grand Tour: The Lure of Italy in the Eighteenth Century' (1996–7) and the Laing's 'Art Treasures in the North. Northern Families on the Grand Tour' (1999–2000).

I would like to thank Stephen Clark, Bill Gibson, Roy Porter and an anonymous reader for their comments on an earlier draft. It is a matter of great sadness that Roy, a friend and scholar whom I greatly admired and who gave me much encouragement, not least for this project, did not live to see it published.

While writing this book, I revisited Naples in order to give a lecture. I had a day free and spent it in the Old Town, rain-swept as Naples can be in January. I was deeply moved for the second time in my life by the sculptures in the Museo Cappella Sansevero, and would urge all those who have not been there to go and see them. If this book encourages others to read the fascinating accounts by tourists of the period, then it will have achieved its purpose.

It is a great pleasure to dedicate this book to two good friends, Marian and Nigel Ramsay.

Political map of Italy, 1713–48. From H.C. Darby and H. Fullard (eds), *The New Cambridge Modern History*, Vol. XIV, 1970, p. 160. Reproduced by the kind permission of Cambridge University Press.

1. Introduction

> "A man who has not been in Italy is always conscious of an inferiority, from his not having seen what it is expected a man should see. The grand object of travelling is to see the shores of the Mediterranean. "
>
> Samuel Johnson, who did not visit Italy, in Boswell's *Life of Johnson*, 11 April 1776

Protracted travel for pleasure was scarcely unknown in Classical and medieval times, but it developed greatly in the sixteenth, seventeenth and eighteenth centuries, becoming part of the ideal education and image of the social élite, as well as an important source of descriptive and imaginative literature and art. As tourism developed, its patterns became more regular and the assumptions about where a tourist should go became more predictable. Literary conventions were also established. The term 'the Grand Tour' reflects a subsequent sense that this was an ideal period in the fusion of tourism and social status, as well as a contemporary desire to distinguish protracted and wide-ranging tourism from shorter trips.

The Grand Tour is commonly associated with aristocratic British travellers, more particularly with the eighteenth century,[1] but travel for pleasure did not begin then and it was not restricted to the British; there was a more general fascination with southern Europe by northern Europeans. The vast majority of those who had travelled to Italy over previous centuries had done so for reasons related to their work or their salvation. Soldiers and those seeking employment had shared the road with clerics discharging the tasks of the international Church and pilgrims. Such travel was not incompatible with pleasure, and, in some cases, it fulfilled important cultural functions as travellers bought works of art or helped spread new tastes and cultural interests. This was not the same, however, as travel specifically and explicitly for personal fulfilment, both in terms of education and of pleasure, the two being seen as ideally linked in the exemplary literature of the period.

Such travel became more common in the seventeenth century, although it was affected by the religious (and political) tensions that followed the Protestant Reformation of the previous century. The war with Spain that had begun in 1585 ended in 1604 and England had only brief wars with France, Spain and the Dutch during the following seventy years. It was no accident that the Earl and Countess of Arundel went to Italy in 1613–14, nor that a series of works on Italy, including Fynes Moryson's *Itinerary* (1617), appeared in the years after the Treaty of London of 1604.

However, divisions culminating in civil wars (1642–6, 1648, 1688–91) in the British Isles forced men to focus their time and funds on commitments at home, and also made travel suspect as in some fashion indicating supposed political and religious sympathies. Concern about Stuart intentions in large part focused on the real and alleged crypto-Catholicism of the court, and this made visits to Italy particularly sensitive.

The situation for tourists eased with the Stuart Restoration of 1660, and Richard Lassels, a Catholic priest who acted as a bearleader (travelling tutor), published, in 1670, his important *Voyage of Italy, or a Compleat Journey through Italy. In Two Parts. With the Characters of the People, and the Description of the Chief Towns, Churches, Monasteries, Tombs, Libraries, Palaces, Villas, Gardens, Pictures, Statues, and Antiquities. As Also of the Interest, Government, Riches, Force, etc of all the Princes. With Instructions concerning Travel.* It was the best work available and new editions appeared in 1686 and 1698.

Britain was involved in two serious wars with France, in 1689–97 and 1702–13, which provided employment for many young members of the social élite and, also, challenged (although without preventing) the routines of peaceful travel. The first war also involved sustained conflict between France and Savoy-Piedmont, while the second saw large-scale warfare in northern Italy until 1706. This period gave way to one that was largely peaceful for Britain, which lasted until 1739 (and until 1744 in the case of formal peace with France). During those decades, the conventions of the Grand Tour developed for British tourists.

This was part of a wider pattern of élite cosmopolitan activity. Throughout Europe, members of the élite travelled for pleasure in the eighteenth century. The most popular destinations were France, which meant Paris, and Italy. Italy had several important advantages over Paris. The growing cult of the Antique, which played a major role in the determination to see and immerse oneself in the experience and repute of the Classical world, could not be furthered in Paris, which, under Louis XIV (reigned 1643–1715), had been a magnet of European attention. Nor did Paris satisfy those tourists who sought travel to the warmth of the South for health and/or pleasure. War also limited or at least discouraged visits to France, without having an impact on such a scale on travel to Italy. Thus, Sambrooke Freeman (*c.* 1721–82), who left Britain in August 1744, during the War of the Austrian Succession, returning in July 1747, was in Italy from November 1744 until April 1747, visiting Switzerland briefly in the winter of 1745–6. A graduate of Oxford, Freeman was subsequently an obscure parliamentarian.

There was no cult of the countryside: tourists travelled as rapidly as possible between major cities, and regarded mountains with horror, not joy. The contrast with nineteenth-century tourism, and its cult of the 'sublime', dated from Romanticism, not earlier. The 'pre-Romanticism' that encouraged a response to landscape was more literary in location than descriptions of élite views, certainly than those by 'brawny beef-eating barons', so called by Sir Robert Murray Keith, envoy in Vienna. The Italian cities offered a rich range of benefits, including pleasure (Venice), Classical antiquity (Rome and its environs; the environs of Naples), Renaissance architecture and art (Florence), the splendours of Baroque culture (Rome and Venice), opera (Milan and Naples) and warm weather (Naples). Once tourism had become appropriate and fashionable, increasing numbers travelled, a growth interrupted only by periods of war, when journeys, although not prohibited, were made more dangerous or inconvenient by disruption and lawlessness.

Travellers to Britain were particularly interested in technological progress and signs of modernity, a process that reached its social and political apogee with the visit of Peter the Great of Russia who went to see a ship being built on the Thames. A Newtonian world of applied science and the dramatic new utilitarian buildings of, for example, Greenwich, the Bank of England and Westminster Bridge, were of interest: tourists did not tend to go to London for the sake of court or culture, ancient or modern. In some respects, the situation was analogous to that of travel today to the United States, as was the reporting of such travel.

Paris and the Mediterranean were different. Tourists visited Paris as the leading European court and as the centre of civilisation, polite society and the arts. The cultural sway of Paris developed from the seventeenth century and received tribute in, for example, the purchase of expensive furniture by German rulers, such as the Electors of Bavaria, or the spread of the umbrella to England. Italy was the potent centre of Classical culture, and travel there was seen as a crucial demonstration, and source, of taste.

Cultural images and influence also spread through publication. They might spread most effectively by personal impression, and tourists, therefore, served as crucial cultural intermediaries, but the numbers involved were necessarily small. Travel literature magnified the impact of tourism. The question is, how far did it also refract it, both by creating a misleading impression of tourist activity and by framing the experience of tourists?

Culture is often at the cusp between cosmopolitanism and xenophobia, between the wish to be part of, and to appreciate, the foreign, the different, the outside world; and concern and fear about just such a process, and about the apparent threats to identity and integrity that they pose. Travel and the recording of travel focus these pressures of attraction and rejection. They present, clarify and bring to all the senses, and, in an uncontrolled fashion, sensations and responses that had previously been controlled or limited. This was certainly the case with the Grand Tour of the eighteenth century. It is less so in the modern age, because there is now greater exposure to the outside world. Foreign sights are purveyed by television and film, recipes by newspapers, foods and drinks by supermarkets. The Britons of the 2000s can buy their pasta at Sainsburys and their Chianti at Oddbins. Abroad is less foreign; indeed one of the complaints is sometimes that that is the problem: that foreign cities have McDonald's. This shift is, like much else, an aspect of consumerism, technology and democratisation; the last that large numbers can now afford to travel. As our experience of tourism is so different to that of the eighteenth century, it is necessary to recreate the mechanics of earlier travel in order to provide the context within which to judge its impact.

Another difference between the Grand Tour and later travel was presented by the organisation of tourism. In the absence of facilities for mass transportation and of paid holidays, tourism was costly and a minority activity. The cost and exclusivity of tourism, especially of travel beyond the Alps, was increased by the length of time it entailed. The average Grand Tour lasted longer than a year.

The democratising and institutionalising tourism that developed in the nineteenth century, with travel companies such as that founded by Thomas Cook, and the possibilities of rail travel, transformed the experience of tourism by making it a mass phenomenon. This ensured that tourists who sought to be distinctive were reacting against other tourists as much as in response to what they were visiting. It also created a problem for modern travel literature, most of which deliberately searches for the atypical, and presents the maverick.

Thus, the eighteenth-century experience of tourism, of the foreign, the 'other', was very different to the modern one, and is difficult to put into context. It is a field in which comparisons of places visited or food consumed can be misleading, because they fail to note the different contexts. In the modern world, food preferences have been depoliticised, and the emotive issues about national identity raised by the beef crisis of 1996 played a smaller role than those focusing on public health and regulation. In the eighteenth century, food was different. Views were expressed within a known and understood context in which food was seen as symptomatic of moral forces and national stereotypes. On the whole, such comments were not made humorously or in a spirit of curiosity, but were a serious response to the pressures of cosmopolitanism.

There was a profound sense of unease and cultural tension on the part of the British which affected responses to the foreign and to those who found elements of foreignness attractive. However, it is difficult to decide where to place the emphasis. It would be wrong to suggest that there was a *Zeitgeist*, a spirit of the age that incorporated, refracted and influenced, if not controlled, all opinions. Far from that being the case, there were a variety of opinions. This is scarcely surprising. It is a condescension to the past to assume that former societies were less complex than those of today. The Don Quixote approach to the past – that seventeenth-century Spanish history and culture are symbolised and summed up by the knight in Cervantes's novel tilting foolishly and unsuccessfully at windmills – is misleading: which character in an Iris Murdoch novel is to be used to sum up postwar Britain?

Eighteenth-century Britain has suffered from this simplification, not least because of the seductive images produced by televised stories. The reification of tourism, as if responses were similar, is as one with this process. In fact, Britain was a complex society and, accordingly, there were different responses to abroad and to tourism. Nevertheless, it is pertinent to note that international tension – political, economic and cultural – played a role in these responses. The cultural and ideological dimension was especially important. To visit France was to visit the national enemy. Italy, the site of Papal government and, for much of the period, the Jacobite court, was also a source of ideological challenge, although not a direct political threat. It was as if the prime destinations of American tourists at the height of the Cold War had been the Soviet Union and China.

The comparison is appropriate because tourism was seen as posing a danger of seduction. Today, we tend to see the artistic seduction of eighteenth-century British tourists, their attraction to Classical sites and ambiences, to Baroque architecture and painting, to contemporary opera, and to artists such as Canaletto. Yet, to contemporary critics, the seduction that posed a threat was that of Catholicism and autocracy: of the turning of the élite through travel to favour foreign ideological and political mores and precepts. The danger was not seen solely in these terms. Foreign cultural preferences could be held to be more widely indicative, and, specifically, to reveal political and ideological tendencies.

This attitude was well established in the discussion of domestic culture, the printed polemic within Britain that was part of the context for the appearance of Grand Tour literature.[2] Criticism of British patrons of Italian opera, for example in the 1720s, and of French theatre, especially in the 1730s and 1740s, focused on their supposed role in spreading alien values. Cultural nationalism was also reflected in a positive direction, with the development of vernacular opera, ballad opera, most famously John Gay's *Beggar's Opera* (1728), and oratorio, the rediscovery of Shakespeare, and the foundation of the Royal Academy. This context was publicly expressed in press discussion about tourism.

The extent to which the tension between xenophobia and cosmopolitanism was internalised by tourists is unclear. The sources for tourist attitudes are problematic. Diaries and correspondence are not theoretical texts. They are bitty by nature, frequently allusive or elusive in content and comment, and do not contain explanations of background attitudes. In addition, there is the issue of the writers of travel literature. Although an increasing number of women travelled, usually in male company, tourism was largely the prerogative of the adult male, with the aristocratic young man in his late teens being particularly prominent. This at once introduces a tension with the literary sources, for the majority of travel accounts were not by aristocrats, and this was even more the case as far as both lengthy and coherent manuscript journals and published literature were concerned. Authorship indeed was a social construction. It was not, of course, unknown for an aristocrat to offer details of his or her breakfast or accommodation, and several aristocrats did publish travel accounts. These included *A Journey through the Crimea to Constantinople* (Dublin, 1789) by Lady Elizabeth Craven, in which she published letters from her tour through northern Italy in 1785.

Nevertheless those who were called 'Jolly-boys' by the clergyman Robert Wharton (1751–1808), who visited Italy in 1775–6, or 'very absurd riotous drunken fellows' by his friend and fellow-cleric, the bearleader Thomas Brand (*c.* 1751–1814), did not often leave accounts, and certainly seldom published them, although their bearleaders, who came from a different social background, often did. Their works included Patrick Brydone's *A Tour through Sicily and Malta* (1775) and John Moore's *A View of Society and Manners in Italy* (1781). In some respects, travel literature paralleled the position in general fiction, with Henry Fielding, Samuel Richardson and Jane Austen writing about their social (but not moral) betters. Differences in social position can be seen in comments on the mechanics of travel. Guidebooks tended to praise public transport, but it is doubtful if many wealthy tourists wished to spend several days in a confined space practising their limited French and Italian with strangers.[3]

At another level, many tourists took servants with them, sometimes several. There are very few records of the experiences of these tourists. Edmund Dewes, servant to Court Dewes on his tour of 1776, and James Thoburn, servant of John Hawkins, who visited Italy in 1788 and 1793, both left diaries which survive.[4]

In so far as broad trends can be discerned in the tension between xenophobia and cosmopolitanism, it is clear that as Italy, and, indeed, other parts of the Continent, became more familiar to many tourists, it seemed, at the personal level, less hostile and, to a degree, depoliticised. Furthermore, as facilities for tourists developed, so they became less alien figures to the Italians, who were used to travellers but not to Protestant British men and women travelling for pleasure.

Tourists were also affected by the growth in British cultural self-confidence that was increasingly apparent from the 1740s. The sources of this were various – the defeat of the Jacobite rising of 1745–6 and British victories over France and Spain in 1758–62 (the years of victory during the Seven Years War of 1756–63) were notable. The British constitution now appeared clearly established, the economy was expanding, and population growth from the early 1740s, after a century of stagnation, was notable. As a result, the British élite became more confident of purpose – a generalisation, but one that describes a key mid-century shift in sensibility. This greater confidence was particularly apparent in the case of British treatment of Italy.

Charles Thompson, the putative author of a travel account published in instalments in 1730–2, and as a book in 1744, explained his decision to visit the peninsula in terms that reflected its artistic reputation:

. . . being impatiently desirous of viewing a country so famous in history, which once gave laws to the world; which is at present the great school of music and painting, contains the

1. *William Weddell, Reverend William Palgrave and his Servant Janson,* by Nathanial Dance, 1765. An avid collector of paintings and sculpture, Weddell, on his tour of Italy, spent longest in Rome, which he travelled to via Turin, Milan, Genoa, Bologna and Florence. From Rome he visited Naples, and he went home via Venice.

> noblest productions of statuary and architecture, and abounds with cabinets of rarities, and collections of all kinds of antiquities.[5]

However, whatever its artistic treasures, compared to the seventeenth century, Italy became more obviously a theme-park of the past, a country de-civilised by a decadent society and, eventually, culture. Italy was held to represent the past, not only the past of Classical splendour and culture, the past that inspired Edward Gibbon (1737–94) when he toured in 1764–5, among others, but also the past of the present. This became more of an issue as a consequence of the growing cult of progress, interest in change and support for tolerance that not only characterised advanced thought in Britain in this period, but was also more widely diffused in that society. Thus Italy appeared outside the process of civilisation, indeed a denial of it, as was made cruelly obvious by the Classical ruins that attracted more

View of the ruins of Agrigentum from the Tomb of Thero.

Temple of Hercules.

Sepulchers cut in the rock detached by age or accident from the Mountain.

Temple of Concord

Temple of Juno

Tomb of Thero.

2. View of Agrigento from Henry Swinburne's *Travels in the Two Sicilies* (1783–5). Swinburne and his friend Sir Thomas Gascoigne visited Sicily from December 1777 to January 1778. The view is taken from the Tomba di Terone. It shows some of the temples built between the late sixth century BCE and the late fifth century BCE. The Temple of Concord, built in 450–440 BCE is in the centre.

attention during the century. This very denial attracted attention, most famously with Gibbon's masterpiece about the decline and fall of Imperial Rome published from 1776 to 1788. Spending the winter of 1789–90 in Naples, Lady Craven was very critical of a situation 'where the Government supplies nothing for the ease of its subjects . . . where public misery is concealed under national pomp'.[6]

In early seventeenth-century Britain there had been a positive response towards Italian republicanism, especially to Venice, seen as a model of republican virtue, civic organisation and Catholic opposition to both Spanish hegemony and papal pretensions. By the eighteenth century, the situation was different. Venice was still seductive as a centre of culture and pleasure, but it was less credible than it had been to present the republican liberty and energy of Classical Rome through its refracting example.[7]

Fashion and convenience restricted most tourists to established destinations, particularly Paris and Italy, and to several well-worn routes, where the whims and wishes of those who travelled for pleasure were appreciated. In contrast, across much of Europe, roads were poor and accommodation for travellers minimal. There were relatively few tourists to the Balkans, Iberia, the Baltic and eastern Europe. Disease, wars and disorder affected travel to the Balkans, and Hellenism and philhellenism, sympathy for Greece ancient and modern, did not become prominent until the 1790s.

Italy dominated the attention of those who travelled south beyond Paris. Travel to the Mediterranean meant travel to Italy. Spain was not regarded as the most interesting country to visit. Madrid lacked the cosmopolitan, accessible culture of Paris and its society was perceived as dull and reclusive. Outside Madrid there appeared to be little to see. There was no vogue for the beach, the mountains lacked the splendour and glamour of the Alps, the Roman antiquities were less well known than those of Italy, and there was little interest in the Moorish remains. Travellers to, and in, Spain also encountered major difficulties. The journey there by land was very long, involved passage of the Pyrenees, and there were poor facilities for travellers. The sea journey to Portugal was a long one, facilities outside Lisbon were poorly developed, and, once there, British travellers did not tend to travel outside Lisbon, except for those going to Madrid who tended to follow the main road. Partly because so few tourists visited Iberia, it was largely experienced through travel literature: works such as Henry Swinburne's *Travels through Spain in the Years 1775 and 1776* (1779) and Joseph Townsend's *A Journey through Spain in the Years 1786 and 1787* (1791). The same was true of Sicily and of Apulia and Calabria in southern Italy, with Patrick Brydone's *Tour through Sicily and Malta* (1773), Swinburne's *Travels in the Two Sicilies* (1783–5) and Brian Hill's *Observations and Remarks in a Journey through Sicily and Calabria* (1792).

Apart from negative factors discouraging travel elsewhere, there were positive reasons for encouraging tourism to Italy. It was fashionable, exciting and fairly pleasant; and the hardships of travel were fewer than elsewhere in Europe. Such hardships were also made predictable and readily understood by the experience of earlier travellers expressed through the medium of print.

Italy was crucial to the Grand Tour, although there was no set course for travel there: preferences and circumstances varied. In a culture dominated by the Classics, Rome was the focus of interest. Indeed, Thomas Pelham (1756–1826), the eldest son of the second Lord Pelham of Stanmer, later an MP and, subsequently, 1st Earl of Chichester, complained in April 1777 that 'at present Rome has too great a resemblance with Brighthelmstone [Brighton]': he thought it crowded with about seventy British visitors.[8] In the sixteenth century, religious schism had made Rome the seat of Antichrist, not culture, as far as

Protestants were concerned, but in the seventeenth century this tension ebbed and in the eighteenth it receded markedly. Furthermore, cultural trends helped to make Rome more important. If the Baroque was the culture of any place, it was the culture of Rome. It was also a culture whose impact was general to Europe and not restricted to lands under Catholic sway. The dramatic new edifices that Baroque rebuilding brought to Rome, and the newly commissioned works displayed in them, both paintings and sculpture, ensured that, until the mid-eighteenth century, Rome's appeal was very much that of a contemporary cultural powerhouse; the attraction of its Classical past was less urgent for many tourists.

Variety, however, is a central theme. Tourism was more varied than is sometimes implied by the phrase the 'Grand Tour'. However much guided by tutors and influenced by their own expectations, and those of parents and peers, tourists were individuals seeking different objectives and following different routes. Sir George Shuckburgh (1751–1804), who spent three years in France and Italy after leaving Oxford, in part on scientific investigations, inherited his uncle's Warwickshire estate and baronetcy, and subsequently became an MP, had different priorities from tourists who chased opera dancers in Paris or those who admired the contents of the Uffizi; and such differences affected itineraries. Shuckburgh is also an interesting example of the difficulty of recreating past itineraries as no correspondence or journal is known to survive.

The age-related pattern of tourism was different from that in the modern world. It was far more concentrated in the period of youth, the most formative period post-childhood, and the average tour was of greater duration than the modern counterpart. This was in part a function of the time necessarily taken up by travelling, but, more significantly, a consequence of the lesser role played by both higher education and employment in the lives of the affluent young in the seventeenth and eighteenth centuries. Many did not go to university and, for those who did, it was unusual to complete a degree course.

Because foreign tourism was principally to major cities, it also emphasised another aspect of the educational nature of travel, to use the term 'educational' in the widest sense, as indeed it would have been understood in this period. Much of the European élite was landed in its wealth and lived in rural seats, although in some, especially Mediterranean, regions the nobility was more concentrated in the towns. In Britain, exposure to urban life did not have to wait until foreign tourism, as the landed nobility travelled to, and sometimes resided for part of the year in, cities in their own countries, but it was, nevertheless, less part of the experience of an aristocratic youth in this period than it would be for a young tourist today. As such, as indeed more generally, the 'foreign' experience has to be understood not as a totality in which the principal measure of novelty for the tourist was that of being abroad, but as a more variable encounter in which what was different was not necessarily a product of what was foreign.

This was also true in a number of specific respects, including, most centrally, escape from a context of control. The aristocratic youth was not only away from parental supervision, but also away from the tutelary control of the educational system. The travelling tutors who accompanied many young tourists were in no position to control them: apart from anything else, many knew that their subsequent career would depend on the patronage of their young charge.

Debate over the value of the Grand Tour is the aspect of travel literature and tourist accounts that tends to be underrated, but it was important, not least in influencing the private and public experience of travel, and the related literature. Published travel accounts tended to advocate the value of travel, unsurprisingly, as they wished to encourage readers and because many were written by bearleaders. In his *New Letters from an English Traveller* (1781), Martin Sherlock (*c.* 1750–97), an Irish clergyman who visited Italy in 1778–9, claimed:

> Nothing is so useful as travelling to those who know how to profit by it. Nature is seen in all her shades, and in all her extremes. If the mind of the traveller be virtuous, it will be confirmed in the love of virtue, and in the abhorrence of vice; because he will everywhere see that virtue is esteemed by the persons who practise it the least. If the traveller has the seeds of one or of several talents, he will find men of the first merit in every line, who will think it a pleasure to encourage and unfold those seeds, and to communicate knowledge … The traveller has, besides, the advantage of making continual comparisons, which strengthen his judgment extremely.[9]

Much of the debate reflected directly on this issue of lack of control and the alleged consequences in terms of heavy expenditure and personal excess; but, as already suggested, this aspect of the impact owed more to the novelty of lack of control than simply to being abroad. Thus the contemporary debate over the value of tourism was in some respects misleading, in that much of it related to a sphere – abroad – in which other pre-existing tensions or disputes, over, for example, the conduct of the young, the appeal of Catholicism, or the issue of élite cultural betrayal, could be discussed. In the case of tourism, these anxieties could be sharply focused, and were so with reason, as the effect of having so many of the young who would later be influential abroad was a sensible issue for discussion. In societies based on hereditary wealth, status and often position, the activities of heirs was a matter of acute concern; not least because, in a way, they presented the future to the present.

Yet criticism of the conduct of tourists in part only served to consolidate the image of tourism as fashion. The eighteenth century was, at least at the higher social levels, becoming a consumer society affected by fashions; news of these was spread by the growing number of ephemeral publications and the literature of social manners. Travel became fashionable as a means of finishing the education of youths, as a source of social polish, and as a pleasant and desirable way in which to spend periods of leisure. Cosmopolitanism was redefined, away from a sense of religious identity – the strident animosities of competing camps – and towards the sense of a common European cultural inheritance. Religious tension remained a feature of the period, but tourism to Catholic Italy ceased to be hazardous, although some inconveniences remained. Intellectual shifts played a role in this process, but in addition, the power of the clergy in much of Italy was increasingly restricted and thus less of an issue.

Political preferences were largely sustained by tourism. This was certainly true of British tourists, most of whom remained convinced that Britain was the best country in Europe. Despite the hospitality they received, and the access they were granted to Italian society at its highest reaches, it would not be unfair to claim that many returned to Britain as better-informed xenophobes. Tourism and travel literature reified and affirmed national identity and values, and confirmed a sense of British exceptionalism. Henry, 2nd Viscount Palmerston (1739–1802), an Irish peer and British MP who was subsequently a Lord of (Member of the Board of) Trade, of the Admiralty, and of the Treasury, considered that one advantage of his tour in 1763–4 was 'a thorough conviction of the superior value of my own country and my friends in it which one cannot so properly have till one has compared them with other countries and their inhabitants'.[10] This was a theme repeated by others, and one that echoed the strictures of much travel literature. The dedication to Sacheverell Stevens's *Miscellaneous Remarks Made on the Spot in a Late Seven Years Tour* (a volume without a publication date, but with the dedication dated 3 July 1756) had a clear ideological agenda:

> The following faithful Narrative will plainly show under what a dreadful yoke the wretched people of other nations groan, their more than Egyptian task-masters having impiously robbed them of the use of that glorious faculty, their reason, deprived them of their properties, and all this under the sacred sanction of religion . . . they thus miserably lie under the scourge of the tyrant's rod and the merciless phangs of ecclesiastical power.

Most of the book was devoted to the mechanics of tourism. Stevens was in Italy from 1739 until 1744 but little is known about him. His *Remarks* were clearly designed to have an additional purpose:

> I beg leave to conclude with the following short reflection, which is, that if, from the foregoing faithful account of the wretched and miserable state of slavery and subjection, both ecclesiastical and civil, both in body and soul, other nations are reduced to by their arbitrary tyrannical governors, one single reader should be made sensible of the ines-timable blessings he enjoys, be upon his guard against any attempts that may be made to deprive him of them, either by wicked ministers at home, or by enemies from abroad, and

become a better subject, or a sincerer Christian and Protestant, it will afford me the highest satisfaction, and I shall flatter myself that I have not altogether laboured or lived in vain.

This attitude contrasted markedly with the Anglomania that affected influential sections of Continental aristocratic and intellectual society in the second half of the century. It is, however, difficult to present Anglomania as a consequence of tourism. Instead, tourists to Britain went expecting to be impressed and accordingly were so: the values they already held received concrete validation in their impression of English society.

British tourists visiting Italy held no such assumptions. However, there was a troubling quality to visiting Italy, for the remains of Roman civilisation prompted speculation that Britain would, in turn, succumb, a view that was strengthened by the strong belief that history had a rhythmic quality. This sense of mutability was given an additional dimension when tourists encountered Greek sites in southern Italy. Impressed in 1764 by the ruins of Paestum, Palmerston noted that it was built 'at a period when Rome consisted of thatched hovels'.

Comparisons with antiquity were pointedly made in the case of modern Italy. Visiting the newly constructed Neapolitan royal palace at Caserta, Palmerston saw a massive aqueduct: 'It equals in greatness the works of antiquity but I doubt its duration'.[11]

Comments on the political situation in Italy were often closely related to reflections on social customs, a practice that responded to the utilitarian tendencies present in the loose bodies of ideas referred to as 'mercantilism', also, subsequently, to those summarised as 'the Enlightenment'. There was an interest in such matters as poor relief and the punishment of criminals. Lady Craven praised the caution shown in dispensing drugs in Venice: 'You cannot buy a drug at the apothecaries here, without an order from a physician. A very prudent caution against the madness of those who choose to finish their existence with a dose of laudanum, or their neighbours with one of arsenic.'[12] Mostly, however, the portrayal of Italian society was hostile. Margaret Grenville (d. 1793), who had visited Italy in 1761–2 while with her husband Henry *en route* to take up his embassy to Constantinople, wrote to Palmerston in 1764:

I find you think of the Italians as I did. I own I never was in any town in Italy that I did not say softly to myself I would not take a large fortune to be obliged to live here. It is astonishing how very ill educated the women are almost in general, a superstitious devotion joined to very dissolute manners are but too frequently the only visible features in their characters. What they call pleasure gave me not the least idea of it. You will find I believe whenever you come to live in France that they understand much better in that country for every one there wears a form of elegance.[13]

In general, tourists devoted more attention to the arts than the politics, society or economy of the Italian states. Artistic criticism can be just as frequently a sign of ignorance or prejudice as of discernment; political and religious biases could colour responses. And yet, it is striking how far tourists sought to counter such prejudices and to respond to paintings as works of art. However, although tastes varied, they were clearly affected by printed art criticism. There was a marked preference for the Classical over the Gothic that led most tourists to slight medieval buildings and to ignore, or criticise, the architecture of some of northern Italy. Old towns and quarters were disliked; the preference was for wide, straight streets, as in Turin.[14]

The strong influence of a Classical education can be seen in the accounts of many tourists. The famous essayist Joseph Addison (1672–1719), who received a government grant of £200 in order to help him use his travels to prepare for a career in public service, consulted Horace and Virgil when travelling between Rome and Naples in 1701, and Juvenal, Manilius, Ovid and Seneca on Rome. Addison was subsequently an MP and Secretary of State. Andrew Mitchell (1708–71), also later an MP, verified Virgil's description of the falls of Terni in 1734.[15] The Italian Classical remains and sites that most tourists saw were Roman. The large number of sites near Naples was the furthest south that many travelled, though, in the second half of the century, an increasing number went from Naples to Paestum on the Gulf of Salerno. The Greek temples there played a major role in the controversy of the late 1760s over the respective merits of Greek and Roman styles. It was only a small number of tourists, and those mostly later in the century, who visited the Greek sites in Sicily.

Yet there were also different views. In 1770, John, 3rd Earl of Bute (1713–92) – formerly the favourite and leading minister of George III and, after his resignation in 1762, a cultured and well-travelled connoisseur, who visited Italy in 1768–9 and 1769–71 buying books, pictures and vases, and seeking health – wrote,

> had it pleased Providence to destroy the works, the writings, the very memory of the Greeks and Romans with their Empires, we now should brag of poets, architects, sculptors, etc. as we do of Newtons, Raphaels and other superior beings, whose vast inventive geniuses have soared to science and arts, that scarce were known before, Milton would have wrote a divine poem, though he had never known Homer; [Robert] Adam would have erected buildings worthy of the British nation, in a British taste, and instead of wandering to Spalato [Split] for the remains of Diocletian's palace.[16]

Bute captured one of the central features of culture, and thus leisure, in the seventeenth and eighteenth centuries: the emphasis on the past. This was true more generally of the period. It was reverential of, and referential to, the past, and, in that, as in so much else, the 'early-modern period' can be seen as a continuation of the Middle Ages. Aspects of novelty – gunpowder, printing, the creation of transoceanic empires, the Reformation schism in western Christendom – were subsumed in a system the basic lineaments of which were very conservative: low-productivity agriculture as the basis of the economy, limited energy sources, an absence of rapid and easy transportation, inequalities in wealth and opportunity, the dominance of birth, status and privilege, the subordination of women, respect for age, limited literacy and education.

The Grand Tour was a reflection of this society, as, more particularly, was the emphasis on the past that characterised much tourism. As already indicated, there was a different set of priorities focusing on interest in social institutions, economic progress and technological developments, but these were minority concerns, as, indeed, they would always be in the history of tourism. Travelling for economic advantage was not at issue here, as commentators on these topics, such as the agricultural improver Arthur Young (1741–1820), who visited Italy in 1789, were primarily motivated by interest and were not being paid. Young's *Travels* revealed that he was unimpressed by what he saw as the lack of dynamism in Italian society. Tourists from Britain, the leading European maritime and economic powerhouse in the eighteenth and nineteenth centuries, wished to visit the Classical sites of Europe, and, in the nineteenth century, added the Alps and the shores of the Mediterranean: they were not in search of industrial plant along the Meuse or Ruhr, any more than modern American or Japanese tourists.

Furthermore, to most tourists, the mechanics of travel were of greater interest than details about the economy or society of Italy. These mechanics played a major role in travel literature, and this served as a pattern for accounts not intended for publication. Travel literature was also seen as providing advice. In some cases it served as an aspect of conduct literature, and there were also more specific suggestions and warnings. Thus, in his *Miscellaneous Remarks*, Stevens described a journey from Marseilles to Genoa in 1739, in part in order to advise future tourists:

> On Sunday, May 31, I embarked in a felucca for Italy, having first laid in a good stock of provision, as cold tongues, ham, bread, wine etc. This precaution will be of service to those who may perform this voyage; for in these feluccas it is uncertain where you may be drove to, which was my case; for we had not sailed above a day and a half, when the weather began to be extremely bad, and the sea became so rough and boisterous, that the waves very near beat over us; the mariners were now terribly daunted, the boat being half full of water; and for want of pails, etc. to fling it out, we were obliged to make use of our hats . . . I grew so sick that I could do no service.[17]

Storms at sea were frightening as well as exciting. This aspect of travel was not characteristic of all travel literature, but adventure was integral to many travelogues, especially if experience with the unfamiliar can be seen in that light. At times, the adventure was more explicit, as in hazardous passages of the Alps or near-encounters with brigands.

In 1770, Bute had grasped another contrast that is also pertinent today: that between tourism focused on the appreciation of the past, and an interest in travel for pleasure that was reverential of the past. In the eighteenth century, the past prevailed under both headings in the goals of tourists, but there were already signs of a shift in sensibility, interest and itineraries. By the 1780s, the volatile William Beckford (1759–1844), a wealthy and notorious writer and collector, was already gushing about wild, primitive scenery. There was greater interest in this type of scenery and sensations. Switzerland became a goal, rather than an obstacle. It was no longer necessary for a mountain, waterfall or lake to have been mentioned by Virgil or Livy for it to attract tourists.

The Romantic sensibility marked the end of the conventional Grand Tour, although not as clearly as the French Revolution would do. When tourists began to visit Italy again in large numbers from 1815, their mental world was different to that of their predecessors. As ever, it would be misleading to exaggerate change, but, after 1815, the past was being looked at from the perspective of a present that increasingly was less shaped by the impact of earlier centuries.

2. Sources

the reflections I have made on that vast variety of things which Italy furnishes
beyond any other country in the world.

Francis Drake[1]

Given the diversity of tourist interests and experience, it is not surprising that the impact of tourism varied. There are, however, serious methodological problems in assessing first experience and then impact. There are three categories of extant tourist writing: manuscript accounts, accounts published by contemporaries, and those published subsequently. The first and third categories are different from the second. They were designed for personal recollection, family or friends. A lack of clarity has arisen from the habit of conflating these types of material and treating them indiscriminately as sources for the Grand Tour. Published travel literature should be differentiated from letters and journals never intended for publication, although a continuum of sorts can be observed. The preface of Patrick Brydone's *A Tour through Sicily and Malta in a Series of Letters to William Beckford* (1773) claimed:

> Had there been any book in our language on any subject of the following Letters, they never should have seen the light. The Author wrote them for the amusement of his friends, and as an assistance to his memory; and if it will in any degree apologize for their imperfections, he can with truth declare that they never were intended for publication: nor indeed was that idea suggested to him, till long after they were written. One principal motive he will own, was the desire of giving to the world, and perhaps of transmitting to posterity, a monument of his friendship with the gentleman to whom they are addressed . . . In transcribing them for the press, he found it necessary both to retrench and to amplify; by which the ease of the epistolary style has probably suffered, and some of the letters have been extended much beyond their original length.

He now presents them to the Public with the greatest diffidence; hoping that some allowance will be made for the very inconvenient circumstances, little favourable to order or precision, in which many of them were written: But he would not venture to new-model them; apprehending, that what they might gain in form and expression, they would probably lose in ease and simplicity; and well knowing that the original impressions are better described at the moment they are felt, than from the most exact recollection . . .[2]

In conclusion he asserts the value of spontaneity. Brydone had visited Sicily in 1770 as bearleader to William Fullarton (1754–1808), a wealthy Scottish landowner who was an MP and a successful army officer. Brydone's *Tour* was very popular, but was found unreliable by some other tourists, as well as by a former consul.[3]

Artifice could, of course, play a role in material never intended for publication. A youth writing home to his parents might have many reasons to disguise his activities and gloss over his responses. Journals were shown to others, letters read aloud and handed around by friends and relations. Sir John Perceval (1683–1748), later 1st Earl of Egmont, who had himself been in Italy in 1706–7, congratulated Edward Southwell junior (1705–55) on the letters he wrote during his tour in 1725–6, and wrote, in response to one giving a 'description of the government and city of Genoa', of 'the pattern it gives my son how to write when it becomes his turn to voyage as you do'.[4] Southwell was subsequently an MP. His own son, another Edward (1738–77), himself travelled to Italy in 1763–4, although by then he was already an MP. George, Viscount Beauchamp (1725–44) was aware that his mother, Frances, Lady Hertford, was collecting his letters for posterity, and indeed she did publish them as a book. It is unclear how far this affected what he wrote. Lady Hertford had written to him expressing the hope that he would enjoy them in later life:

what I said to you in jest about the pleasure you would find when you grew old in making one of your grandchildren read them to you, will I am persuaded be very seriously accomplished. It will be a satisfaction to you to find in them that in so early a part of your life you had not run heedlessly through foreign countries but had made judicious observations on their curiosities, people and customs.

The last was also a form of admonition as to what was expected.[5]

Even if the written record was somewhat contrived, there was a difference between writing for an intimate circle and producing a work for a large anonymous market, in which the sole identifiable readers would be publishers and booksellers concerned about commercial appeal, although it is not clear how far the coverage and style established by published works affected more private accounts. There were also works that fit into neither category. Thus, *A Journal of a Summer's Excursion by the Road of Montecassino to Naples, and from there over all the Southern Parts of Italy, Sicily and Malta, in the Year 1772* by William

Young (1749–1815) appeared in a privately printed edition limited to twenty copies. Young visited Italy after university. He subsequently became an MP, succeeded his father as a baronet, and was Governor of Tobago.

The conventions expected by the market, reviewers, readers and writers themselves definitely had to be respected in published work. This can be seen in the correspondence of James Russel (*c.* 1720–63), whose *Letters from a Young Painter Abroad to his Friends in England* (2 vols, 1748–50) were, in part, influenced by the demands of his family, specifically his father and his bookseller brother. Demands upon James, who was in Italy from 1740 until his death, included a trip to Herculaneum, as well as 'some short account of Loreto, Bologna, Ancona and Venice: and some relations of diverting events', and, later, details of the ceremonies in which the Jacobite Pretender James 'III''s younger son, Henry (1725–1807), became a priest and a cardinal and more material on the Jubilee Year (1750). James Russel thanked his father for his role in improving the letters: 'I am truly sensible of the favour you have done me in touching them up, in such a manner, as has made them so acceptable to the public'. He also referred to 'writing letters, in order to supply matter for a second volume'.[6]

New works were in many senses explicitly or, more commonly, implicitly commenting on what had come before. In her *Observations and Reflections Made in the Course of a Journey through France, Italy, and Germany* (1789), Hester Piozzi (1741–1821; earlier Hester Thrale), who visited Italy in 1784–6, cited Addison, Brydone, Burney, Chesterfield, Cork and Orrery, Hamilton, Howell and Moore. Borrowing was common, as indeed in many other aspects of the culture of print, such as cartography. It was not always welcome. The well-travelled John, 3rd Earl of Bute, who visited Italy in 1768–9 and 1769–71, noted that travel writers drew heavily on other works, and was unhappy with what he found in their books. He thought many of the subjects useless or improper, which he blamed on the fact that 'writing is become a trade'.[7] William Coxe (1747–1828), who was to be a noted travel writer, although not of Italy, complained from Venice in 1779: 'it is as little known as Pekin – almost all the accounts that have been published being extremely erroneous'. Coxe, who was there as a bearleader for George Herbert (1759–1827), later an MP, a general and 11th Earl of Pembroke, specified inaccurate comments on the difficulty of visiting Venetian nobles and foreign envoys.[8]

Most of the well-known accounts of seventeenth- and eighteenth-century tourism fall into the category of travel literature. They vary in their methods, tone and areas covered, but they share a concern for impact and style. It is not surprising that scholars have concentrated on these writings, some of which were by major cultural and literary figures, such as Joseph Addison, who published *Letters from Italy* (1703) and *Remarks on Several Parts of Italy* (1705), which were much read by other travellers, and which influenced the conventions of travel writing.[9]

The views expressed in travel literature are more accessible, through being printed, and the texts themselves are easier and more attractive to read than subsequently printed accounts that were never intended for publication. In addition, much of the work on tourism has been done by amateurs lacking the time or resources to search for manuscript sources, and by scholars of literature whose forte has generally lain elsewhere. Both groups have concentrated on readily accessible published material by prominent figures, without appreciating that such accounts should be seen not as necessarily typical of the writings and views of tourists, but as works of literature. To a certain extent, however, the modern fashion for studying discourses or 'hegemonic concepts' ensures that the coherent constructs of travel literature are actively preferred to the more bitty and amorphous responses presented in manuscript sources. It has been claimed that 'the established itinerary of statues and paintings as well as cities unified English visitors in a controlled common experience'.[10] This was true of many (although far from all) visitors, but not necessarily of their responses.

Travel literature could, and can, provide an ideological slant on what was reported and the way in which it was discussed. Writers were not neutral figures. Their works commonly sought to make specific as well as general points for a readership that did not recognise any barriers to partisan viewpoints and political images. There was no more reason why travel literature should be immune from these influences than history or religious writings, both of which were frequently heavily politicised in this period.[11]

Travel literature can be seen to be removed from the experiences of ordinary tourists, not least because, in some cases, it is probable that it was written to be read as much as a form of fiction, as interesting works at times similar to picaresque novels, rather than as objective descriptions of the travels of individual tourists. Travel literature provided an opportunity for autobiography and literary amateurism, often in the readable context of a heroic or mock-heroic journey. Such literature was of course not uniform, but one of the more pertinent shifts occurred in the later eighteenth century: a move from the supposedly objective to the frankly subjective.

Apparently objective travel accounts were consulted by later tourists, and cannot therefore be seen as completely distinct from the experience of the latter. Richard Lassel's *Voyage of Italy* (1670) was given as an authority sixty years later by a Catholic writer seeking to refute the notion that the Pope profited from prostitution in Rome. In 1730, Joseph Atwell (*c.* 1696–1768), bearleader to William, 2nd Earl Cowper (1709–64), cited Addison and Misson on Vesuvius. William Lee (*c.* 1726–78), who visited Italy in 1752–3 shortly before succeeding his father who was a prominent judge, mentioned reading Addison on Venice, and, in 1754–5, W.H. Sneyd read Addison and Misson on Florence.[12]

It was normal to take guidebooks. Thus, Ambrose Phillipps (1707–37), who visited Italy in 1731–2 and was later an MP, took the *Gentleman's Pocket Companion for Travelling into Foreign Parts ... with Three Dialogues in Six European Languages* (1722). In addition, manuscript accounts, both diaries and correspondence, were affected by the availability of travel books, which lessened the need to cover what was already described. John Holroyd

3. *Sir Gregory Turner* by Pompeo Batoni, 1769. Turner (1748–1805), who took the name of Page before Turner in 1775 when he succeeded to the property of his great uncle, Sir Gregory Page, was a wealthy Oxfordshire landowner who had succeeded his father in 1766. He visited Italy in 1768–9, travelling from Geneva to Turin, Milan, Parma, Reggio, Modena, Bologna, Florence, Naples, Rome and Venice before leaving for Vienna. He sat to Batoni in Rome, where he also saw the funeral of Pope Clement XIII.

(1735–1821), later an MP and Earl of Sheffield, who travelled extensively after leaving the army at the end of the Seven Years War in 1763, wrote a detailed letter about his crossing of Mont Cenis in 1764, adding:

> I have been very tedious in the description of my six days Alpine journey, apprehending that particulars of such an uncommon country might entertain you, great cities and polished, improved countries being much alike and in general well known do not encourage an attempt towards such exact accounts of them.[13]

Other tourists critically compared what they saw with what they had read or been told. George, Viscount Villiers (1735–1805), later an MP and 4th Earl of Jersey, wrote in 1756,

> Florence is said by all travellers to be a very handsome town, and indeed it is called *la bella*: there are certainly some fine palaces scattered up and down, but in general the look of the houses is by no means handsome.[14]

As a related problem, there are issues of selection in printed sources and secondary liter-ature. It is understandable that scholars wishing to make reference to Palmerston's two tours in Italy should use Brian Connell's *Portrait of a Whig Peer. Compiled from the Papers of the Second Viscount Palmerston 1739–1802* (1957). Yet to turn, for example, to his description of Venice, he cites Palmerston's discussion of the arbitrary quality of the government,[15] but makes no reference either to Palmerston's remarks on the limits to this arbitrariness nor to his assessment of the government's popularity (see p. 148).

By ignoring the vast bulk of unprinted material, and concentrating on a relatively small number of familiar texts, a somewhat narrow conception of tourism and of the range of responses to travel has developed. In particular, it is necessary to understand the conventions of the genre. Writers' comments frequently suggest a sense of artificial interjection and a conscious striving after effect, not least with some of the paeans to nature that occurred towards the end of the century.[16] There could also be a striving after a more partisan effect, as in attacks on foreign food. Both should be quoted with due qualification.

If there are methodological problems in assessing the tourist experience, that is even more true of attempts to evaluate the impact of tourism, although it is clear that one effect was to encourage interest in travel literature. The general impact of tourism was debated at the time, but much of the contemporary printed criticism of tourists was misguided, a product more of the hostility shown in Britain to signs of cosmopolitan activity than of any reasoned response to the experience of travel. Tourism did play a significant role in encouraging the openness of the upper orders of European society to cosmopolitan influences and this left some commentators uncomfortable. Let us turn, however, to the tourists.

3. Into Italy

Italy was framed for tourists by the experience of travelling to and from it. This was far from easy, and it is necessary to understand that in order to appreciate the sense of achievement felt on arrival at the first major city, whether Venice, Milan, Genoa or, more usually, Turin. The extent to which tourists wrote at length about their approach to Italy, especially across the Alps, is noteworthy, and it is important to devote due attention to these accounts in order to obtain a rounded impression of their travels.

There was no set route to Italy. Most tourists visited the peninsula as part of a tour that also focused on Paris. In addition, France lay athwart the major route from Britain to Italy. For these reasons, the majority of tourists came through France. There were, however, two alternatives. The first was to travel overland via the Low Countries and the Holy Roman Empire (Germany and Austria). That entailed entering Italy via the eastern Swiss Cantons and the St Gotthard Pass, or via Bavaria, the Tyrol and the Brenner Pass, or via Vienna, Austria and the Tarvisio Pass.

By sea, it was possible to sail from Britain via the Straits of Gibraltar, but that was an uncommon route. The trip across the Bay of Biscay was rarely pleasant, the sea passage to Italy was long, and it was not easy to secure adequate shipping. In the absence of passenger services, the most pleasant way to sail to the Mediterranean was in a warship, as captains' and admirals' cabins provided comfortable berths. British garrisons at Gibraltar and Minorca ensured that warships did sail to the Mediterranean, but there were few reasons for them to call at Italian ports. The absence of diplomatic relations with the Papacy ensured that they could not call at Civitavecchia, the port for Rome. Many British merchant ships sailed to Livorno, but most could not provide comfortable accommodation.

Diana, Duchess of Bedford was terrified about the idea of sailing to Naples in the early 1730s as her husband John, the 4th Duke, wished: 'I have the greatest dread imaginable of it; going by sea I know would kill me, the least retching in the world gives me a pain in my side and breast, and to be so sick as almost everybody is at sea.' Sir William Hamilton (1730–1803) did indeed sail direct to Naples when he took up his embassy in 1764: 'We had a very rough

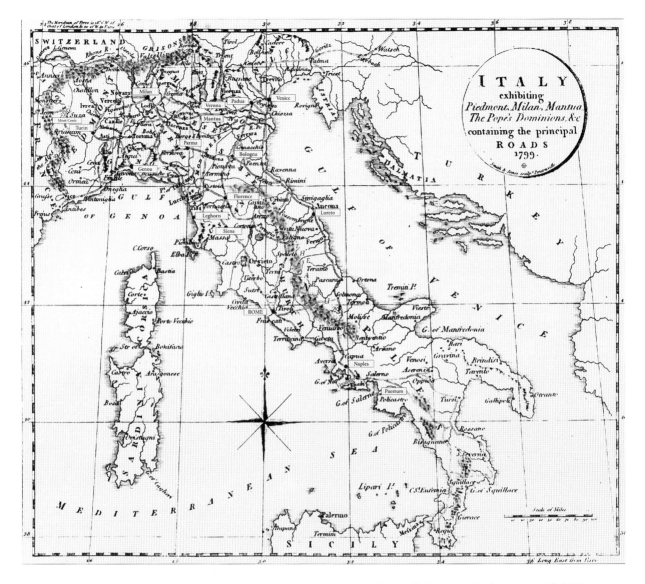

4. Map of Italy in 1799 adapted from Mariana Starke's *Travels in Italy* (1802). Starke (*c.* 1762–1838) left Nice for Italy in 1792, accompanying her elderly parents. Her father died in Pisa in 1794. Mariana stayed until 1798, returning after the Napoleonic wars.

passage and for Mrs [Catherine] Hamilton to whom the sea was quite a new object it was dreadful. I found it very unpleasant though I was more used to it.'[1]

Travelling to Italy from France, it was necessary to face the Alps. They had to be crossed or to be bypassed by sea. As yet there was no good road along the Mediterranean coast. Neither the Alps nor the Mediterranean was an attractive prospect for tourists. By sea, there was the risk of storm and shipwreck, and the lesser risk of Barbary pirates, which Lady

Craven was warned of in 1785, as well as the major inconvenience of contrary winds or being becalmed, and the minor one of the accommodation available. The boats used, feluccas, were small, vulnerable to storms, and dependent on the wind. In 1723, John Molesworth (1679–1726), envoy in Turin and later 2nd Viscount Molesworth, wrote, 'No mariners in the world are so cowardly as the Italians in general, but especially the Genoese; so that upon the least appearance of a rough sea, they run into the first creek where their feluccas are sometimes wind-bound for a month.' At Florence, two years later, Alan Brodrick (1702–47), later 2nd Viscount Brodrick, found there remained nothing left in Italy that he wanted to see 'but Genoa, Milan and Turin. My shortest way had been from Leghorn [Livorno] to Genoa by sea, but that way I could not go, having promised my aunt both before and since I left England, not to make any part of my journey by sea.'[2]

Andrew Mitchell (1708–71), later an MP and an influential diplomat, had a troublesome passage from Genoa in 1734 when northern Italy was racked by the War of the Polish Succession: 'I was detained some weeks longer at Genoa than I intended, and that by bad weather, for if it blows the least or if there is anything of a sea, the feluccas won't go out. I hired a felucca with 3 men from Genoa to Antibes for 3 pistols and a half.' On 1 November, he sailed from Genoa to Savona. The next contrary wind obliged Mitchell to put into Loana and have the felucca hauled onshore as there was no harbour: 'I was detained here a whole day by the laziness of the Italian sailors who chose rather to lie in the port and take their chance for a wind afterwards than to put to sea in fair weather. If there is the least swell in the sea they will by no means venture out'. Later in the trip, he was delayed for another two days by adverse winds and indolent sailors.[3]

The situation did not improve in the second half of the century. There was no comparison to the transformations produced by steam travel during the nineteenth century. In October 1754, W.H. Sneyd who hired a felucca and eight men at Nice to take himself, his companions, servants and a coach for six louis, wrote:

> it is much better for those who go this way into Italy to come by land from Marseilles to Nice and there take a felucca . . . in the winter it is so bad a way of going that I would not advise anyone to go in one of those boats: not that there is any great danger at any time in them from the sea; the Genoese being so great cowards: but there is danger of being put on shore and being obliged to continue several days where you can neither get house to cover you, bed to lie on, or bread to eat. Then again they are in continual apprehensions from the Barbary corsairs . . . I would not advise any one to defer his passage by sea into Italy later than the middle of September.

A contrary wind so hindered his rowers that they had to put into Menton, as well as Bordighera, where he stayed for four days, at first 'in a little fisherman's hut', and, subsequently, Savona, where the delay lasted for three days. Bad weather subsequently delayed him a week at Genoa when he was ready to sail for Lerici. In the late spring of 1773, George Romney (1734–1802) and his fellow painter Ozias Humphry (1742–1810) were thwarted by the weather when they tried to sail direct from Nice to Livorno, and subsequently encountered a storm *en route* from Genoa to Livorno. The problems of travel by sea encouraged voyages that were as short as possible. In 1771, William, 2nd Earl of Shelburne (1737–1805), travelling after the death of his first wife, sailed from Monaco to Genoa before continuing overland into Lombardy.[4] John Mitford (1748–1830), later an MP and Baron Redesdale, noted in 1776:

> From Genoa to Lerici travellers usually pass in a felucca to avoid the fatigue of a mountain journey along roads where mules only can keep their feet. These Mediterranean vessels are not formed for bad weather and they are manned by no very skilful mariners. Scarcely ever an oar's length from a shore they creep under the rocks, and trembling at every wind are always afraid to hoist a sail. If the wind is very fair, eight hours will carry the felucca from Genoa to Lerici, But if the wind is the least contrary, or if it is so high that these timorous seamen dare not trust a sail, twenty hours rowing will hardly suffice to double every projecting rock, and bring the bark to its destination. The beauty of the rocky coast, and the variety of its scenery afford some recompense for the tedious passage.[5]

In 1778, Phillipina, Lady Knight (1726–99), an impecunious widow travelling with her daughter Cornelia (1757–1837) who was later governess to Princess Charlotte, sailed from Marseilles to Civitavecchia: 'our voyage was somewhat tedious, as we were, after seven weeks waiting for a wind, thirty days on our passage, putting into different ports'. George, 9th Earl of Winchelsea (1752–1826), who had already succeeded his uncle and was later an army officer, took a week to sail from Nice to Genoa in November 1772, and another to sail on to Livorno the following month. Lady Craven was so fed up in September 1785 that she cut short her passage from Genoa to Livorno and landed at Viareggio.[6]

Indeed, the continued problems of sea travel contrasted with the gradual improvement in overland journeys over the century thanks to improved roads. Tourists could cope with discomfort. It was the uncertainty that storms, contrary winds and calms brought to timetables that was the crucial problem. Although there was a lot to do in Genoa, tourists generally did not wish to wait for any length of time in the other ports – Antibes, Livorno and Civitavecchia. In addition, some of the fishing towns and villages on the Ligurian coast that feluccas could be driven to seek shelter in were less than inviting.

Travelling by boat, however, was not without its compensations. The trip could be quick. It also offered an alternative to passes closed by snow. The tourist who wanted to head south in Italy as soon as possible could sail direct from France to Lerici, Livorno or Civitavecchia. There were also visual attractions. Sir Francis Head Bt. (*c.* 1696–1768) was most impressed by the beauty of the Ligurian coast, and the approach to Genoa was generally regarded as very appealing.[7] This route might also be the only one available for the winter months, as snows could close the Alpine routes and the cold make them unpleasant, while it also provided an opportunity to visit Marseilles, Nice and Genoa. In January 1791, the painter William Theed (1764–1817) took this route on his second trip to Italy. In Nice, 'I could almost fancy myself in Paradise; when I looked out of my chamber window I saw oranges growing in abundance, and all along the coast from Marseilles to Genoa, myrtle, thyme, lavender and many other sweet herbs grow wild'.

Theed was open, however, about the disadvantages of the journey:

We left Nice . . . about 8 o'clock in a beautiful moonlight – the time for contemplating – but I assure you I contemplated on nothing but the disagreeableness of my situation; for I was starved almost to death with the cold and most consumedly sick, could not eat or drink for seventeen or eighteen hours; but at last attempted it, which only served to kick up fresh disturbances. The next night we were forced to put into a small fishing town as the weather grew rather bad, and if there is the least appearance of blowing weather they always put in, for these boats cannot keep the sea or the people are afraid . . . from this place we set out again at 1 o'clock in the morning and sailed on pretty well till noon and had got Genoa in sight, where we should have arrived in two hours but behold you it began to blow very fresh; the sea began to be very rough, and a Frenchman began to be very frightened; so we were forced to bout ship and go on shore in a paltry place within fifteen miles of Genoa, and nothing to be got; therefore we eat up what we had got and trudged off for the next town – four miles – before we could get horses to carry our weary carcasses to Genoa, where at least we arrived safe and well, for all those perils and dangers – O the glorious scenes in travelling![8]

Most tourists preferred the Alpine route. This was less hazardous and unpredictable than travelling by sea, and there were opportunities to break the journey, although the road was even more affected by seasonal factors. The most common route into Italy was from Lyons to the Franco-Savoyard frontier at Pont-de-Beauvoisin. Until ceded to Napoleon III in 1860, the Duchy of Savoy (like the county of Nice) was part of 'Italy', as its ruler was also ruler of Piedmont. From there, tourists crossed the Alps over the Mont Cenis pass to Susa, and thence to Turin, the capital of Savoy-Piedmont, the ruler of which became King of Sicily in 1713–20 and King of Sardinia from 1720.

As the Mont Cenis pass was not suitable for wheeled vehicles, it was necessary to dismantle carriages near its foot. These were then transported over the pass on mules, while the tourists were carried in a type of sedan chair by porters. The means of transportation did not change during the period, as the route did not become a carriage road until the following century. Crossing in 1734, Richard Pococke (1704–65), a clergyman in the (Protestant) Church of Ireland and an assiduous and observant traveller, was 'carried down in a chair without legs, with poles to the sides, carried by two men'. He was delighted by the 'speed of the crossing' and observed 'it is nothing at all'.[9] John Holroyd crossed the pass in 1764. Although it was summer, his party was glad 'to put on worsted stockings and muffle ourselves up in great coats'. At the top, Holroyd found 'a tolerable public house where I drank the richest milk I ever tasted'. He was more worried by the descent:

> The descent of the mountain on the Piedmontese side is extremely difficult and would be impracticable but by means of traverses zigzag in the side of the mountain. The road is horribly rough and is often stopped up by huge fragments of rocks fallen from the higher passes, on one side of the road a considerable river tumbles over prodigious rocks and rages most magnificently especially in one part where it falls from a great height. Halfway down this descent is the dangerous part where during winter but more particularly in the spring travellers are overwhelmed by immense bodies of snow sometimes 100 feet deep which falls or rather slides from the mountain. Many people are carried on an indifferent sort of seat on poles over the whole mountain. I rode my mule and walked all but the last half of the descent when being obliged often to dismount and it beginning to be very hot and also an inclination to try the method of conveyance induced me to suffer myself to be carried on one of these machines. Was astonished to see with what ease and how quick the men went without slipping or stumbling. I was carried a league of this difficult road for a shilling and the men only stopped twice for a very short time each.

The entire experience was part of the delight of the trip for Holroyd, a view that gathered currency in the second half of the century as mountainous regions came to play a more positive role in the collective imagination: 'I was much amused passing through a country so wild and more in a state of nature than any I had seen'.[10] Thomas Pelham wrote in early 1777:

> crossing Mont Ceni is certainly a great undertaking in point of conveying the carriage etc, but as to our own persons there is neither danger nor inconvenience; it was so hard a frost that when we came to the top of the mountain we left our chairs and descending in sledges which though very trying to the *nerves* was not unpleasant. It was the clearest day imaginable and our view beyond all description.[11]

There was no decent route further south. East of Monaco, the Ligurian mountains fell sheer to the sea, the corniche road on the Riviera was not opened until Napoleon's time, and it was not practicable to go by land to Genoa via Oneglia, Finale and Savona. It was possible to go inland, crossing the Alps between Monaco and Turin through the Col (pass) di Tenda/de Tende. Edward Thomas described the journey in vivid detail in 1750. He had intended sailing from Antibes to Genoa, but, instead, went overland, finding the most 'Romantic' prospect he had ever seen:

I took a felucca at four louis or guineas to carry me to Genoa . . . The sea was as smooth as a looking glass when we took boat, but in less than half an hour it began to swell in such a manner as that several waves broke over the boat especially at the three mouths of the [River] Var where there was a great swell at that time. But the boat was very good and we had ten stout rowers. However I made them land me and my things at Nice resolving never to set my foot in another felucca and I thought myself well off to get to shore at the loss of the four louis.

Instead, Thomas set off from Nice for Turin with two Sardinian officers:

I hired 3 mules to carry me to Coni, one for myself, another for my servant, and another for my baggage. These creatures are the surest footed in the world; and nature has calculated them for these wild passages where no horse can possibly go. It was at first a frightful thing to me to ride on the very edges of stupendous precipices without daring to touch the bridle which must hang loose on the creature's neck . . .

The first day we travelled through a dreadful wild naked rocky country by the sides of horrid precipices where the mules had but just holes to put their feet in, sometimes through snow, and if the hole happened to be too deep and the creature came down on his breast, it lay in that posture till you got off and till the muleteer spoke to it. This day on a mountain near us we saw a wolf hunting, the wolf run just by us and several shepherds and dogs after it. We soon got into the bowels of vast rocks which were of a stupendous height above us on each side and of a vast depth below us. Here the road was cut in the side of the rock and very narrow.

Thomas began his climb of the pass at 3 a.m. in order to be through by 11 a.m.:

for it is exceeding dangerous to be caught there at midday, at which time the tempests begin almost every day and carry off with vast depths of snow both men and mules . . . I was almost in one continual agony not daring to take my eyes off the mule's neck or the side of the mountain which was like a wall on one side; for the stupendous precipice at the other would have turned my head . . . the most difficult and perilous passage of all the Alps and I several times wished myself at Framore while making it. But there was something so Romantick and different from what I had ever seen before that when it was over I would not for £50 not have seen these wild and extraordinary scenes of nature. But it is impossible to give you any kind of an adequate idea of the prospect we had from the top of this mountain into an immense basin on the other side below us surrounded with mountains of the same kind and edged with snow which as the sun melted run down the sides in the most beautiful and vast cataracts my eyes ever beheld, and would put all the waterworks of the world made by art out of countenance. We had also the prospect of clouds a great way below us hovering on the sides of the mountains, which made a most Romantick appearance.[12]

Thomas's contrasting of natural with man-made splendour, and his preference for the former, was indicative of a general shift in taste. An anonymous traveller in the mid-1770s found:

> the road is utterly impracticable for a carriage, and scarcely to be found travelled by an
> ordinary horse; mules are chiefly used on it; and tender ladies and infirm men have no
> succedaneum but a sedan chair. It is three days journey over the mountains to the plains
> of Piedmont for a mule, and five for a sedan chair. The narrow rugged path which is called
> the road, is conducted up the courses of different torrents.

A carriage road was then being built to Turin. It was to be opened the following decade: the first complete opening of an Alpine pass to wheeled traffic. The anonymous traveller, concerned more with the convenience of tourists than the interests of Victor Amadeus III (r. 1773–96), who wished to link his dominions, regretted that the road was not being built from Nice to Genoa.[13] Indeed the Mont Cenis route continued to be the preferred route for tourists, not only because it was the quickest between France and northern Italy, but also because the far longer Col di Tenda route involved the poor roads in the county of Nice. The new route, however, was used by some tourists. James Buller (1766–1827), a member of a prominent West Country landed family, left a description in 1788. Having travelled through France, he journeyed from Antibes to Nice, where he bathed in the Mediterranean, before crossing the pass in June: 'very little snow on the top but the road bad for carriages. Winds up the mountain like a cork screw.' On the descent, he recorded that work had begun on a three-mile tunnel through the mountain, adding 'indeed the whole journey across the Alps gave evident proof of the public spirit of the Princes of this country'.[14] Samuel Boddington (1766–1843), Edward Rigby (1747–1821) and two friends followed in 1789. Like Buller, they were to visit Turin and then leave Italy.[15] The route thus rounded out their itineraries, rather than leading to a tour of Italy.

Other passes varied considerably. Charles Hotham (1693–1738), a member of a Yorkshire landed family, later a baronet, MP and a colonel, reached Turin in 1711 'after a very tedious journey of eight days through the Alps. The fifth day we got to the foot of the highest mountain called St. Bernard; we were six hours getting to the top of it; we found the snow so deep, it being in most places the depth of four horses, and no track made that we were once or twice upon the point of going back; but at last with the help of some men with shovels who made the way before us we got through.'[16]

In contrast, Henry Oxenden (1721–1803), who later succeeded to his father's Kent estates and baronetcy, found that his journey from Venice to Vienna over the Tarvisio through Styria in early 1749 was on 'excessive good roads'.[17] George, Viscount Villiers (1735–1805), who travelled with George, Viscount Nuneham (1736–1809) and Villiers's tutor, William Whitehead (1715–85), later Poet Laureate, had spent a while in Germany and entered Italy in

5. *Lord Boyne and Companions*, by Bartolomeo Nazari. Gustavus, 2nd Viscount Boyne (1710–46) visited Italy in 1730–1, embarking from Venice in April 1731 in order to sail to Malta, Minorca, Gibraltar, Cadiz and Lisbon.

1754 after a long journey by good roads from Vienna via Graz and Ljubljana to Trieste. From there, they found that

> The road is very mountainous along the shore of the Adriatic, and as rough and rocky as can possibly be conceived. As this is not a common road, the post is not established, so that we were obliged to take our horses on two stages to Monfalcone, where we entered the Venetian territories. The road from thence . . . was much better and more pleasant; there was great plenty of vines on each side the road.[18]

They were in Italy.

Sambrooke Freeman (*c.* 1721–82) found the approach to the Brenner less easy: 'Chiusa a very bad pass'.[19] Due to the French Revolutionary War, Sarah Bentham (d. 1809), widowed stepmother of the philosopher Jeremy Bentham, travelled to Italy via Harwich, the United Provinces (Dutch Republic), Munich, and the Brenner and Bolzano. She found Trent (Trento) a 'dirty town with narrow streets and wretched looking houses' and the route down the Adige valley frighteningly precipitous.[20]

There was also a sea route to Venice to parallel that to Genoa. Simon, 2nd Viscount Harcourt (1714–77), subsequently a general, envoy to Paris and Viceroy of Ireland, sailed from Venice to Trieste in June 1734, *en route* for Vienna. On the return journey in 1748, Lord Garnock was detained two days at Trieste by a contrary wind. The subsequent journey took two days.[21] The increased popularity of travel to Venice and the improvements at the port of Trieste ensured that the Trieste–Venice run, which had attracted few tourists early in the century, was quite busy by the 1780s. In 1786, Adam Inglis found it:

> a pleasant journey as far as Trieste where we were obliged to remain three days the wind though fair being so high that we could not put to sea. We were two days on the passage which was rather disagreeable. By what we now hear of the new road by Klagenfurt we regret that we did not come by it as we should then have shunned the uncertainty of a sea passage.[22]

Indeed, the 'tempestuous' weather had enabled the bearleader John Moore (1729–1802) to persuade his charge, Douglas, 8th Duke of Hamilton (1756–99), to take the land route in October 1775.[23] Once within Italy, however, the choice was only rarely between land and sea routes. Instead, it was necessary to tackle the problems of land transport.

4.   From the Alps to the Arno

Turin was the first major Italian city reached after crossing the Cenis. Tourists were able to travel there easily and speedily and most were impressed by what they saw. From Susa, Holroyd

> passed through a most beautiful country and well cultivated to Turin. The approach to the town is extremely magnificent. The last nine mile is as straight as the Mall at St. James, and as regular. The road is very wide and on the sides exactly planted. There are no suburbs to that part of the town where we entered. The environs are delightful and some neighbouring hills covered with villas.[1]

Some tourists rushed through Turin on the way to other Italian towns, but many lingered. Aside from the attractions of the city and, more particularly, its court, many tourists were tired after their crossing of the Alps, and Turin was often their first real stop after Paris. The Reverend Patrick St Clair hoped that Ashe Windham's son, William (1717–61), on the Grand Tour in 1738, would 'stay a fortnight at least at the King of Sardinia's court, which is now the politest in Europe'. Ashe Windham had himself been on the Grand Tour in 1693–6 with St Clair as his bearleader, and, as with many other tourists, the young man's plans were in part shaped by these earlier experiences. Augustus, 3rd Duke of Grafton (1735–1811), later Prime Minister, spent six weeks in Turin in 1761. The rulers were patrons of the Academy, a kind of finishing school, which attracted a fair number of British youths: there were seven there in September 1737, although only one other in 1762 when Frederick, 5th Earl of Berkeley (1745–1810) arrived for a two-year stay. As a reminder of the extent to which tourists were linked, Berkeley was brother to Elizabeth, Lady Craven, while their mother, Elizabeth, Countess of Berkeley (1720–92), travelled in Italy in 1778–9 after her second husband, Earl Nugent, had rejected her because of her prominent interest in men. In 1775, Sholto Douglas found the Academy more expensive and less impressive in the 'quality of the masters' than he had anticipated, and he added, 'the principal advantage I shall reap here is I fancy an *easier air* in company, as I am to be introduced to the king and the principal nobility at the return of the court, and being in the Academy am in some measure obliged to give constant attendance at the Drawing Room'.[2]

The court of Turin was regarded as pro-British, and Sardinia fought with Britain in anti-French coalitions in 1690–96, 1703–13 and 1743–8. Many British tourists liked the city, its rectilinear street plan, and the spectacular new buildings erected under Victor Amadeus II (r. 1675–1730). William Freeman found Turin 'an handsome large town, the streets wide and the houses finely built . . . the Duke's palace is large and richly furnished and the apartments lie well together'. George, Viscount Sunbury (1716–71), later 2nd Earl of Halifax and a major politician in the 1750s and 1760s, was less impressed in 1737: 'I have heard much in praise of Turin and, if I mistake not, it is called one of the finest towns in Europe. I own it falls short of my expectations, and though its regularity is beautiful, I can't think it deserves extravagant encomiums'.[3] Such contrasting of anticipation with experience was very common in letters and journals. In 1763, Margaret, Lady Spencer noted:

> The chief things thought worth seeing at Turin were, the King's Palace, the great Theatre, a hunting house of the King's, and the Church of the Superga from whence there is a glorious view, bounded on one side by the Alps and a high mountain called Monte Viso from under which the Po takes its course and on the [other] side an extensive prospect of almost all Piedmont, with the Po running through it and if it was clear they assured us we might distinguish Milan and the Appenines.[4]

In 1779, Nathaniel Wraxall (1751–1831), who had made his money in India, was touring with the Honourable Robert Manners (1758–1823), later a general, and was, like Manners, to become an MP, and found Turin 'a very elegant, well built, pleasant city'. On the other hand, some tourists found the amusements there limited: Philip, 2nd Earl Stanhope (1714–86) writing in 1733 of 'so mournful a place as Turin';[5] Robert Lowth (1710–87), later Bishop of London, bearleader of Lords George (c. 1727–94) and Frederick Cavendish (1729–1803), both later MPs, complained in 1750 that there was little to do in Turin. But, that summer, the marriage of the king's heir, later Victor Amadeus III, to Maria Antonia, a Spanish infanta, drew many British visitors attracted by the prospect of spectacles and impressive ceremonies.[6] Like other cities, Turin also provided an opportunity for acquiring or developing accomplishments. Thomas Pelham took lessons in dancing and perspective in Turin.

From Turin there were several routes for tourists going into Italy: to Milan, Parma or Genoa. There was no set course for the Italian section of the Grand Tour. Tourists were influenced by their point of arrival and of expected departure; the season of the year, which was important because of summer heat,[7] and the onset of malaria near Rome; the inclinations, if any, of their travelling companions; their desire to meet friends; and their wish to attend specific events: particularly the opera in Reggio, Bologna and Milan, the Carnival in Naples and Venice, and religious, especially Easter, ceremonies in Rome. George Lyttelton (1709–73), who had been to Italy in 1729–30, and went on to become an MP, a Lord of the Treasury and the Chancellor of the Exchequer, inherit the family estate in Worcestershire and baronetcy, and be created Lord Lyttelton, in 1763 gave Elizabeth Montagu, 'the Queen of the Bluestockings', his advice on the route she should follow. The surviving portion starts in mid-sentence:

> Tivoli, Frascati etc. Go from thence through Umbria and along the beautiful coast of the Adriatic to Venice, see the Doge espouse the Gulph at the Feast of the Ascension, and then follow my route through the southern parts of Germany and the Swiss Cantons to Geneva . . . If you can't be so long from your business or pleasure in England, you must give up the thoughts of seeing Rome; for without great danger to your life, it can't be visited in hot weather, nor can you pass the Alps in winter or early in the spring. But you may set out next year about the middle of May, stay at Paris a fortnight, and pass Mount Cenis about the middle of June, and then go by Genoa and Lucca to Florence, where I hope to join you before the end of July. From thence, after I have stayed about a week in that city and its charming environs, we will go together through Parma and Piacenza to Milan, and make excursions from thence as far as to Vicenza, till about the last week in August, at which time my son and I must take our leaves of you if you propose seeing Rome; and your best course will be to stay in the Milanese all the month of September, return to Florence in October, and stay there, or at Siena, till the cold of November makes it safe for you to go to Rome. But if you find it not convenient to pass the winter out of England, then we will go all together from Vicenza to Venice, from thence to Munich . . . By this plan the great heats of summer and autumn will be passed in the coolest parts of Italy, and the whole tour will be made with as little inconvenience as a lady can suffer in so long a journey . . . If your heart is set upon seeing Rome without passing a winter out of England it will be possible to do it thus. Be at Calais the first of March, go as fast as you can from thence to Nice, embark there for Genoa, at which place you may arrive by the beginning of April, in part of which month, and in May, you may see Rome and Naples tolerably well. But the worst difficulty is to secure a good passage from Nice to Genoa at that time of the year. To trust yourself in a felucca I think is too dangerous, and an English or French ship may not easily be found. I therefore revert to my former plan, which is safe, easy, and delightful.[8]

In the event, Elizabeth Montagu did not visit Italy and Lyttelton did not accompany his son Thomas (1744–79), later an MP and 2nd Lord Lyttelton, to Italy in 1764. Nevertheless, his letter showed the factors that were considered when planning itineraries. The weather was also important. It affected both the attractiveness of particular locations and the routes that could be followed. On 27 November 1725, Edward Southwell wrote from Genoa that he had been detained in Turin for an extra week by poor weather, and that:

we have waited ten days here for a fair wind to transport us to Leghorn, which we have but little hopes of amidst the present thunder, lightning and rain, and yet the roads are impassable to Milan and it is so late in the year, that we are resolved to choose the straight road to Rome, and not to visit the other courts of Italy till after Easter.

Richard Edgcumbe (1764–1839), Viscount Valletort, later an MP and subsequently 2nd Earl of Buckinghamshire, left Italy early in June 1785, travelling from Mantua to Munich, because of the 'violent heats'. George, Lord Herbert (1759–1827), later an MP and then 11th Earl of Pembroke, complained from Milan in July 1779 that his father had rejected his wish to put off his southern tour: 'I now find myself obliged to descend into the broiling heats of Rome and Naples, and shall think myself well off if I get clear of them unbaked'. In May 1728, the Reverend Gaspar Wetstein, the Dutch bearleader to Lionel, 4th Earl of Dysart (1708–70), was informed that, 'If my Lord finds the climate at Genoa more agreable to him than that of Turin during the heat of the summer, he may stay there till the heats begin to be over and then return to Turin.'[9]

In addition, the role of festivals, ceremonies and other events was certainly prominent in itineraries as they could make cities far more interesting. In 1729, William Freeman found at Parma 'a very handsome large court it being at a time when there was acting the completest opera in Italy. The town was full of strangers.' In 1740, Frederick Frankland MP (*c.* 1694–1768) wanted to see the forthcoming papal coronation in Rome and the liquefaction of the blood of St Januarius (Gennaro) at Naples, but his nephew, Thomas Worsley (1710–78), warned him 'that he must not think of quitting Rome till the heats are over, if he stays there till they begin'. Frankland, a member of a Yorkshire landed family, who had become a merchant, had separated from his recently married second wife. Worsley had been in Florence with Frankland, and was later an MP. Francis, Viscount Beauchamp (1743–1822), later an MP, an ambassador and Marquess of Hertford, planned in 1765 to go to Sicily after the summer heat was over, returning to Florence for the accession of Archduke Leopold as Grand Duke of Tuscany. Sir John Fleming Leicester, Bt. (1762–1827), a member of a Cheshire landed family and later an MP, noted in Rome in 1786, 'Everybody is going to Venice for the [Feast of the] Ascension.'[10]

Actual itineraries often differed from what had been planned. Spending longer in one place left less time for others, and tourists often found cities they were visiting more or less interesting than they had anticipated. Much depended on how long the tourist had to spend in what Robert Wharton in 1775 termed 'the land of ancient virtue and modern virtù (otherwise called taste)'. Sir Francis Head (*c.* 1696–1768), who visited Italy in 1723–5, observed that the country was 'like a fine mistress which is always the more agreeable on a larger acquaintance'.[11]

The three major sights in northern Italy were Genoa, Milan and Venice. Many tourists went direct from Turin to Milan, although they found much of Lombardy unappealing. Lady Spencer wrote in 1763, 'From Turin to Vercelli is a fine road but most part of it over a dead flat which ugly though it was bounded on the left by the Alps and on the right by the Appenines.' Charles Abbot (1757–1829), a lawyer who was later an MP, was also unimpressed by the countryside east of Turin:

> The country very uninteresting, the road through a plain with trifling inequalities. The Alps on the Italian side are by no means so picturesque as on the Swiss side. They are perpendicular and black, with only a ridge of snow on the tops – on the Swiss side they rise in numberless chains above each other, and present to the eye a endless plain of snow.[12]

Much of Lombardy belonged to the Duchy of Milan, which was held by the Habsburg family, and, as elsewhere in Italy, crossing a frontier made it possible to make contrasts. Tourists sought to match what they saw to reflections on government ethos and methods. Entering the Milanese from the west in 1776, John Mitford (1748–1830), a lawyer who was later an MP, Speaker of the House of Commons and 1st Lord Redesdale, readily discerned

> the change of government. The Sardinian monarch, supporting with difficulty a large military establishment, and a numerous royal family, draws from the hands of the peasant every farthing which the ingenuity of the farmers of the revenue can find means to extort. The imperial family, supporting their state with less difficulty, do not bear so hard upon the inhabitants of the Milanese. A traveller soon perceives a labour bestowed upon the cultivation of the lands, a neatness in the various habitations, and a comfortableness in the appearance of the peasants which he does not meet with in Piedmont.[13]

Milan was not noted for artistic treasures to rank with Genoa, Florence, Rome or Venice, but most tourists found it pleasant. Milanese society was welcoming, especially during the administration of the Anglophile Count Carlo/Karl Firmian in the 1760s, and there was a good opera. La Scala was opened in 1778 with a new opera by Salieri. Richard Creed, a half-pay officer accompanying John, 5th Earl of Exeter (*c.* 1648–1700), visited the cathedral, citadel and Ambrosian library in late 1699, as well as hearing 'a great deal of good vocal music' performed by nuns, and commenting on the attempts made in Milan to avoid the plague: 'they take so much garlic to prevent it for the future that they are fit to poison one'. The response of British tourists to garlic was unfavourable, and it was an aspect of Italian foreignness that many commented upon. The varied appeal of Italy was captured by Palmerston at Milan in August 1764, on his departure from Italy: 'I am now quite to the door of Italy and am taking my last leave of it at a place which has but little to make one regret it. I mean as to objects of curiosity; the inhabitants seem to be more agreeable than those of any other Italian town.'[14]

6. *The Bucintoro Departing from the Bacino di San Marco*, by Luca Carlevaris (1663–1730), 1710. Carlevaris was the key figure in the development of eighteenth-century Venetian view painting and he concentrated on animated scenes.

From Milan there were two major routes further into Italy. Tourists could go east, via Brescia, Verona, Vicenza and Padua, to Venice; or south-east, via Piacenza, Parma, Reggio and Modena to Bologna. From there, they could continue to Pesaro and the Adriatic coast, or turn south across the Apennines to Florence. In planning their itineraries for this part of Italy, Florence and Venice were the major attractions, but many of the cities of Lombardy, the Veneto and, in particular, Emilia-Romagna offered much to see. Parma and Modena were the capitals of duchies, and Bologna a major centre of artistic treasures. William Freeman found 'many palaces of Palladios' in Vicenza, and 'many antique remains' and 'many original fine paintings of Paolo Veronese' in Verona. At the latter, Palmerston was impressed by the 'amphitheatre which has all its inner part and the seats very entire; though upon enquiry I was sorry to find that great part of the seats had been replaced rather than preserved and that in the doing it some gross mistakes had been committed'. Sarah Bentham was more critical: 'The want of sewers made the streets often very offensive from the stench of the filth.'[15] The development of sewer systems in British cities, particularly by improvement commissions, made such a situation more noteworthy and more a sign of primitiveness. Not all tourists commented on the state of public cleanliness, but women were apt to do so.

Venice offered a very different phenomenon to other Italian cities; one that tourists were well prepared for by guidebooks and pictures, but still one that was surprising, if not amazing. The city also attracted interest with its splendid treasures, pleasures and spectacles, most notably the Carnival on the Feast of the Ascension of the marriage with the sea, for which the Doge used the *Buccentoro*, his spectacular ship of state. In 1729, William Freeman noted, 'The description of the situation of Venice every one knows but still it surprises when you first enter the town.' In his three weeks in the city, Freeman was disappointed by the Rialto, offering an unfavourable comparison with Sir John Vanbrugh's very new palace at Blenheim for John Churchill, 1st Duke of Marlborough, but was impressed by the marriage with the sea, describing the galley as 'the richest that can be made. Everything gilt above water adorned with exquisite covering and statues and covered with gold inside and out'. Three years earlier, Edward Southwell had described it as 'a fine gaudy entertainment'.[16] Other festivals included that of Giovedì Grasso on the last Thursday of Carnival, and that of the Redentore when the Doge paid his annual visit to the Giudecca and a bridge of boats was built to link it with the town.

7. *The Entrance to the Arsenal, Venice*, by Bernardo Bellotto, *c.* 1743. Born in 1722, Bellotto was Canaletto's nephew and his work was frequently said to be by the latter. Working alongside Canaletto probably helped Bellotto gain access to important commissions, providing a link with Joseph Smith, a British merchant, banker and art dealer in Venice who became Consul there in 1744 and who owned four works by Bellotto.

The number of British tourists in Venice varied by year and during the year, but there were usually quite a few. Charles Wyndham (1710–63), a member of a Somerset landed family, and later an MP, 2nd Earl of Egremont and a secretary of state, found 'about thirty English in town' in January 1730.[17] Some British visitors, however, were critical of the pleasures of Venice, and found that the novelty of the city rapidly palled. One in 1730 grew 'sick of the insipid diversions of the carnival' and preferred a trip to visit the Roman amphitheatre at Pola in Istria, a Venetian-ruled area of Italy visited by very few tourists, and now part of Croatia.[18] Sir John Perceval (1683–1748) grew 'heartily tired' of Venice in 1706. In 1764, Palmerston noted, 'The appearance and customs of the place are at first very striking and agreable at least from their novelty; but I think one should soon grow tired of them and then it must be of all places the most disagreable because it has the least variety.'[19] In 1787, the bearleader Thomas Brand was not keen to return a second time to 'row through stinking canals in those coffin-like gondolas in the heats of that unwholesome climate'. Lady Craven was also disappointed.[20] Leaving in 1793, Sarah Bentham presented a contrast that other tourists also noted:

> The day was calm and serene and the city of Venice looked beautiful rising from the sea, but there appears a great mixture of meanness with magnificence in the buildings. The window shutters being generally a white board hanging on the outside of the house against the stone or plaistered house without being painted and this is customary throughout the route to Padua.[21]

More generally, Venice was not a city that permitted tourists to commune with Classical civilisation. A medieval city, greatly embellished with the products of sixteenth-century Italian culture, Venice offered a different set of perceptions and in many respects was a distinct civilisation, certainly compared to the Classical–Baroque interaction of Rome.

To the south of the Lombard plain, the Apennine chain posed a major problem for tourists seeking to enter Tuscany or, further south, to move between the east coast and Rome. There were few passable routes across it and these could be blocked by winter snows. The latter kept the Reverend Norton Nicholls (*c.* 1742–1809) in Milan in the winter of 1771–2. The usual crossing was the road from Bologna to Florence, although, in the 1780s, the routes from Modena to Pistoia and Lucca were improved. The Bologna–Florence route was not regarded as attractive by most tourists until Florence came into view, having no snow-capped magnificence and no great forests. In 1792, Samuel Drew, a doctor who attended the sickly Henrietta, Viscountess Duncannon (1761–1821) on the Continent, was unimpressed by the route as far as Loiano: 'I was much dissatisfied with these Apennines, a long lingering ascent up barren sandhills … dreary, barren and worthless'. The following year, Sarah Bentham, whose coach from Bologna required six horses and three postilions, described Loiano: 'nothing is in view but high barren rocks with beds for torrents lying between them'.

Drew at least found the later stage better: 'Thank heaven and the government of Tuscany, we have entered a more cheerful country and a better inn.'[22]

A frequently used route, the major alternative to that from Bologna, was from Ancona via Loreto, Foligno, Spoleto and Terni. This served tourists travelling to or from Venice. In 1734, Jeremiah Milles (1714–84), later Dean of Exeter and President of the Society of Antiquaries, found this road 'disagreeable, along the sides of hills, and in some places dangerous'.[23]

Palmerston's letters offer a particularly valuable account as he was wide-ranging in his interests and clear in his prose. Travelling from Rome to Venice in 1764, via Spoleto, Loreto, Ancona, Bologna, Ferrara and Padua, he wrote:

> The journey was very pleasant through a country which afforded as much variety and as many fine views as any I ever passed. The prospects among the Apennines are very romantic and beautiful but the misery of the inhabitants is excessive . . . the Treasury or the absurdities of Loreto which are both very extravagant. I think Addison observes justly that to repeat the follies of the Roman Catholic religion is about as wise and as entertaining as telling one's dreams. At many of the towns in this journey I found capital pictures by Raphael, Buroccio and Guerchino particularly by the last at Cento his native place.

Palmerston, however, was less attracted to the Apennines when he crossed them three months later, albeit by a different road, *en route* from Florence to Bologna, and it is worth quoting the second passage in order to indicate the variety of the individual response and also because it reflects the interest of tourists in natural phenomena. This was more prominently seen in their response to volcanoes and to the country near Naples:

> as this journey is entirely over the Apennines I had full enough of them before I got there. These mountains are considerable enough to incommode and retard the traveller but not to amuse him with fine romantic views. In this journey I saw one great natural curiosity which is a bright clear flame about as considerable as what might rise from a common faggot constantly burning on a spot of ground where there is no apparent openings and crevices. The soil is dry, dusty and stony but does not seem to consume or to be affected by the flame so that it is plainly not the fire which feeds it. I should imagine it to be some vapour that finds vent there of such a nature as to be inflammable on communicating with the free air and this I fancy the chemists might explain though in me it is mere conjecture. What confirmed my notion was observing some smaller fainter flames detached from the great one and which with some difficulty one might extinguish for a time but which immediately catched again on holding a burning paper about a foot from the ground as a candle blown out may be lighted again from the smoke.[24]

Aside from across the Apennines, Florence was also reached from the Tuscan coast. The latter route was favoured by those who had journeyed by sea to Italy, as well as those who

8. *Grand Canal, the Rialto Bridge from the South*, by Zuanne Antonio Canal, called Canaletto (1697–1768), the prime moulder of the British pictorial memory of Venice.

had travelled south-east from Turin via Asti and Alessandria to reach the Mediterranean at Genoa. This was a city very different to Turin. There was no royal court to serve as a focus for activities, but Genoa had a richer history and more artistic treasures. These were held in aristocratic palaces to which access was readily granted. William Freeman was struck by the opulence: 'the palaces of the noblesse which make up whole streets are very magnificent and large and . . . rich with ancient figures and paintings and everything tending to luxury'. Lord John Pelham Clinton (1755–81), who visited Italy in 1776–7, becoming an MP soon after his return, noted, 'I have been to see some of the beautiful palaces of this place, which infinitely exceed the ideas I had formed of them; I have just taste enough to admire a good picture, when it is pointed out to me, but not judgment enough to find it out by myself.'[25]

Genoa was also a compact city that could be seen quickly. Unlike Turin, Rome and, even more, Naples, there were no important tourist sites in the surrounding countryside. Arriving in Genoa in September 1788 on their whistle-stop tour, Charles Abbot and his friend Hugh Leycester hastened to view the city: 'We dressed immediately and set out in chairs to see the different objects pointed out to us in our plan. We continued our round till it grew dark. Dined between seven and eight in the evening, and walked afterwards to see the effect of the buildings by night.' The following morning, they finished their sightseeing: 'We went about in chairs to save ourselves from the heat and fatigue of walking.' Abbot's comment on the bright colour of Genoa captured the difficulty of interpreting everything in terms of British concepts of taste, but he added a practical note:

> The painting the outside of the houses at Genoa has certainly a very uncommon effect to an English eye. To see green, blue, and strawberry coloured walls, shocks at first sight, and with reason, as those colours resemble nothing that properly belongs to any known

9. *The Arno in Florence with the Ponte Vecchio*, by Bernardo Bellotto, who visited the city in 1742, painting six surviving canvases, five of which focus on riverside scenes.

materials for the construction of building, but perhaps it may be less exceptionable to colour their stucco with plain solid colours such as belong to durable stone, this however may be still a doubtful question of taste. What I think must be universally condemned is the painting the outside of their finest palaces with columns, cornices and entablatures in imitation of real architecture. If the reality would be proper, the imitation offends, by reminding the spectator of what is wanting, and the reproach is the stronger in a city boasting of its marble and prodigal of expense in other articles of building. As soon as this mimickery becomes partially defaced by weather, or the stucco peels, nothing can be more ragged, shabby and ridiculous. Certainly it is not for the outer decoration of their houses that the Genoese have a right to extoll Gênes le Superbe.

It is the magnificence of the natural situation of Genoa and the great abundance of immense palaces constructed upon a scale of grandeur unknown in other cities, which truly intitles it to that appellation.[26]

There were other criticisms of Genoa. In late 1729, one tourist was surprised by the liberties of married women and their male companions, the *cicisbei*, which, he felt, set a bad example for British women tourists, while Philip Yorke, later an MP and 3rd Earl of Hardwicke (1757–1834), who was there in 1778 and described the government and history of the city in his diary, observed: 'The police is ill regulated at Genoa and murderers are frequently left to escape with impunity.'[27] Francis Drake (1721–95), a fellow of Magdalen College, Oxford, who visited Genoa in 1750, complained that the Genoese defrauded strangers.

It was normal to sail from Genoa to the Tuscan ports of Lerici or Livorno (Leghorn), and thus avoid the Ligurian mountains which come down to the Gulf of Genoa. William Freeman noted, 'From Genoa the mountains to Lucca were so bad we were forced to hire a felucca which passage is very hazardous. They are built like a London wherry and the least storm oversets them. We lay every night ashore, the auberges tolerable; the wind being against us it was two days and half before we came to Viareggio.'[28] In contrast, Holroyd reported in 1764 that it took only 32 hours to sail the 120 miles from Genoa to Livorno.

With his dismantled carriage on the boat, Francis Drake went by felucca to Lerici in 1750, although, due to the weather, it was necessary to seek shelter in Portofino. He found the journey enchanting:

As we were never a mile from shore, these rugged rocks, which hang over the sea, with the falls of water, which rolled down the sides in so many natural cascades, with the goats, and other wild animals, skipping from rock to rock, afforded a most enchanting scenery. Where there was any little valley or hollow amongst the mountains, there was always a village or hamlet, with groves of oranges and olives and vineyards, that nothing can be imagined more romantic or more delightful.[29]

Travelling overland along the coast could be very difficult. Metcalfe Robinson (*c.* 1683–1736), a member of a Yorkshire gentry family, did so in 1705 because his companion disliked the sea. He found the journey 'very bad and unpleasant' as far as Massa, but the Duchy of Massa, between the republics of Genoa and Lucca, 'the fruitfullest and pleasantest I ever saw. It is generally corn, all covered with olives, walnuts, orange trees and other fruits, those that bear none of their own, have vines engrafted on them, so that it is a perfect garden'.[30]

Tourists pressed on from the Tuscan coast to Florence via Lucca and Pisa. Florence stood for art, 'a most agreeable place abounding in every species of virtu that one can wish to see, sculpture, painting and the arts carrying to the greatest perfection', in the words of William Lee in 1752.[31] The Renaissance treasures of the Uffizi were regarded as the single most important artistic site in Italy, but, in addition, the city offered a social life, not least with other tourists. While staying in the city from December 1739 until March 1741, Thomas, 1st Earl of Pomfret (1698–1753) and his wife Henrietta (*c.* 1700–61), attended *conversazioni* or balls twice weekly. Sir Horace Mann, who represented British interests from 1738 until his death in 1786, offered hospitality, not least at the *conversazioni* he held in the Palazzo Masnetti, where he lived. These were doubly attractive as Florence's more prominent married women attended. Mann played a far more active role than other British diplomats in introducing tourists to the local social and cultural life and in helping make arrangements for them. Recommendations played a major role in Florence and other cities. Arriving at the end of 1751, Colonel Henry Seymour Conway, MP (1719–95), later a secretary of state and commander-in-chief, was, for example, in part due to Horace Walpole's recommendation, given hospitality by Mann and introduced by him to Giovanni Buonavita, the Keeper of the Uffizi, with whom he was to take a 'course' on antiquities.

Evenings could be passed at the opera, when open,[32] but Florence was not without its drawbacks, one tourist complaining in 1778: 'If it were not for the resources of the Gallery and the advantages of having so good an Italian master as the Abbé Peloti [Antonio Pellori] Florence would be readily unsupportable, but with these one might pass a couple of months here with profit and pleasure. There is not a single house that receives strangers.' George, Viscount Villiers, who visited the city in 1756, thought it did not contain 'much society'.[33] In 1764, Palmerston described the Florentines as 'the lowest of the Italians'; although others enjoyed their visits, not least because, as Chapter 11 indicates, some of the women were particularly accommodating.[34]

The relative appeal of Florence to the average tourist (in so far as such a term can be employed) faded as the century proceeded, not least because of the growing determination to visit Naples and its environs on the part of tourists. This was very important to the southward reorientation of the Grand Tour discussed in the next chapter.

5. Rome and the South

There is a grandeur, a dignity, and a taste in it, far beyond all the cities I ever beheld, even in its present condition . . . were I to be gratified in a wish to see anything under Heaven, it should be to see Rome in its ancient splendour and adorned with her heroes, instead of the D—ls [Devils] incarnate she is now generally replenished with. She must have then looked like the mistress of the world . . . even now she makes a most charming figure in her ruins, which strike me more than her gorgeous churches, fine paintings and charming music; though . . . I believe St. Peter's Church to be the most beautiful fabric that ever was built on the globe.

Edward Thomas, 1750[1]

Pressing south from Florence towards Rome, many tourists felt that they had entered another Italy. Charles Abbot commented in 1788: 'The hills grow scabrous and dingy. The soil is brown and stony and the mean oil tree and stinted vine give it an appearance of poverty.' The approach to Rome across the Campagna dismayed many tourists, Abbot writing: 'Wretched, barren, sandy country all the way to the very gates of Rome – hardly an attempt to cultivate . . . We were repeatedly exclaiming all the way upon the miserable appearance of the country.'[2] Abbot also noted a change in the wildlife, with lizards appearing frequently upon the walls. This was very much a sign of a different world. The absence of zoos ensured that British tourists were not familiar with the wildlife of Italy.

The towns on the journey appealed to few tourists. Simon, 2nd Viscount Harcourt thought the women in Siena very beautiful in 1733, but those, such as Anne Miller (1741–81) and Philip Francis (1740–1818), who passed through the city in 1770 and 1772 respectively, found it disappointing, the latter commenting: 'The Piazza is trifling, and the cathedral, built of brick and white marble, looks like a church in second mourning.'

There was also a border to cross, and one that helped define a very different political realm. The Papal territory was the sole ecclesiastical state in Italy and it was a novelty for most tourists, as few had visited the ecclesiastical states in the Empire (Germany), such as the Archbishop-Electorates of Cologne, Mainz and Trier. Abbot noted:

> At Passignano we entered the Pope's territories, and by producing our Lascia Passere which had been sent us from Rome to Florence we got rid of a very troublesome custom house officer who would not take the usual bribe.

Rome was the goal of many tourists, the furthest point of numerous tours, and both reality and symbol of what was desirable about foreign travel. William Vyse spent the winter of 1769–70 there, noting that he found 'such a fund of entertainment from the many objects of curiosity at Rome'.[3] In a culture dominated by the Classics, Rome was the focus of interest, and British tourists responded accordingly. 'The town is perfectly filled with English', Sir John Fleming Leicester observed in 1786. In March 1788, John Hawkins (1761–1841) reported 'one hundred and seventeen English travellers of fashion are now in this city', his qualification 'of fashion' reflecting the social lineaments of tourism.[4]

Philip Francis had suggested in 1772 that 'to a man really curious in the polite arts, Rome alone must be an inexhaustible fund of entertainment',[5] while Charles Cadogan, who visited the city in late 1784, thought 'it is as impossible for a person to dash through it, as it is for him to fly. I stayed a full fortnight there, and only had time to get just such a general idea of the numberless wonders both of modern and ancient times, as to determine me to spend 2 or 3 months there before my return to England.' He indeed returned in 1789 for 'a regular and most interesting course of antiquities'.[6] The best-known course from 1764, provided by the antiquarian James Byres (1734–1817), lasted six weeks and was regarded as hard work. Colin Morison (1732–1810) was his major rival. Earlier, Mark Parker (*c.* 1698–1775) and James Russel (*c.* 1720–63) had been the leading antiquarian guides.

One of the attractions of Rome was that it was readily possible to find such edification. Rome, like Paris, had the facilities a tourist could wish for, but the greater importance of tourists to the economy of the city[7] helped ensure that they played a more central role there than they did in Paris. Tourists purchased paintings and antiquities, hired antiquarians, and sought artistic advice, Thomas Pelham turning to Anton Mengs in 1777.[8] Rome's cosmopolitan artistic colony made the city's marvels readily accessible to the tourist, and the range that it had to show increased the city's appeal. Rome offered Classical and Baroque sculpture, architecture and painting, and many tourists treated it as the cultural goal of their travels. As artistic and cultural interests and appreciation shifted, this helped to ensure that Rome was culturally recreated. Thus, for example, the works of Bernini, rated with Michelangelo and the Classical world at the beginning of the eighteenth century, declined in reputation. Mitford, who was in Rome in 1776, indeed commented on 'all the affectation and flutter for which he is remarkable'.[9] The Classical sites that were being excavated in the second half of the century contributed to a major re-evaluation of taste.

10. *Rome Seen on a Grand Tour*, attributed to John Frearson (*c.* 1762–1831), who set out for Italy with the painter William Theed in 1790 but travelled from Florence to Rome alone later that year when Theed was recalled to England. Frearson stayed mostly in Rome, but also visited Naples and Venice before returning to England in 1796. This picture captures the fascination with the light of the South seen in many paintings, as well as the closeness between city and countryside.

At the individual level also, tourists experienced the different cultural worlds offered by the city. Many commented on the Classical remains. Viscount Palmerston wrote in 1764:

When one first comes to Rome one is not equally struck with everything at once, but the different objects make their impressions successively at least I found it so and thought it very lucky as I should have been otherwise too much divided to have attended properly to anything. The great remains of antiquity such as the Pantheon, Coliseum etc. are what naturally attract one's admiration first and their effect depends upon the disposition of the mind and not upon any particular skill or practise in the arts. On the contrary a Person not much versed in Sculpture or Painting receives at first but a small degree of

Pleasure from Pictures and Statues compared with what they afterwards gave him when his Taste is formed and his eye has acquired by Practise the faculty of readily distinguishing Beauties and defects.[10]

Later that same year, to more lasting effect, Edward Gibbon (1737–94) was inspired by the Antique: 'It was at Rome, on the fifteenth of October 1764, as I sat musing amidst the ruins of the Capitol, while the bare-footed friars were singing Vespers in the temple of Jupiter that the idea of writing the decline and fall of the City first started to my mind.'[11]

11. *A Caprice Landscape with Ruins*, in the style of Bernardo Bellotto. These popular works, which brought ruins into prominence presented Italians as living literally in the shadows of the past.

This interest in ancient Rome did not contribute to the reputation of modern Italy. In 1764, 'regularly going the round of antiquity', Palmerston wrote:

It is deplorable to see what havoc has been made by barbarians and bigots. Little has escaped but what by its vast solidity has withstood their efforts or by being converted to some use has served the purposes of avarice. One is struck with astonishment when one considers from the size of the fragments that remain and the nicety of the workmanship what those buildings must have been.

Palmerston's cultural sensitivity was certainly affected by his visit, although his political assumptions were not shaken:

I never had any idea till I came here what a good statue was or what effect it was capable of producing . . . I am concerned to find that there are scarce any remains of buildings so old as the time of the Republic: if there were any such however plain and unornamented they would be much more interesting than the most magnificent works of slaves and tyrants.[12]

Roman society was less open to British visitors than that of Turin or Milan. Its ecclesiastical character did not provide the British (with the exception of Catholic tourists) with many points of access, and the activities of the Papal court were less interesting and approachable to the British tourists than those of the lay courts elsewhere. John, 2nd Lord Boringdon (1772–1840), from 1815 1st Earl of Morley, who was there in 1793–4, spending six weeks 'viewing different parts of the city' each morning, noted: 'There was little or no society at Rome. I waited one morning by appointment upon the Cardinal de Bernis, and saw one day the Pope and Cardinal York',[13] the last Henry (1725–1807), the younger brother of Charles Edward Stuart.

Rome did, however, also offered a range of secular entertainments, including the Carnival, which lasted twelve days, spectaculars, especially the *Girandola*, and the display seen in the show of carriages, particularly in the Piazza di Spagna. The *Girandola* was the annual fireworks at the Castel Sant' Angelo at Easter and for the festival of St Peter and St Paul. The fireworks, fired from a *girandola* (revolving wheel), created the impression that St Peter's was glowing red. The *Girandola* was seen by the painter Joseph Wright of Derby (1734–97), who witnessed the display for the inauguration of Pope Pius VI in 1775, as the counterpoint of Vesuvius.

Rome was generally avoided in the summer when it was hot, but some tourists who were there then found it bearable. On his return from Sicily in 1785, Sir James Hall Bt. (1761–1832), who was later an MP, wrote from Rome on 2 August: 'I thought it impossible to live here for the heat but I find it very tolerable especially as this is reckoned a mild summer.' In contrast, Thomas Pelham had written from Rome on 9 August 1777, 'We have a very hot air today that incapacitates one to do anything.'

Sarah Bentham was less than impressed by Rome. Like many other tourists, she was disappointed by the approach across the Campagna, writing that the city 'appeared to be situated in a desert'. Once in Rome, she found the churches magnificent, but, as with Venice, contrasted magnificence with meanness:

> I was much disappointed in seeing Rome. The streets are narrow, dirty and filthy. Even the palaces are a mixture of dirt and finery and intermixed with wretched mean houses. The largest open places in Rome are used for the sale of vegetables. The fountains are the only singular beauties . . . Rome has nothing within, nor without its walls, to make it desirable for an English person to be an inhabitant.[14]

Whatever the merits of the city, Rome was the base for trips into the surrounding countryside, in particular in search of Classical reference along the Appian Way and also to the scenic towns in the nearby hills. William Freeman noted 'the most remarkable places are Frascati and Tivoli, the first for its beautiful villas and prospects over to Rome and the sea, the second for the cascade as well as charming villas'.[15] The volcanic crater-lakes of Albano and Nemi in the Alban hills were another attraction. The appeal of the region in part stemmed from the lustre of the paintings of Claude Gellée, better known as Claude Le Lorrain (1600–82) who provided golden blues in sky and water and golden stone to light his landscapes with their timeless pastoral scenes. There were other reasons for trips into the countryside. In October 1748, James Russel wrote to his sister: 'As the vintage approaches, every one is preparing to go into the country; and really we have had the longest run of fine weather I ever saw in this place. Mr. W. and other English are at Albano; if I can possibly spare a day or two, I shall take a ramble myself towards those delightful places, as Tivoli, Frescati, Albano etc.'[16]

From Rome, many tourists pressed on to Naples, especially in the second half of the century. The route lay via Gaeta on the coast, and was not the inland route followed by the modern motorway. John Hawkins's servant, James Thoburn, described the journey in 1788: 'The country from Rome to Naples is a pleasant and good road to travel. The accommodations indifferent; the lands which are cultivated have a rich soil and very fruitful . . . much of the land lies uncultivated, as the Italians in general are a lazy, dirty set of people.'

In the spring of 1729, William Freeman found Naples 'a great seaport exceeding well peopled, streets clean and large', although the climb up Vesuvius was 'exceeding laborious'.[17] After Don Carlos, son of Philip V of Spain, conquered Naples from the Austrians in 1734, it became the capital of an independent kingdom first under him and then, after he became Charles III of Spain in 1759, under his son Ferdinand IV (r. 1759–1815). This provided tourists with a court that could be visited. Not all were moved by the majesty of kingship. Edward Thomas noted in 1750:

12. *The Bay of Naples seen from Mergellina*, i.e. from the North, by Claude-Joseph Vernet, *c.* 1740. Popular with British tourists, Vernet offers a lively view of a panorama that enchanted visitors.

No one dined with his Majesty except the Queen and two great dogs. They had their feet several times upon the table and were ready to snatch the meat from it. But two great greasy fowls were thrown on the floor to them just at the King's feet, a servant came and wiped their mouths after they had devoured them.[18]

The court was based in Naples, but in 1752 Luigi Vanvitelli began a splendid palace at Caserta to the north of the city. This was to be a Neapolitan Versailles, and included a dramatic sequence of fountains and basins closing with a monumental cascade in the gardens. There was nothing to equal the palace in Britain, and the cascade could not be matched at Versailles. George III preferred to buy the far less imposing Buckingham House than to build such a palace.

There was 'a great concourse of English gentlemen' in Naples in December 1749, ten in total,[19] a reminder of what were, by modern standards, the small numbers that created such an impression. Palmerston, who was at Naples in the winter of 1763–4, 'stayed . . . longer than I intended but I was tempted to it by the agreableness of our society and by the constant amusement which the place afforded'.[20]

The lively sun-drenched harbour views that tourists purchased from painters, especially Pietro Fabris (*fl. c.* 1756–1804), captured the attraction of the city. The combination of city and water was of great visual appeal. Fabris consolidated the visual impression of Naples when he exhibited views in London in 1768 and 1772. Naples was generally presented as more fluid and sunlit than Venice. The prospect of Genoa was favourably mentioned by some tourists, for example John, Lord Boringdon in 1793, but it did not compare to that of Naples, and was not celebrated in the pictures painted as tourist souvenirs.

Not everyone appreciated the city. Frederick, 2nd Viscount Bolingbroke (1734–87) wrote to his uncle, Lord Luxborough, in 1753,

> My stay at Naples was not very long, nor does it deserve one's attention above a fortnight or three weeks. The town is very ugly but finely situated. The natural curiosities of the place and some few inconsiderable remains of antiquity amused me for a few days; being presented at Court and dining with some of the chief persons employed the rest of my time. I then quitted that city with as little regret as I shall do every city in Italy. I still persist in thinking Italy a country worth seeing but by no means worth living in. The ignorance and pride of the people of fashion, their manners and their customs destroy all society and where there is none I shall never choose to live. I hope soon to quit this metropolis [Rome] and approach France where I may, if I take the proper methods, both amuse and improve myself.[21]

13. *The Bay of Naples seen from the Marinella*, i.e. from the South, by Claude-Joseph Vernet, *c.* 1740. This scene of bustle includes well-dressed individuals, presumably tourists.

Many tourists attended the triennial miracle when the blood of St Gennaro, Naples's patron saint, liquefied. This was generally presented as a fraud by British commentators. Yet such ceremonies were impressive. John, Lord Brudenell (1735–70), later MP and Lord Montagu of Broughton, who thrice visited Naples in 1756–8 during a tour of Italy that lasted from December 1754 until February 1760, commissioned Antonio Joli to paint a series of views including the Festival of the Four Altars.

The Neapolitans were not popular with all tourists, William Blackett (1759–1816), a member of a Yorkshire landed family who was to succeed his father as baronet, writing in 1785, 'I never saw a rougher, more unpolished people both in countenance and manners in my life. They have a vulgarity and ignorance about them which is particularly disgusting.' Francis Drake (1721–95), who was there in 1751, offered a harsh ethnographical view, employing a language that was not shared by most tourists:

> a race of puny animals that shiver at a gentle tramontane wind, and in winter when the cold constipates the pores and prevents that plentiful perspiration they have at other seasons, they appear most mean and miserable objects.

A similar approach was taken by Thoburn: 'in general the Neapolitans are a saucy, savage race of people and regard a person's life little more than a dog's . . . must be proved that a man has killed three persons before the laws will condemn him to death'.[22]

That far south, the heat was particularly notable. In his *Travels through Italy* (1766), John Northall (*c.* 1723–59), an artillery officer who had toured Italy in 1752, referred to 'the usual method of going to see Naples before the weather grew hot'. Norton Nicholls (*c.* 1742–1809) wrote in July 1772 of a city where 'the nights are so delightful and the days so hot' that no one slept at night: 'I am become a greater friend of the moon than the sun.' Two months later, Philip Francis found it hot and close, adding 'Oh, for a deluge of rain.' In contrast, in the winter of 1766–7, Dodwell Tracy (1747–68), the only son of a Gloucestershire MP, found 'the climate and air most heavenly'. William Blackett was similarly delighted in early 1785 and Brand in December 1791.[23] Naples had a milder winter climate than Rome.

Nearby tourist destinations were among the major attractions of Naples. Vesuvius was one of the great sights of the century. It was a natural phenomenon close to a city and it was therefore possible to see it without making the special expedition that most such phenomena usually required. Many tourists climbed the volcano. William Bentinck (1704–74), a member of a prominent Anglo-Dutch aristocratic family, reported to his mother:

> the climbing up is the hardest work I ever did in my life, not only the steepness, but the quantity of cinders and hot ashes, which make one fall back again above three quarters of each step one takes. There is at present a great river of fire running down which we have been up to see, but could not stay long by it because the heat is just like that of a glasshouse

and takes one's breath away; we could not neither go to the mouth, because of the quantity of large red hot stones that fly out at present. Another troublesome thing is that when one is half up, one must do the rest all out of breath, because the fire that is under one's feet hinders you from standing still an instant in the same place. The people of the country are glad to see it burn because then there is no danger of earthquakes.[24]

Vesuvius could also be viewed from a distance. Margaret Grenville, who spent the winter of 1761–2 in Naples *en route* to Constantinople where her husband was taking up his post as Ambassador, subsequently recollected:

there was a magnificent eruption at Mount Vesuvius which created two streams of lava that winded down the hill a considerable length and from our windows at night it was really a glorious sight, and perfectly answered Mr. Burke's idea of the Sublime,[25]

the last a reference to Edmund Burke's *Philosophical Inquiry into the Origin of our Ideas on the Sublime and the Beautiful* (1757). Italy could validate the new sensibility, as the frequent images of Vesuvius testified. Its natural power appeared particularly potent when presented on canvas as erupting by night. Picture collections frequently included such works, for example Giovanni Lusieri's *Mount Vesuvius by Moonlight: the Eruption of 1787* at Attingham Park.

Mary, Lady Palmerston, who visited Naples with her husband in 1792–3, saw an eruption in March 1793:

The different tints and forms of the different lavas has a most picturesque appearance and looking into the mouths of these craters you see all the different colours which are formed by the sulphurous matter . . . dark . . . the view was superb. The mountain continually throwing out red hot stones which resemble the stars of a number of rockets and the stream of lava which was considerably increased and fallen very low illuminated great part of the side of the mountain made the valley quite luminous and all dispersed over the mountain you saw light which looked like stars which were the torches of the different parties who were wandering about.[26]

Although far less dramatic, and incapable of animation, the Greek remains at Paestum south of the Amalfi peninsula became a major tourist sight. They did not rival Vesuvius, but they made Classical Greece graspable. These remains were profoundly influential for the formation of Neo-classical taste. Paestum was the Latinisation of Poseidonia, a Greek colony founded in about 600 BC by colonists from Sybaris in Calabria. The town had been abandoned under the Romans because of malaria. The building of a road across the site led to the discovery of the temples in 1746. They swiftly excited interest. The combination of the Basilica, the Temple of Neptune and the Temple of Ceres was far more impressive and

14. *The Two Great Temples at Paestum*, by John Robert Cozens (1752–97), who visited the site in November 1782 while on his second visit to Italy. Paestum was a very popular subject from the 1760s, and this contributed to the Doric revival. Cozens had gone to Italy on his second visit as draughtsman for the difficult William Beckford, but they parted in September 1782.

certainly grand than the excavations at Herculaneum and Pompeii. At the same time, the pastoral setting with grazing anlmls, cypresses and oleanders helped make Paestum seem a real version of the idyllic Classical scenes depicted by painters. Joli painted the scene in about 1758 for John, Lord Brudenell, and a large number of views were produced over the following decade. Cork models were also produced. Palmerston visited the remains in 1764:

> I was more struck with them than with anything I ever saw except the first view of Rome. They stand quite solitary upon a deserted plain by the seashore at the bottom of a large bay behind them runs the chain of the Appenines. The remains consist of the walls which are pretty entire, one of the gateways, many foundations of old buildings, and three large public edifices with all their outer columns with which they were entirely surrounded and many of the inner ones and the whole entablature standing. The largest has above 70 columns of

the Dorick order of a short and inelegant proportion, which however gives an air of grandeur and solidity and is a proof of their great antiquity. These buildings are the more curious because there are no others of that form with porticos on every side remaining in Italy except we reckon Sicily where there are some of the same kind but not so well preserved. One circumstance which often takes away half the pleasure of seeing the remains of old buildings is the number of modern ones which generally surround them often join them and are even built upon them. When one sees fine Corinthian pillars on a narrow dirty street serve to ornament a pigstye or half an ugly Gothic church tacked to half an old temple the effect of the scene is destroyed and one loses that enthusiasm which is the pleasantest companion one can carry with one to these spots. There is no mixture of this kind at Paestum and nothing but here and there a solitary cottage appears near the ruins.

To Palmerston, Paestum was exotic, and an imaginative outlier of the Orient: 'When one comes into the plain one is struck with the idea of Palmyra, Baalbeck or some of those forsaken places.' By going to Paestum, it was possible to comprehend this distant world which was becoming better known from mid-century. Palmerston also went on an excursion to Benevento, where he saw Trajan's triumphal arch.[27]

British tourists were also attracted to Naples by the social life that owed much to their own company, to the foundation of a royal court, and to the hospitality of Sir William Hamilton (1730–1815), envoy from 1764 until 1800. He entertained at the Palazzo Sessa in the city and at the Villa Angelica at the foot of Vesuvius.

The region was made more interesting by the excavations at Herculaneum and Pompeii. Covered as a result of the destructive eruption of Vesuvius in AD 79, both were excavated from the first half of the eighteenth century, although the process was slow. By 1738, the theatre of Herculaneum had been excavated. Horace Walpole (1717–97), later an MP and, eventually, 4th Earl of Orford, described the excavations there two years later. Official excavations at Pompeii, begun in 1748, were pressed from the 1760s. The theatre there was unearthed in 1764 and the Temple of Isis in 1764–6. Views produced in that decade helped spread knowledge of the excavations. These discoveries of Roman remains played a major role in the development of European taste, in part thanks to the relative inaccessibility of Classical remains across much of the Mediterranean, especially in Turkish-ruled Greece and Asia Minor.

They also led to a shift in emphasis away from the Classical sites west of Naples, particularly Solfatara, Pozzuoli, Posillipo, Baia, Lake Miseno, Cumae and Lake Avernus. The Classical Phlegrean (burning) Fields was an area made exotic and mysterious by the hot springs, steam-jets, sulphurous gases, mysterious caves and brooding craters that reflected its volcanic character. At the Solfatara, a still active volcanic area, Lord William Mandeville (1700–39), later 2nd Duke of Manchester, discovered in 1719 that 'the crust of earth upon

15. *Ruins of Pompeii*, by Jakob Philipp Hackert (1737–1807). Painted in 1799, this was commissioned by Thomas, 2nd Lord Berwick (1770–1832) who had visited Naples in 1792–4, returning there in 1797.

which one walks, is generally not above a foot thick, and wherever one pierces it, as I did in several places with my sword, there comes out a sulphurous vapour, hot enough to burn one's hands or feet, if in the way'.[28] The crater indeed had a hot surface with spitting hot mud and strong-smelling, sulphurous jets of steam. The Phlegrean Fields was also the area of the Cumaean Sibyl and the entrance to Hades, the Underworld. For some tourists, it retained a sense of mystery. Virgil, who had lived at Naples, and other Classical authors were read as sources, and tourists compared their accounts with what they saw themselves. Paintings of the region were purchased and commissioned.

The response to the new excavations varied. Joseph Spence (1699–1768), an Oxford academic who was bearleader to Henry, 9th Earl of Lincoln (1720–94), wrote of Herculaneum, which he visited in 1741, when the excavations were still very new: 'I have walked two miles about the streets of it . . . one is obliged to creep almost all the way through narrow passages

. . . with two or three smoking flambeaus before you; and I don't see anything really worth seeing, perhaps for half a mile together. It is a journey fitter for a mole than a man . . . I had much greater pleasure in seeing the collection of pictures, which had been taken out of it.' On the other hand, Spence noted the appeal of the excavations, writing in 1752 of one tourist setting off for 'Naples and the underground town'.[29] Cadogan visited the excavations in 1784–5 and wrote from Naples:

> This is also a wonderful place, or rather its environs are so. The town itself except the great street of Toledo [Via Toledo] is beastly, but the Quay (on which I live in an excellent hotel with a noble view of the Bay), Mt. Vesuvius which is all red hot every night, Portici, Pausilippum, and the rest of the towns on the sea coasts, form one of the most wonderfully delightful scenes I ever saw. The carnival is now begun, and the town full of plays, masquerades, operas, pickpockets etc.[30]

In 1772, Philip Francis planned to travel down the east coast of Italy, but he only got as far as Ancona:

> Our original intention was to have crossed the kingdom of Naples in order to avoid the Campania di Roma; but upon inquiry we found that the roads were impracticable, without posts or inns, and the people to the last degree brutal and barbarous. So we took the high road to Rome.[31]

Of the few who went further south, most travelled from the city of Naples and were interested in Classical architecture and archaeology. St George Ashe (*c.* 1698–1721) visited Apulia in the late 1710s, with George Berkeley (1685–1753) as his tutor. Berkeley, who was very impressed by the Baroque architecture of Lecce, which he attributed in part to the influence of Classical Greek culture, went on to visit Sicily, including the 'Valley of the Temples' at Agrigento.[32] John Breval (*c.* 1680–1738), who claimed to have travelled abroad on ten occasions, and who certainly accompanied George Cholmondeley (1703–70), later 3rd Earl of Cholmondeley, as bearleader in 1721 and John Crawley (1703–67) in 1725, included in his *Remarks on Several Parts of Europe* plates of Agrigento, Selinunte and Taormina which encouraged interest in Greek remains in Sicily and southern Italy. John, Lord Brudenell (1735–70) went to Paestum in 1756 and such remote sites as Agrigento (1756) and Taranto (1757). William Young (1749–1815), later an MP, visited Apulia and Calabria in 1772, before sailing to Sicily, visiting Malta, spending a month in Palermo and returning to Naples. Sir Richard Colt Hoare (1758–1838), who had inherited the Hoare banking fortune, visited Classical sites in southern Italy and Sicily in 1789–90. In 1819, Hoare published *A Classical Tour through Italy and Sicily*. One of the most successful

16. *Lake Avernus and the Island of Capri*, by Richard Wilson (1713–82), *c.* 1760. Wilson had arrived in Italy in 1750, and stayed there until 1756 or 1757, mostly in Rome, but with a visit to Naples during which he saw Lake Avernus, a site rich in Classical resonances.

works set in southern Italy, *The Castle of Otranto: A Gothic Story* (1764), a brooding mystery, was written by Horace Walpole, who visited Naples in 1740 as part of his tour, but did not, in fact, travel on to Otranto. Indeed, in 1786, when Lady Craven gave Walpole a drawing of the castle there, made the previous year by Willey Reveley (1760–99), the delighted Walpole responded, 'I did not even know that there was a castle of Otranto'. The book's descriptions of the castle and its environs are extremely sparse. In Italy, in 1784–8, Reveley travelled south from Rome in 1785, visiting Capua, Benevento, Salerno and Paestum, before travelling to the Adriatic coast where he visited Barletta, Trani, Bari, Brindisi, Lecce and Otranto.

Sicily could be reached by sea from Naples or Rome. To go there was an adventure. Distance ensured that relatively few tourists visited the island, which had a semi-civilised reputation. Messina was the last city in western Europe to have an outbreak of the plague, in 1747. Some tourists visited Sicily as part of a wider swing through the Mediterranean by sea. John, 4th Earl of Sandwich (1718–92) toured the Mediterranean by ship in 1738–9, visiting Sicily, Greece, Turkey, Rhodes, Cyprus, Egypt and Malta. He had taken a conventional tour hitherto, seeing Turin, Florence, Rome and Naples in 1737–8, and sailed in the *Cliston* from the last with his bearleader, three friends, including William Ponsonby (1704–93), later an MP and 2nd Earl of Bessborough, and a French artist, Liotard. Having sailed to Malta, Sicily, Greece and Constantinople in 1738, returning to Livorno, he sailed again to the Levant in 1739, visiting Egypt.[33]

Other tourists also sailed the Mediterranean. Towards the end of an epic journey that had taken him from Vienna through the Balkans to Constantinople, and thence to Cyprus, Crete and Greece, John Hawkins (1761–1841), in February 1788, underwent a month's quarantine at Messina on his way from Zante to Naples after his 'compleat tour of Greece'.[34] In December 1793, he travelled via Venice to Greece.

Some tourists visited Sicily as part of a less far-flung tour. Neville, 6th Lord Lovelace (*c.* 1708–36) and John King (1706–40) sailed there from Naples in 1728 on an English merchantman. John Frederick (1704–77) and Roger Kynaston (*c.* 1710–88) sailed round the island in May 1749, taking Richard Dalton (*c.* 1713–91) with them as a travelling draughtsman. Sir William Stanhope, MP (1702–72) went from Naples to Sicily in 1754. Sir Thomas Worsley (1728–68) made a six-week visit in 1766, although he left his family in Naples. On his second trip to Italy, Richard Payne Knight (1750–1824) visited Sicily in 1777. He sailed from Naples, stopped at Paestum and the Lipari islands, landed at Milazzo, toured the Classical remains at Segesta, Selinus, Agrigento, Syracuse and Taormina, climbed Etna, and sailed back to Naples from Messina. His companions, the German painter Jakob Philipp Hackert and Charles Gore, made sketches from which copies were commissioned from John Robert Cozens and Thomas Hearne. Later an MP, Knight was a Herefordshire gentleman whose family had become rich through the Shropshire iron industry, as well as a prominent Classical scholar, numismatist and connoisseur. Gore (1729–1807) was a Lincolnshire landowner who had sailed to Italy in 1773 with his wife Mary and three daughters after spending the winter of 1772–3 in Lisbon in an effort to repair her health. He was a close friend of Hackert and an amateur artist.

Charles Cadogan toured the island and climbed Etna in 1785, reaching the crater at dawn, having walked eight miles over the snow.[35] Sir James Hall (1761–1832) was also in Sicily in 1785, although he was 'stormstay'd' a week in Stromboli on the way there.[36] This probably did not bother him as he was very interested in geology, particularly the formation of volcanoes, which led him to study rocks in Italy and Sicily. Active volcanoes were not found in Britain, and were a great curiosity.

In 1792, Thomas Brand accompanied Charles, Lord Bruce (1773–1856), later an MP and eventually Marquess of Ailesbury, to Sicily. From Palermo, where they found 'great

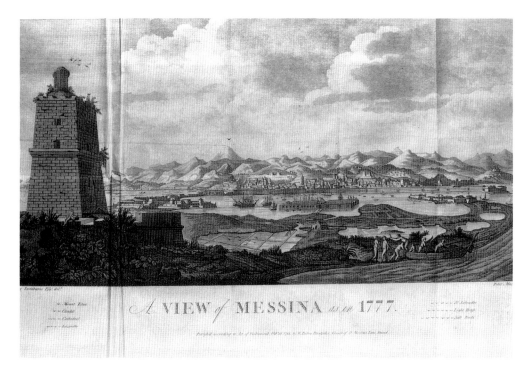

Mount Etna
Citadel
Cathedral
Lazaretto

ℒ VIEW of MESSINA as in 1777.

St Salvadore
Light Hoyse
Salt Pools

Publish'd according to Act of Parliament, Oct.r 30 1793, by T. Dobie Strahan's, Corner of S.t Martins Lane, Strand.

MONREALE.

View of AMALFY and its Coasts.

19. *View of Amalfy and its Coasts*, engraving from Swinburne's *Travels in the Two Sicilies*. Swinburne visited Paestum and Amalfi in September 1777. The Amalfi coast became popular with tourists in the nineteenth century, but earlier interest in Paestum led to visits to Amalfi.

(facing page)

17. *A View of Messina as in 1777*, engraving from Henry Swinburne's *Travels in the Two Sicilies*. Swinburne (1743–1803), the fourth son of Sir John Swinburne Bt., was a Catholic who was educated in Paris, Bordeaux and the Academy of Turin. The population of Sicily rose from one to one and a half million during the century.

18. *Monreale*, engraving from Swinburne's *Travels in the Two Sicilies*. Monreale grew up around a medieval abbey and included a majestic cathedral, impressive cloisters and terraces providing dramatic views over the Conca d'Ora (Golden Conch Shell), the plain near Palermo.

hospitality', they took a trip to the Classical remains at Segesta, before moving on towards Messina. Bruce climbed Etna. Brand was unimpressed by the quality of Sicilian roads and of accommodation outside the cities: 'There is not a wheel in the whole country, the roads are mere paths for a single mule and the few huts scattered round are as bad as Hottentot kraals'. Brand wrote of the road to Segesta: 'it is rugged and precipice or mud'. The journey out from Naples to Palermo had been good, but they were delayed at Messina by 'very contrary' winds: 'Our original intention was to have returned to Palermo and have taken the packet there but we are sick of Sicilian roads and accommodations and as the north side of the *triangle* contains nothing worth seeing we determined to take the opportunity of a Neapolitan brig of good character.'[37]

The Classical remains in Sicily received attention from artists, tourists and government alike in the late eighteenth century. The first excavations on the theatre at Syracuse were carried out in 1756, while the temple was restored in 1781, and those of Juno and Concord at Agrigento in 1787 and 1788 respectively. Many tourists, however, felt that Sicily was too much. In 1764, Palmerston explained:

> such an expedition would have disconcerted every other part of my plan and would have been very uncomfortable at that unsettled season and alone and as I must have gone by sea the whole time I should most likely have lost much of the pleasure by sickness. The port of Syracuse is I think the most interesting thing in the island but of that there are scarce any remains and as to Mount Etna and the temples and amphitheatres I flatter myself I shall have seen things as curious of the same kind before I return home.[38]

Sardinia never enjoyed the vogue that Paoli's resistance to French annexation and occupation in 1768 brought to Corsica, and it lacked important Classical sites. British warships had helped in the conquest of Sardinia in 1708, but subsequently it was largely ignored.

Greater interest in southern Italy in the second half of the century produced a limited number of guidebooks and journals. The most important was Henry Swinburne's *Travels in the Two Sicilies in the Years 1777, 1778, 1779, and 1780*, a work published in 1783–5 that described Sicily and southern Italy. Swinburne (1743–1803), the fourth son of Sir John Swinburne of Capheaton Hall, Northumberland, was a Catholic, educated in a monastic seminary in France, who was well received at the courts of Paris and Vienna. Also author of *Travels through Spain in the Years 1775 and 1776* (1779), he played an important role in spreading information about travel in southern Europe. A different perspective was offered by Patrick Brydone (1736–1818), the bearleader who accompanied William Fullarton in 1769–70, who, in 1773, published his *Tour through Sicily and Malta*. Three years later, *A Voyage to Sicily and Malta* by John Dryden (c. 1667–1703) was published; this journey had actually been made by the famous poet's second son, accompanying William Cecil, second

20. *Ruins and Figures, Outskirts of Rome near the Tomb of Cecilia Metella*, attributed to Bernardo Bellotto. This capriccio combines architectural fragments from Rome and Padua. The composition exists in many versions and copies in the style of Canaletto or Bellotto.

son of the 5th Earl of Exeter, in 1700–1. In 1792, Brian Hill's *Observations and Remarks in a Journey through Sicily and Calabria in the Year 1791* appeared.

Despite this greater interest, most tourists still turned back at Naples. The variety of sights around the city provided much to see and what was known of facilities for travellers further south provided scant encouragement for tourists.

Having turned back, tourists returned to Rome, generally again via Gaeta. Thereafter, there was a variety of routes, as there had been on the journey to Naples. If, however, as was frequently the case, tourists had travelled out via Turin, Genoa and Florence or Turin, Milan and Florence, many sought to return via Loreto and Ancona in order to see Venice. Via this route, or via Florence, it was also common to visit Bologna, whence it was possible to travel to Venice or back to Milan via Modena, Reggio, Parma and Piacenza. From Venice, it was common to return to Britain via the Mont Cenis pass, and this usually involved travelling via Padua, Vicenza, Verona and Milan. It was possible to return (as it was to go out) via passes east of the Swiss Confederation, especially the Brenner and the Tarvisio, but this was unusual.

As a result, the part of the Venetian terra firma north of the line from Venice westwards via Vicenza, received few tourists. This included Friuli and the towns of Belluno, Udine and Treviso. Other territories now part of Italy were then under German princes: the Prince-Bishop of Trent, who ruled the area around that city, the Prince-Bishop of Brixen, and the Count of Tyrol, who ruled Bolzano, Merano and the surrounding lands. This county was held by the head of the Austrian branch of the Habsburg family who, as Duke of Carniola, also ruled Trieste. The Brenner route did, however, lead to some descriptions of the region. Thus, Sarah Bentham noted in 1793 that at Bolzano she saw frogs and snails on sale in the market, and provided some description of the frogs.[39]

On the eastern shore of the Adriatic, Venice ruled Istria and most of the Dalmatian coast, including Spalato and Zara, as well as islands such as Cherso, but none of these featured in the travels of the vast majority of tourists. However, the architect Robert Adam (1728–92), at the close of a tour in Italy in 1755–7, sailed from Venice to Pola and then Spalato where he drew the ruined Roman palace.

The journey back towards Britain was frequently a rush, not least because of the determination to cross Mont Cenis before the weather deteriorated. Venice was often the last city in which tourists lingered for any length of time. Some who did so had visited the city on their way out, but for others it was their first visit. For tourists travelling north from Naples and Rome, Venice, with its Gothic architecture, ambivalence towards the Papacy, opportunities for libertinism, and otherness, was a very different environment to that which they had recently encountered. In place of the Classical world as both backdrop and foreground, came a bustling and crowded urban environment. This broke the mood between Classical Italy and the more contemporary world also seen in Milan and Turin.

The contrast cannot be pushed too hard. Verona was a major Roman site and there were other Roman remains elsewhere in northern Italy, for example at Susa. However, the shift was essentially clear. Northern Italy, under the Romans Cisalpine Gaul, lacked the Classical intensity and resonance of central and southern Italy, let alone the remains of Magna Graeca in southern Italy and Sicily. At the same time, tourists received a different impression from Venice to that of Milan and Turin. Venice was exotic in a way that the remainder of northern Italy could not hope to be.

If tourists, naturally independent, ended their journeys with different experiences, this diversity increasingly accorded with a stress on personal intellectual and emotional responses to travel that became stronger in the closing decades of the century. The standard itinerary, the guidebook and the bearleader had never shaped the perception of Italy as closely or rigidly as is sometimes suggested.

6. Accommodation

We lodged at the Bonne Femme where had quite a fine apartment furnished with yellow damask, large looking glasses etc.

Lady Spencer, Turin, 1763[1]

A major factor encouraging tourists to spend as much time as possible in large towns, and, in between, to rush from one to the next, was the nature of the accommodation available elsewhere. Small towns, villages and rural areas over most of the Continent could not offer acceptable accommodation for tourists who had been accustomed, at least since leaving their boarding-school in Britain, to a modicum of comfort. There was no international or national network of inns or hotels to match the post-roads of Europe, limited and varied as the latter were. Accommodation in Italy on any scale outside the major cities was only provided on a few of the leading routes. Even then, it was frequently found inadequate by tourists. In 1741, Henrietta, Countess of Pomfret (*c.* 1700–61), travelling with her husband and two daughters, stopped at Radicofani in Tuscany, a regular stop on the route between Rome and Siena:

We are to sleep this night at a very good or rather fine house erected by Cosimo the First for the reception of strangers. I wish he had furnished it, for it is without windows and with very few doors, the furniture just enough to sit down to supper and lie down to sleep, for which our rough and dismal journey has prepared us.[2]

Tourists were frequently disappointed by the accommodation outside the major Italian cities. Richard Creed spent a night 'in straw' at a posthouse between Siena and Livorno in May 1700, although such bedding became less common during the century. Richard Pococke was dissatisfied with the inns on his descent from the Alps into Savoy in 1734, while James Buller (1766–1827) recorded in 1788 'I slept at Tende a dirty miserable village'.[3] Andrew Mitchell found his inn at Ancona 'exceeding bad'.[4] Stopping at Piperno on his way from

Rome to Naples, Sacheverell Stevens observed 'the town affords but bad accommodations for travellers', and, on the way from Florence to Bologna, he spent a night at Scarparia where he 'found but very indifferent accommodations'.

On the same route later in the century, leaving Florence on 29 December 1776 and arriving at Bologna on 2 January 1777, Mitford wrote:

> the road has few charms in a winter's journey . . . At all times this is a tedious journey, and in the winter it is dangerous from the vast quantities of snow collected in drifts among the mountains, and often raised by sudden gusts of wind and almost overwhelming the travellers. The unexpected delays these whirlwinds of snow occasion have produced many little inns upon the road, for a traveller is often arrested in his journey, and unable to proceed a mile one way or the other, and is therefore constrained to take the first shelter he can find. Miserable, however, is this shelter, for a cold uncomfortable house with paper windows is his usual defence from the storm.[5]

The Rome–Naples route was also criticised by other tourists, Villiers writing in 1756, 'The inns and accommodations on this whole route are so very bad that it seems certainly the best way to go through without stopping.'[6] In 1764, Palmerston 'lay in a miserable hovel' at Monte Sancto.[7]

Many tourists had to seek shelter in other accommodation. In 1768, the antiquarian Charles Townley (1737–1805) was the guest of a canon of the cathedral of Salerno when he visited Paestum, but he found this unsatisfactory as there was a lack of sheets, cutlery and glasses. However unsatisfactory, such stays were necessary where there were no inns, as was often the case off the major tourist routes. Travelling round Sicily in 1790, Sir Richard Colt Hoare stayed in monasteries. Peter Beckford advised: 'Accommodation at the inns is so bad that you should order your banker to provide you a lodging before you arrive.'[8]

Bugs were a major problem throughout Italy. Thomas Brand complained of 'some distresses from abundant vermin and from the indifferent accommodations of the *castles* of Piedmont'. At Cadenabbia on Lake Como, the situation was sufficiently different to be worthy of comment: 'found an inn clean as in England, a supper that would have done honour to a [diplomatic] residence, cook and people civil and *honest*. Did you think there existed such a place in Italy?'[9] On his way from Siena to Viterbo in 1787, Adam Walker (?1731–1821) stopped the night at Aqua Pendenta and complained of 'the bugs and fleas of this filthy town'.[10]

Bugs were not the only animals with which accommodation had to be shared. In 1793, Lady Palmerston stopped at Loreto *en route* to Ancona from Rome, which reminded her of Ramsgate: 'The inn was rather uncomfortable as the horses occupied the lower apartment and the smell was excessively disagreable.'[11]

Fortunately, the situation was very different in the major Italian cities. Good accommodation was available there and, in general, tourists were satisfied by the quality. Robert

Sharp lodged 'very well' in 1702 at the Cross of Malta in Genoa. Pococke found 'a very good English public house' in Venice, and Henrietta Pomfret 'a very good inn' in Siena. Stevens was impressed by the accommodation in Naples.[12] Tourists stayed in well-established hotels, such as the Corcelli hotel near the bay in Naples. This owed much to recommendations as well as availability. Thus, having stayed the winter of 1791–2 at the Corcelli, John Villiers (1757–1838), later MP, envoy to Lisbon, and an earl, and his newly married wife Maria (*c.* 1759–1844) recommended it to his father-in-law, the banker Sir William Forbes (1739–1806), who stayed there the following winter with his wife Elizabeth and another daughter. The hotel was kept by a Frenchman, formerly butler to the Duke of Gloucester. The bookseller James Robson (1733–1806) was similarly pleased with his accommodation in Venice in 1787 at 'the *Escudo di Francia* near the Rialto . . . a very good inn and civil people. Paid dear for my apartments, being upon the Grand Canal, where the English generally go to'.[13]

In Florence, the major hotel was English-run. Charles Hadfield, a Mancunian from an affluent background, who came to Florence in about 1746, was unimpressed by what travellers were offered in Italy and, having acquired a large house, furnished it like an English hotel. He eventually had two hotels in the city, one close to Horace Mann's Palazzo Manetti. Hadfield was also an agent for acquiring works of art. After he died in 1776, his widow Isabella ran the hotels until she returned to England in 1779, when one was taken over by Megit, who had been a servant to Charles, 2nd Viscount Maynard, who visited Florence in 1778 and 1780. He was much praised by British travellers, including Charles Parker in 1782 and the Earl of Pembroke in 1785. Like Mann's hospitality, this was a little England. Watkins noted in 1787 that everything was served up in 'the English manner'. Thus, Charles Abbot and Hugh Leycester, who toured in 1788, stayed at Megit's hotel and in Margherita's hotel in Rome. At least in the 1760s, Vannini's hotel on the Piazza Soderini in Florence was considered as good as Hadfield's. Maria Vannini, the hotel keeper, was English. Her position appears to have been inherited by her son. In 1790, the painter William Theed stayed at Vannini's, 'a very capital hotel . . . board with the family at a very reasonable charge. They are agreable and sensible people and I think I shall profit by their conversation.'[14]

Abbot's mother, the recently widowed (for a second time) Sarah Bentham (d. 1809), left accounts of everywhere she stayed on the tour she made in 1793–4 with her eldest son, John Farr Abbott, and his invalid wife Mary. These provide an indication of what was deemed necessary and acceptable. At Bolzano, the Sun was 'a very clean house' and very comfortable, but with no curtains to the beds. At Trent, the Europa was full: 'we were obliged to submit to stay the night in a most miserable apartment, the windows broken, the beds and rooms so dirty that I could not venture to undress, but stretched myself on the outside of the bed with my cloathes on'.

Building, like other tourists, on experience:

We doubted whether it would not be advisable to stay the night at Volarni, but the post house accommodation appeared [so] much like those we had had at Trent, that we determined to go on to Verona, where we arrived at eleven o'clock but were kept so long at the gates before we could procure admittance, that it was two o'clock in the morning before we got to bed at our inn, *Le Due Torri*, which we found a good house, though the floors were brick, and beds without curtains, and no rooms to sit in without a bed in it, and charges extravagant . . . we found upon our beds cotton coverlets, instead of feather or down beds, which we had throughout Germany.

The rooms in the inn were large and lofty, but the furniture dirty. At Vicenza, L'Ecu de France was 'very indifferent', but, at Padua, L'Aigle d'Or was 'very comfortable', and, at Venice, the party had a 'very comfortable apartment'. Returning to L'Aigle d'Or, Sarah Bentham offered more of an explanation of what was desirable: 'we again found a most comfortable house: the floors of composition, the beds clean and good. The people very attentive and the whole much better than any we had yet seen in Italy.'

Situation was also important. Both the Three Moors in Ferrara and the Pelegrin in Bologna were comfortable but their situations were bad as they were in narrow streets, which made access difficult and affected the view. Far worse was at store at Cubillario, *en route* across the Apennines from Bologna to Florence, a route that tested most tourists:

a single house situated in the midst of high craggy mountains and it being the close of the day when we arrived it was thought advisable to stay the night, though the accommodations were bad, the floors of brick, the rooms very small with two beds in each and no curtains and the bread was black, but as we had always provided ourselves with bread, cold chicken and grapes on the days we took long journeys that we might dine in the coach or at some post house while horses were changing it now happened that we had some bread left which with our tea and some milk gave us a good supper – though the boiling water was brought us in a brown earthen pipkin, and the warming pan for the beds was only iron bars over wood embers laid into an earthen dish with a very dirty female to wait upon us but our own sheets were our comfort.

At Trent we had first found brick floors and Italian dirt which continued at Verona, Vincenza, and throughout except at Padua where the floors were a composition and the inn by far the cleanest we had seen in Italy.

Next day, they saw at Mashere 'the house we ought to have reached last night, it being the only tolerable sleeping place between Bologna and Florence; the situation delightful, the apartments decent and the people obliging'. Some tourists, such as Henry Nassau in 1732, Philip Francis in 1772 and Adam Walker in 1787, were able to make the journey sufficiently

21. *An Inn at Barletta,* by Louis Ducros, 1778. Barletta, on Apulia's Adriatic coast, was visited by very few tourists. Ducros captures the crowded bustle of the inn and the absence of privacy.

fast not to have to stop for the night, but this required both determination and luck, as a very early start, favourable posting arrangements, and good weather were all necessary.

Pressing on to Florence in 1793, Sarah Bentham's party stayed at Megit's, where they were driven upstairs by other British tourists who were already there: 'a very good apartment from which we had a view of the River Arno; but we had 72 steps to ascend to it . . . Here we first found nets put over the beds, and curtains which we had not seen since leaving Munich.' The nets were against mosquitoes.

At Livorno, as James Thoburn noted in 1788, there was also the option of staying in English-run accommodation, the London Tavern. At Siena, the Hôtel d'Angleterre proved 'a

tolerable good inn' for Sarah Bentham, but that at Radicofani was less satisfactory: 'beds
without curtains and cold and uncomfortable but cleaner than many we had slept in – a
large glass in shape like that we call a tumbler and covered like a flask with straw having a
lid or cover to it was placed by the sides of the beds for use at night'. Details of the accommodation were lacking from many accounts, and it is therefore useful to have the physicality
offered by Sarah Bentham's descriptions. Thus, at Rome, she commented on 'a very dirty
stone stair case like every other house in Italy'. However prosaic, and lacking in literary flair,
such descriptions may seem to some, they were the stuff of travel. Thoburn also commented
on every place he stayed.[15]

Sarah's second son, Charles Abbot, who made a speedy tour with his friend Hugh
Leycester in 1788, took sheets with him. It was clearly a family habit to be both concerned
about the accommodation and to comment on it. Charles criticised what was offered,
although less acerbicly than his mother was to do. For example, the Petit Turin at St Michel
on the way up to the Mont Cenis pass was 'a very clean large inn. We slept very comfortably
. . . The floors were earthen . . . the beds very good'. At Turin, 'our inn should have been the
Albergo Reale, but that being full we went to the *Bonne Femme* – where our accommodations were but indifferent'. At Novi, the Sign of the Post provided excellent rooms but was
'infamously dear', while, at Genoa, the St Marthe offered very satisfactory apartments, and
at Pisa there was 'an excellent inn'. Abbot stayed at Megit's in Florence,

> where our accommodations were very decent. Our table well served in a clean manner
> with good articles. Megit himself behaved very civilly, his intelligence accurate for all the
> common matters of the place, but not much acquainted with the houses at Florence, nor
> the circumstances of the road to Rome . . . His bill was reasonable.

En route for Rome, Abbot stayed 'in a miserable inn, no milk, and oil lamps instead of
candles', and thought it was worth noting that he could get 'clean beds' at Perugia.[16]

Compared to modern tourism, with its commercial chains and government regulation,
there was a lack of predictability and therefore more to comment on. This included many of
the factors that concern people today. Some tourists, such as Walker in Milan in 1787, were
angered by the cost.[17] An anonymous tourist complained about the three hotels in Turin in
1782, not least the absence of lavatories: 'all three seem on an equilibre as to inferiority, for
excellencies they have none'.[18] Difficulties could arise if it was impossible to get into the best
inns, as happened to George, Viscount Nuneham (1736–1809) and Thomas, 7th Viscount
Bulkeley (1752–1822) at Trieste in 1755 and 1785 respectively.[19]

Nevertheless, the wealthy British tourists in Italy rarely had problems with availability in
the major towns, although the accommodation was not always what was wanted. In Naples
in the winter of 1766–7, Dodwell Tracy (1747–68) could not get a view of the Bay as those

rooms in his inn had been taken by Lord Holland's family.[20] The situation would probably have been worse had the number of tourists approached that of those visiting Paris, but Italy remained a largely exclusive area of tourism. Most of the British tourists there were reasonably wealthy and did not share the concern about the cost of accommodation voiced by Walker or Norton Nicholls. Nicholls indeed complained that aristocratic travellers had pushed up prices.[21] As with other aspects of the practicalities of travel, the availability, cost and, in particular, quality of accommodation needs to be borne in mind when considering the tourist experience.

7. Food and Drink

In eating and drinking, tourists faced a far less predictable experience than their modern descendants. If eighteenth-century Europe was a continent of shortages of particular kinds of food, it was also one of a variety of food. This variety was both geographical and seasonal, and was primarily a result of the limited nature of refrigeration available. When food was available all year round, it was worthy of comment. Cold cellars and the use of natural ice could provide a measure of refrigeration, but this was not easy to provide and it was anyway difficult to use these techniques for the long-distance transport of food. Similarly, smoking and salting could increase the range of food available in a specific place at any one time. However, the primitive nature of transportation, both vehicles and routes, and the lack of adequate storage facilities created significant difficulties for preservation, and ensured that food distribution was localised, the reverse of the situation today for most tourists. As a result of eating locally available fare, tourists had a varied experience, and travel writers told them to anticipate regional specialities.[1] Interest in such specialities is also an important characteristic of modern travel writing, but today such dishes are not unfamiliar to most tourists.

Tourists in the eighteenth century faced two food regimes. In rural areas there was a lack of variety, and often a shortage of food, although the former was far more of a problem for tourists. In towns, especially large towns, in contrast, quantity and variety were less of a problem for those who could pay, and tourists did not usually trouble about others. However, in Naples in 1764, Palmerston noted that the situation was very different for the bulk of the population.[2]

Towns were commonly surrounded by a zone of market gardens whose productivity was enhanced by the use of night waste. As a result, vegetables, fruit and dairy products were readily available, and the first two in seasons in which they could not be obtained in Britain. In addition, as centres of consumption, towns were the markets for agricultural regions, and, as centres of communications, they were better supplied than most rural areas. Both food regimes – rural areas and towns – were affected by seasonal variations, as well as by irregular harvest and weather conditions, and by events that affected communications, such as floods and the freezing of waterways.

The contrast between the two regimes should not be pushed too hard. Crossing the Mont Cenis pass in 1776, John Mitford noted:

> among these wild mountains are to be found good bread, good butter, and good milk; three good things not to be met with in many of the more frequented inns, in the rich plains of France; good fish, flesh, and fowl, and bon vin de Montmelian, much superior to the bon vin de Bourgoyne of most of the French auberges.[3]

Conversely, there were difficulties in some towns. Henrietta, Countess of Pomfret supped badly in Ferrara in 1741, later writing, 'considering it is Italy we have supped very well at Verona'. Her dinner at Parma was very good. Anne Miller was unimpressed at Viterbo in 1771:

> our supper consisted of a soup, the chief ingredients of which were all sorts of livers and gizzards, collected from various birds, and I believe were of as various dates, sailing after each other in a muddy pool; very unlike the lake of Bolsena; broiled pigeons with oil, and a friture of livers, etc . . . You may be sure we are in no danger of a surfeit this night.

This description was printed in her *Letters*, and, like other such descriptions, invites consideration as to how far it was made for effect. At this point, Anne Miller appeared to be writing in the splenetic tone employed and made prominent by Tobias Smollett (1721–71) who recorded his stay in 1764 in his *Travels through France and Italy* (1766).

A decade after the publication of Smollett's book, the painter Thomas Jones (1742–1803), on arriving at the posthouse in Modena, found that 'after fasting all day we could get nothing for supper but a few small fish fried in oil',[4] a more factual description than that employed by Anne Miller. Charles Abbot was disappointed in 1788 with breakfast at Foligno: 'a large town, but no milk, nor loaf sugar to be had. We used fresh eggs instead of milk.'[5]

Insufficient or bad food were not the sole problems. Different cooking techniques and methods of preparation were also significant. Members of the social élite were usually familiar only with French cooking, and even that was known in just a few circles in Britain. A liking for French food was criticised by opposition newspapers, especially in the 1720s. As public eating houses played a minor role for the élite, who were, instead, used to eating in each other's houses, there was not a buoyant restaurant world to introduce the wealthy to foreign cuisine. Furthermore, this was not a culture that greatly prized the quest for the unfamiliar in cuisine.

Italian food was a novelty for most travellers. A number of shops existed in late seventeenth-century and early eighteenth-century London specialising in Italian food and drink, especially Parmesan cheese, pasta and Italian wine, but it is clear from their comments that most tourists were not familiar with Italian cuisine. The use of olive oil and garlic was particularly different, and oil was greatly disliked. In addition, meat was not prepared in the English manner with its focus on joints. In 1717, George Carpenter (*c.* 1695–1749) complained, 'all over Italy oil and garlic are put in every dish and are the chief ingredients'.[6] Peter Beckford was unimpressed by Italian meat: 'Butchers' meat is but indifferent; you must entirely forget my good Sir, the Roast Beef of Old England, for they have neither jacks nor chimneys.'[7] Beckford (?1739–1811) was a Dorset gentleman and keen hunter (thanks to family wealth from Jamaican sugar production), who became an MP and Lord Rivers, and was not only to visit Italy in 1765–6, but to live there from 1783 until 1799.

Presentation of food could be as unfamiliar as its preparation. Another obvious difference arose from the conventions and regulations relating to Lent and Fridays, and this could lead to criticism of the role and power of the Church. Tourists needed certificates to eat meat in Lent.

Anne Miller was willing to praise Italian food, if better than English, as with Piedmontese fennel, but she left her readers in no doubt of her delight when she found English dishes, as with the 'excellent British minced pies' she obtained in Florence. At Rome, she wrote:

> Our table is served rather in the English style, at least there abounds three or four homely dishes (thanks to some kind English predecessors who have taught them), such as bacon and cabbage, boiled mutton, bread-puddings, which after they have been boiled, are cut in pieces, fried and served with a wine sauce strongly spiced, etc. so don't think we are likely to starve here.[8]

The distinctive arrangements of Italian meals also attracted comment, as by Peter Beckford:

> An Italian dinner usually consists of a soup, which never fails winter and summer; a piece of bouilli; a fry of some kind or other; a ragout; and the *roti*, which, whether it be a piece of meat or a few small birds, is served up last. The soup is no better than broth, being the essence of the bouilli only, which, of course, is boiled to rags; and the roast meat being usually soaked in water before it is put to the fire, loses all its flavour . . . Raw ham, Bologna sausages, figs, and melons are eaten at the first course. Salt meat, unless it be hams and tongues, is totally unknown. No boiled leg of pork, and peas-pudding; no bubble and squeak; – vulgar dishes, it is true, but excellent notwithstanding: nor have they the *petits plats*, in which the French so much excel, to supply their places.[9]

Others wrote of the differences in individual dishes or of unknown foods. Tancred Robinson found that 'Italy abounds much with swine's flesh; they are generally fat and black; in some places they are extremely fat, thanks to chestnuts etc.',[10] on which they were fattened. Travelling through Sicily in 1788, Thomas Watkins (1761–1829) ate a 'cake of bread, whiter than any' he had hitherto come across. He also wrote that the pigeons 'in this country are so much superior to any I have ever eaten, that they seem a different kind of bird. They are as large as grouse, as fat as ortolans, and so agreable to the taste, that if some of our English epicures were to feed upon them, they would probably eat themselves to death.' Watkins's Italian servant cooked for him in Sicily. Five years later, at Padua, Sarah Bentham found 'some excellent small birds roasted for dinner, which they called thrushes – and sheeps brains fried in small pieces . . . sorrel generally made a side dish and meat pounded in a mortar and baked in a mould often appeared like a pudding and macaroni in a variety of forms'.[11]

Aside from marked regional variations in the availability of fish, fruit and wine, the availability and type of meat varied greatly. Standardised scientific breeding had not yet reduced the number of animal breeds, nor that of types of fruit, and, in addition, local traditions of preparation were strong. Remarks such as Andrew Mitchell's at Spoleto, 'Be sure you eat mutton here', or Norton Nicholls's that Sorrento was famous for veal and butter, had considerable point to them. Visiting Genoa in 1731, the Reverend John Swinton (1703–77), English chaplain at Livorno, wrote:

> The pork and mutton are very good here, but not to be compared with the beef and veal, which is certainly the finest in the world. The beef is exceeding tender, most of the cattle being drove out of Piedmont to this place, and coming over many high and rugged mountains. The fatigue which they undergo is long and gradual, which is the reason the beef is so very sweet and tender at Genoa, though it is extremely tough and hard in Piedmont. The veal is very white, sweet, juicy, and of a very delicious flavour.

Swinton also had broccoli for the first time:

> so tender and fine-tasting that no greens in England or elsewhere can come up to it. They have here likewise a sort of sprouts with a root partly in and partly above ground, which very much resembles a turnip, insomuch that many of our English people have been deceived, and bought them for turnips. They are called radici, and the chief use of them is to make soup . . . They have likewise here a sort of food which they call ravioli which is a collection of cheese, sweet herbs (to which some add flesh) and oil or butter enclosed in a sort of paste, something resembling fritters, but smaller, fried and so served up. There is a great variety of fish brought into the Fish-Market here, some having four legs like a dog, others being of a monstrous size, all which the Genoese eat.[12]

In Genoa in 1788, Charles Abbot also commented on ravioli, as well as on other dishes:

> The bread of Genoa is celebrated for its excellence. Here we eat a small fruit like a little crab apple in shape . . . it had an exquisite taste of ripe acid, like a high flavoured White Hart cherry. Ravioli is a known dish here. It looks like boiled tripe, but is made of a paste resembling maccaroni. We had some afterwards at Florence but served in a totally different manner.

Abbot preferred the Florentine type.

Such comments are worth noting alongside the more critical response to foreigners and their food in English caricatures and on the stage. Sir John Fleming Leicester, who was unimpressed by the milk in Nice in 1784, thought that Turin had 'the finest cream and the best butter in the world', which he attributed to its being surrounded by grassland. William Lee sent his father a Parmesan cheese from Milan and a liqueur from Venice to moisten it.[13]

Local variety was also the rule with drink. It was easier to move beer, water, wine and spirits without significant loss of quality than it was to move most foodstuffs. However, the technology for bottling and transporting liquids was relatively unsophisticated, and financial considerations only justified local distribution, except for expensive and well-known drinks, such as brandy, champagne, claret and port. As a result, tourists frequently encountered wines that were new to them, and were often delighted by the quality, although the critical Francis Drake claimed that they were worse than those both of the ancients and of France, his explanation contributing to the general impression of decline: 'either for want of proper culture or that the vines are degenerated'.[14] According to Abbot:

> The Florence wine which is esteemed the best in Italy is only fit for desserts. It partakes of that aigre-doux taste, which is supposed to proceed from the growth of their vines to unequal heights, by which the grapes ripen at different times and the ripe and unripe are mixed together when gathered at the vintage.[15]

Nevertheless, local Italian wines aroused particular interest and their quality, variety, quantity and cost were praised by many tourists, including Beckford, Carpenter, Garmston, Robert Gray, Sacheverell Stevens and Walker. As most tourists had travelled to Italy through France or southern Germany or Austria, they were used to encountering local wines, but that did not greatly lessen the appeal of Italian wines. Swinton wrote from Genoa in 1731:

> The common wine that is drunk here and throughout the territories of this republic is called Vino Bruscio ie tart or sharp wine. It is of an amber colour, not unlike English beer, though some is of so deep a colour that it inclines to a red. Its tartness is very agreable, and in my opinion the taste of it is not unlike that of Herefordshire cider. It is looked upon here as a wholesome wine, and I must confess that it has agreed perfectly with me though I have drunk pretty plentifully of it.

At Montefiascone in 1756, Villiers had 'some excellent wine of the country, known by the name of the est'. Near Etna, Watkins drank 'a flask of wine that was a perfect cordial', and he wrote of Syracuse: 'the environs of the city produce thirteen kinds of excellent muscadine wines; all of which we had before us every day at dinner'.[16] Such were the pleasures of travel. Other drinks were also welcome. Francis Drake noted the use of snow in Naples in the making of sherbet and lemonade, and also mixed with fruit juices.[17]

Wine, like food, could be transported in carriages, so as to permit meals *en route*. This was particularly necessary as it was common to set off very early in the morning, ensuring that a break for breakfast had to be made on the journey. It was also useful to have food for the stops arising from obtaining fresh horses or waiting for ferries. Thus, crossing the Tesino in June 1734, Richard Pococke noted, 'here, waiting for the boat, we breakfasted on the bank of Bologna sausages, and drank the clear river water'. By Lake Trasimeno in 1788, Charles Abbot and Hugh Leycester 'gathered grapes from the road side and dined in our chaise upon the field of battle where Hannibal defeated the Romans'.[18]

British food and drink were missed. In 1750, James Russel, then in Rome, asked for 'a good large Cheshire cheese'.[19] It was, however, possible to encounter some echoes of Britain. Although not at the leading inn, Charles Abbot noted in Turin in 1788: 'supped at our inn and were surprised to find Staffordshire plates and dishes instead of the ordinary earthenware of the country'.[20] Nevertheless, the length of absence forced tourists to grow accustomed to a very unfamiliar cuisine. Food and drink contributed greatly to the foreignness of the Grand Tour.

8. Transport

I was not hurried with the alarming rapidity of Italian postillions nor shut up in a
close cramp carriage but mounted on a safe easy horse.

Thomas Brand, excursion to Lakes Como and Maggiore, 1793[1]

Transport again can appear a prosaic subject, and one that offers little opportunity for literary
flair on the part of travellers or later scholars. It would, however, be very mistaken not to
devote considerable space to the issue. Travelling took up much of the time of tourists, far
more so than for their modern counterparts who can travel far faster than the speed of a
horse-pulled carriage or a wind-driven boat. Furthermore, although modern transport
systems are affected by problems, not least labour difficulties and operating breakdowns, they
are designed to work in a more predictable fashion than their eighteenth-century predecessors: the latter required frequent stops for fresh horses or, at sea, were dependent on the
wind. Furthermore, eighteenth-century travellers usually did not travel by night.

The details of transport also provided much of the experience of travel as well as many of
the experiences of tourists. This was a matter not only of particular sounds, smells and
sights, but also of the physicality of individual sites and regions. This physicality owed much
to the impact of these sites and regions on transport routes, specifically through road conditions. The bulk of tourist travel was by road, and a major difference between eighteenth-
century and modern comment on European travel was the stress in the former on road
conditions. A wealth of information about these can be found in tourist accounts and in
those of other travellers, such as diplomats. The vulnerability of coaches, the relative
frequency with which they broke down, and the limited comfort of passengers on poor road
surfaces, made the state of the roads of considerable importance. Tourists appear on the
whole to have borne the situation phlegmatically. The major effect of the nature of the roads
was to encourage further the tendency for tourists to travel along a relatively limited number
of routes.

First, they had to cross the Alps by routes likely to be affected by the weather. Approaching the Mont Cenis pass in 1764, John Holroyd noted: 'torrents from the mountain occasioned by the sudden melting of the snow had done much mischief, many of the bridges which had been broken down were but just repaired'. However, he added a valuable and pertinent comparison, 'The inns and roads through these Alps though the former in general are very bad are full as good as those in North Wales.'[2] Thus, travelling in what was seen as the most arduous section of the Italian part of the Grand Tour was presented as not dissimilar in its convenience to that in the more marginal parts of the British Isles.

Thereafter, travelling in northern Italy was also not without its problems. In September 1776, John Mitford found the roads bad between Turin and Novara, because the rivers were often changing course, so that 'the traveller is continually dashing through water, or dancing in a ferry boat'. Mitford wrote of Novi:

> This spot of junction of the Sardinian and Genoese dominions is often dangerous to the benighted traveller. The neighbouring mountains afford a shelter for robbers, and the difference of government renders the police of these borders very inefficient for the purposes of extirpating these banditti. Possibly a traveller may never reach this place of danger; for about two miles from Tortona the road necessarily passes the Scrivia. This rapid stream is very uncertain in its motions. Sometimes merely a swift rivulet, it is passed without difficulty. At other times a vast torrent, no one dares attempt to stem it. These changes are so sudden that the unwary often fall a sacrifice to this treacherous stream, which, appearing shallow, invites the inexperienced to venture the ford, and then overwhelms them with its flood of waters or sinks them in its quicksands.[3]

The reliance of road conditions on the weather was a reiterated theme. Road surfaces were far more varied than is the case today. Instead, there was a close dependence on geology, soil, drainage and terrain. Thus, rain on poorly drained clay soils made road surfaces intractable. The clay became gluey, and ruts filled with rain. Progress was slow and uncomfortable. Villiers was well aware of the role of the soil. Passing the Tagliamento, *en route* from Trieste to Venice in 1754, he noted: 'This is a very tedious stage on account of the deep sand and gravel.' From the Piave to Treviso 'the road is narrow but like an English turnpike road . . . From thence to Mestre is a paved causeway, but very ill kept up.'

Villiers subsequently commented on the roads from Padua to Vicenza – 'the worst I think I almost ever met with, without their being dangerous'; and on to Verona – 'reasonably good'; before linking the pleasure of varied terrain to the quality of the roads, and noting that the most fertile soil was not only less interesting to traverse but also harder. Travelling from Verona to Mantua, he observed a great difference in the country as soon as I came out of Verona, from that on the side towards Vicenza; the soil was not so good, but the hills and variety of ground made the prospect more agreeable. In the two first posts the road was reasonably good, but the last to Mantua, it was excessively bad, the soils extreamly fertile and productive of everything, and the country quite like Friuli, flat but richer . . . At Borgoforte I was obliged to go on with oxen instead of horses on account of the deepness of the soil . . . It was almost one continual slough from thence quite to Guastalla, so that . . . I did not get there until some hours after dark . . . The road went for a great part of the way on high, broad causeways like Roman roads, but not paved, and a deep strong clay.

In contrast, in the Duchy of Modena, the road improved as the soil was a 'light gravel'.[4]

Tourist complaints about the major routes in northern Italy, those from Turin to both Genoa and Parma, and from Milan via Parma to Bologna, were limited. Indeed, the road system was best in Piedmont and Lombardy, both territories with reasonably effective government. The Venetian system was not regarded in as favourable a light, and this offered a perspective on the comparative values of monarchies and republics that was different from that of abstract theorising. Having crossed the terra firma *en route* from Innsbruck, via Bergamo, to Milan in 1792, Brand wrote, 'We have paid the usual tribute to Venetian roads that of broken carriages and broken *commandments*. A *curse* on all republics say I.'[5]

There were also complaints about some other roads in north Italy. Stevens thought the Bologna–Ferrara road 'generally very bad' and Andrew Mitchell wrote of it in 1732 'very bad when it has rained . . . if one days raining in summer was enough to spoil the roads, what must they be in the winter?'[6] 'A journey in miserable roads and bad weather from Venice' to Milan took Norton Nicholls nine days in November 1772; and Lady Craven thought it too easy to fall off the causeway on that from Cento to Ferrara. She also complained about the slowness of the journey caused by the clay soil. This was certainly an issue in the Po Valley. The Bologna–Ferrara road ran over poorly drained clay. An anonymous tourist left Milan for Piacenza, generally a good road, on 3 December 1782, 'with three horses and bribery to take so few, but found the road so deep, that we made a virtue of necessity the third post, and acquiesced to taking four horses which the Postmaster insisted on'. Five years later, Richard Garmston complained about the road from Bergamo to Verona.[7]

In general, however, tourists praised the quality of north Italian roads, which were indeed better than those further south. Richard Pococke was unhappy about the road west from Brescia, but noted that it was rare for him to be thus dissatisfied. Mitchell described the road from Voghera to Tortona as 'excellent', and Thompson praised that from Modena to Bologna.[8]

Further south, there was a deterioration in quality both of major and of minor roads. This reflected more mountainous terrain, the relative poverty of these areas, and the limited effectiveness of their governments. However, some efforts were made to improve roads near Naples after the Bourbons acquired the kingdom in 1734, and this helped tourists between Rome and Naples, who were able, as a result, to travel rather speedily.

Opinions of the Apennine roads varied. Sir Francis Head was very unimpressed by the Bologna–Florence road in 1723, and Sacheverell Stevens thought that the best way to travel it was 'in a litter', as the mountainous road was bad for wheeled carriages. On the other hand, John, 5th Earl of Cork and Orrery (1707–62), who travelled in Tuscany in 1754–5, praised the road.[9] Travelling from Siena to Rome in 1741, Lady Pomfret complained of a 'rough and dismal journey . . . obliged to get out and walk several times for fear of breaking our necks',[10] a reference to the hazards of travelling downhill. Stevens had noted of the same road, two years earlier, that rain and snow affected its quality.[11]

The Tuscan roads were certainly not as good as those in Lombardy, but those in the Papal States were regarded as far worse. Philip Yorke, entering the Papal States from Tuscany in 1778, 'soon began to find that everything changed for the worse, for though they forced us to take six horses at Centeno we waited an hour and an half at the bottom of a hill without being able to get up. Two oxen which happened to be passing by were harnessed to the chaise but had no effect until a little pony was sent for from Acquapendente which drew the carriage up the hill.'[12]

A major problem affecting road travel in Italy was the need to cross rivers, many of which flooded during the spring thaw and the autumn rains. Furthermore, there were very few bridges. As was the case in most of Europe, rivers were usually crossed by ferries or fords which were difficult to operate or use if the river was in spate. Pococke found the system working well on his way from Milan to Turin in 1734:

> before we came to Novara we passed over the Tessino, very rapid . . . a horse drew the boat half a mile up the river, then being carried down in crossing a horse drew us up again to the landing place . . . a boat goes down again to the landing place . . . a boat goes down 12 miles an hour without rowing.

At Alessandria in 1788, Charles Abbot was 'ferried across the Tanaro in a large double boat'. Mitchell was less fortunate crossing the Trebia near Piacenza, 'by reason of a very small quantity of rain that had fallen the day before'. The river had a very wide channel and followed a varying course. There was no bridge, as was the case with most of the rivers that flowed from the Apennines to the Lombard plain. Villiers was ferried across the Panaro between Modena and Bologna. Abbot crossed the beds of the tributaries of the Arno *en route* from Florence to Arezzo. Mitchell also observed that many Apennine roads followed river beds and, after it had rained, often could not be used. This again was a common situation in Italy.

The overflowing of the rain-swollen Tiber affected Henry, 9th Earl of Lincoln (1720–94) on his journey from Florence to Rome in late 1740. Sneyd set out from Florence to Bologna in 1755, but had to turn back because rain swelled a stream; while an anonymous traveller from Turin to Vercelli in late November 1782, wrote: 'The road very good as is generally the case in his Sardinian Majesty's dominions; but two or three large rivers to pass which if flooded may give delay, or what is worse than delay its general companion danger.' Indeed, in 1727, William Freeman had been 'forced to shift the road' between Susa and Turin, the road 'being in some places washed away'. In December 1785, Lady Craven found that the ferryman was unwilling to cross the Trevisa because of storms. Eighteen months later, Robert, Viscount Belgrave (1767–1845), later an MP, 2nd Earl Grosvenor and 1st Marquess of Westminster, travelled from Trieste to Venice:

> The weather was so bad that we were obliged to give up all thoughts of going by sea, so continued our journey on a road, which was very tolerably good, except where the rivers Tagliamento and Piava had overflowed their banks, and almost deluged the neighbouring country, which delayed us considerably.[13]

Villiers had more luck on that route in November 1754, ferrying over the Isorno, Tagliamento and two branches of the Piave: 'the stream is very rapid and full of whirlpools'. Flooding on the Milan–Turin road could lead to detours as far as Lake Maggiore, while, in 1791, Sir Richard Colt Hoare had to make long detours on his tour round Sicily in order to cross rivers swollen by heavy rains.[14]

All too frequently, the alternative to heavy rains and their effects were the dusty roads of the summer. These could throw up choking clouds of dust that were very unpleasant for tourists. In addition, travel in the summer could be uncomfortable as it was difficult to lessen the impact of heat. British tourists were unaccustomed to such temperatures. Travelling from Viareggio to Pisa in mid-September 1788, Charles Abbot forded the Serchio and noted: 'The postilions frequently got off their horses to scrape off the sweat with their knives.'[15]

There were improvements to the road system during the century. Mitford travelled from Campomorone to Genoa in 1776 along a new road that was protected from the River Polavera, and Abbot noted a good new road being built to replace the sandy one near Castello d'Annone in 1788.[16] However, there was nothing to match the process of improvement in Britain. This reflected the absence of the combination of entrepreneurial energy, commercial activity and property rights that lay behind the turnpike boom. By 1750, a sizeable network of new turnpikes, radiating from London, had been created, and by 1770, when there were 15,000 miles of turnpikes in England, and a network radiated from major provincial centres, most of England was within 12.5 miles of one. In Ireland, an Act of 1729 established turnpike trusts, a number of new arterial routes were constructed in the 1730s–50s, and, after a Road Act of 1765, there was a major expansion and improvement of the rural road network. In England from the mid-eighteenth century, the road system was further enhanced by a marked increase in the number of bridges. Stone bridges replaced wooden ones and ferries, improving the load-bearing capacity and reliability of the system. Existing bridges were widened, and new and wider bridges erected with large spans.

The contrast with Italy was readily apparent. In Britain, local charge-levying bodies, authorised by Parliament and drawing on the strength of the local economy, in both investment capital and likely return, provided a degree of dynamism that was absent in Italy, and this contrast became more apparent during the century as the Italians failed to match the British in road construction.

Few tourists travelled on roads in southern Italy aside from the road between Rome and Naples, and most found this route of a reasonable standard. Elsewhere, the situation was less promising. In 1728, William Freeman returned to Rome from Naples by a side route in order to see Monte Cassino, 'which well paid the fatigue of bad roads and no lodging . . . it is large and magnificent and the church finer than any at Rome or Naples which to find in such a miserable country makes it still more surprising'.[17] Philip Yorke, who went from Naples to see the triumphal arch of Trajan in Benevento in 1779, commented: 'the road is for a great part of the way exceedingly bad, and in many places scarcely passable for a carriage'.[18] Seven years later, Sir William Hamilton, the envoy in Naples, reported on the 'want of communication from one province to another' in the kingdom of Naples: 'in winter the roads are impassable and scarcely passable in summer, even on horseback; in most of the provinces in this kingdom, and in Sicily, except in the city of Palermo, wheeled carriages are unknown'.[19] Travel depended on mules.

Most tourists, however, did not tour that far afield. Instead, they travelled in areas where the roads were better. They were, indeed, praised, although the failure to travel all over Italy made this necessarily selective and misleading. Swinton observed that the roads 'almost all over Italy' were good. Walker was very impressed by the roads from Ferrara to Bologna, Rimini to Fano, Siena to Florence, and Bologna to Milan. He claimed that the road near Reggio was 'as good as our best turnpikes'.[20] There were complaints, but no one was put off a trip by the state of Italian roads.

River transport was far less common than in France or the United Provinces (Netherlands). There was no equivalent to the Saône, Rhône and Canal du Midi as tourist routes. Few Italian rivers had been canalised, and many suffered from rocks, shoals or shallows. Irrespective of the state of the waterway, canal and river transport was a slow and inflexible means of communication. In addition, it was frequently interrupted by drought or flood, while it was difficult to travel on many rivers against the direction of the current.

The river that was used most frequently in Italy was the Brenta from Padua to Venice, a route that satisfied most tourists who took it. William Lee made the journey in 1753: 'the number of the country houses and the beauty of the country on each side of the river made

22. *Venetian Postal-boat (Il burchiello)*, by Giandomenico Tiepolo. The absence of a causeway to Venice obliged tourists to rely on boats with all the unpredictability that that entailed.

our little voyage very agreeable. When I came in sight of this great city I never was more surprised in my life. At a distance the whole town appears to be built in the sea.' Taking the boat with three friends in 1787, James Robson recorded that it took eight hours with one horse and, with everything included, cost £6.[21] The journey proved a pleasant one for Leonard Chappelow, Charles Shard, Bertie and Ann Greatheed, and Gabriel and Hester Piozzi on 8 May 1786, helped by music, cold chicken and Cyprus wine.

Not everyone, however, took this route to or from Venice. Villiers, instead, in 1755 took a barge to Venice from Mestre, 'a dirty shabby looking village', but

after we left the canal and got out to open sea, the wind was so strong that we lost our oars two or three times and were hurried down beyond the proper place of entering into Venice, so that we were obliged to go in where the wind would let us. This delayed us so much that it was quite dark, and the appearance of the town was not so strikingly pleasing as I expected.[22]

Travelling in Italy could also involve short voyages by sea. There were few very short trips, but it was possible to sail to the islands in the Bay of Naples, and a few tourists, like Villiers in 1756, coasted along the shore of the Bay to Baia rather than going overland. Other voyages were designed to avoid longer overland routes, rather than to see particular sites. In February 1721, George, Viscount Parker (*c.* 1697–1764), later an MP and an earl, wrote from

23. *James Caulfield, 4th Viscount Charlemont, later 1st Earl of Charlemont,* by Pompeo Batoni, *c.* 1753–6. Charlemont (1728–99) arrived in Italy in 1747, enrolling at the Royal Academy in Turin for a year. In 1748–9, he pressed on to visit Bologna, Rome and Naples, before sailing from Livorno to Messina and the Eastern Mediterranean. Returning to Rome in 1750, Charlemont stayed in Italy until late 1754.

Venice to his father, the 1st Earl of Macclesfield, 'The roads between this place and Ravenna being most extraordinarily bad, we determined to go to that place by water, and have been obliged to stay here longer than we intended by the bad weather.' John Holroyd had a pleasant journey from Genoa to Livorno in 1764:

> A felucca is a large sort of open boat which makes use of sails and oars. There was an awning to protect us from the sun and I had a good bench for a bed during the night. The expedition was very pleasant as we went close to the coast our Genoese boatmen having a very becoming bashfulness as to meeting the corsairs at sea.[23]

It was also possible to sleep in their carriage if tourists took it with them on the felucca.

An increasing number of tourists took longer voyages as part of their tour to Italy, although this number remained a distinct minority. Sir Edward Gascoigne (1697–1750) sailed from Naples to Livorno in 1725 as part of a tour of Italy that was otherwise on land.

Venice to his father, the 1st Earl of Macclesfield, 'The roads between this place and Ravenna being most extraordinarily bad, we determined to go to that place by water, and have been obliged to stay here longer than we intended by the bad weather.' John Holroyd had a pleasant journey from Genoa to Livorno in 1764:

A felucca is a large sort of open boat which makes use of sails and oars. There was an awning to protect us from the sun and I had a good bench for a bed during the night. The expedition was very pleasant as we went close to the coast our Genoese boatmen having a

24. *A Post-House near Florence*, by William Marlow, *c.* 1770. Marlow (1740–1813) visited Italy in 1765–6, producing a large number of sketches that were the bases of pen and ink drawings used by patrons when ordering versions in watercolours and oils.

Few, however, sailed further south down the Adriatic from Venice than Ravenna: the Po delta could be readily circumvented by travelling through towns thought worth visiting – Padua, Ferrara and Bologna, the coast road from Rimini to Ancona was good, and there were disadvantages to sailing. Philip Francis, who did take to the water, noted in 1772:

> embarked [at Venice] on board a Roman trading vessel bound to Ancona . . . passed the night in a hogsty (which the captain called his cabin) on a mattress, in the utmost misery. The vessel full of goods and stinking passengers. Calms or contrary winds all night . . . continuance of misery. Godfrey eating, Francis spewing,[24]

the last a reminder of the variety of tourist responses. The Adriatic coast of southern Italy was toured by very few. Facilities for tourists were scarce and there were no well-known sites south of Ancona. Apulia remained part of unknown Italy as far as most tourists were concerned.

There was no alternative to sailing if tourists wished to visit Sicily. In 1792, Lord Bruce and Thomas Brand

> had a most prosperous sail of four nights and three days and a half cross Hesperian seas from Naples to Palermo. You will conclude that it was nearly a perfect calm – indeed it was much fitter for the revels of Amphitrite and her maids of honour than for any mortal expedition – I saw a few porpoises which I suppose are the Dolphins of the ancients but not a Nereid or Triton . . . The Sicilian packets are the most convenient things you can imagine. Each passenger has his cabin – they have a good dining room and the captains of both of them have had an English marine education.[25]

The Classical reference in this description was a typical flourish.

Tourists could hire vehicles or use the transport available to the local inhabitants. Or many took their own carriages, particularly later in the eighteenth century, but most did not do so and preferred to hire them on the Continent once they had crossed from Dover, often at Dessein's, the leading inn at Calais. The carriages were to be returned at the end of the tour. These carriages had to be dismantled in order to be carried across the Mont Cenis pass. Alternatively, carriages could be bought in France or Italy or hired for shorter stretches of a trip. Second-hand carriage buying and the hiring of carriages were normal practice in Britain, and many coach builders there ran repair and hire businesses as much as manufacturing businesses.

Many tourists were impressed by what they bought or hired. Edward Thomas was very pleased with the second-hand carriage, lined with flowered velvet and with very handsome glass, that he bought at Genoa for 34 sequins. It 'thundered over the mountains of Genoa, as well as the vast rocks and uneven roads between Bologna and Florence without the least damage . . . I never was carried so comfortably or was more in love with any other carriage'.[26]

James Robson was impressed by the carriage provided by 'our old Voiturino' to take his party from Milan to Parma in 1787: 'His carriage was quite an English post coach, with glass windows and blinds open all round, proper for the climate, as well as commodious for four.'[27]

Whatever the means employed to obtain a carriage, it was necessary to hire coachmen and to rely on the system of posting, by which fresh horses could be obtained at the posthouses that were situated at regular intervals along major routes, or, failing that, hire a set of horses for a specific journey. The quality of posting – the availability of horses, and the cost and the speed with which the horses could be changed – varied greatly and was of major concern to tourists. The number of post-horses was often inadequate. Yorke recorded in 1778: 'set out from Lucca immediately after the Ball in order to be the first on the road, without which precaution we should have been stopped for want of horses, the number of carriages that were going that day to Florence'. *En route* from Turin in 1763, Lady Spencer did not reach Milan until 'it was quite dark' as she 'had very bad post horses'. In 1788, Charles Abbot noted, 'Although three days in general suffice for the journey from Florence to Rome, we were delayed for want of post-horses between Florence and Perugia and did not reach Rome till the fourth day ... waiting at the post houses'. Sir Richard Colt Hoare was similarly unimpressed with the availability of sufficient post-horses both on that route and on the one from Lyons to Turin.[28] Edward Thomas wrote from Florence in 1750,

> Though I have a chaise of my own, I find it the most convenient, as well as cheapest, way to hire horses is a voiturino, whom I agree with to maintain me on the road the whole journey. I did this from Milan to this place for 15 sequins, and had I travelled post it would have cost me above 40 ... I only travelled post from Genoa to Milan and it cost me near 14 sequins; for postage runs higher there than anywhere else, and I was not only abominably cheated by the postilions and plagued, but also imposed on at the inns, as most of the English are.[29]

Judging from other comments, this does appear to have been the case. On the final part of his journey from Trieste to Venice, in 1754, Villiers found 'the posts very indifferently supplied and the postilions insolent and never satisfied'.[30] Furthermore, reiterated complaints and warnings led tourists to expect that they would be cheated.

In Italy, the price of posting varied by principality, being especially expensive in the Papal States. Travelling from Milan to Florence in 1790, Brand was dissuaded from the new road from Modena to Pistoia and Lucca, in part because he was told 'that the posts were ill served and the accommodation very bad', but he was not satisfied with the alternative he chose via Bologna, which was in the Papal States:

> Nothing can exceed the ill behaviour both of men and horses at the posts between Bologna and Florence. *Sa Sainteté* [the Pope] had certainly some Jewish ideas of retaliation and

thinks it but right that as he gives us one tremendous annual curse, he should receive thousands of daily maledictions from all those unfortunate heretics who travel through his patrimony and territories.[31]

Conversely, Swinton praised the posting system in Italy, and the resulting ease and speed of travelling, although he was extrapolating from his own limited experience in Tuscany.[32]

Tourists rode on horseback on excursions where carriages were not suitable, for example to see the Marmore waterfall east of Terni. However, the same problem of availability occurred, as Garmston noted in 1787: 'There were no horses to be had at Narni, and therefore we were obliged to stop whilst the horses we brought from Terni ate their oats.'[33] Tourists sometimes had to rely upon mules, either to ride upon or to pull their carriages. Walker stressed the advantages of the mules used to pull his coach between Viterbo and Siena in 1787:

> Our mules held out very well; they will travel for twelve hours together without a bait; but this we did not suffer. Their pace is but slow; but then it is all alike, uphill or down, rough and smooth. . .When we arrive at the post, the driver takes them into an open place, spreads a little straw; the mules then lie down, and begin to tumble over their backs, in a diverting manner, for several minutes. They then get up, shake themselves, and, after a small feed, are as fresh as the hour they set out. It is an excellent animal, and so sure-footed, that I find myself much more at my ease then when horses are in the shafts.[34]

Invaluable as mules might be in mountainous regions and difficult terrain, not least because they did not require frequent stops for food,[35] their lack of speed was a problem, and most tourists preferred not to rely upon them. In addition, travel by mule lacked the appeal and image of horseback riding. *En route* from Cadenabbia on Lake Como to Porlezza on Lake Lugano in 1791, Brand and Lord Bruce, 'for want of horses were obliged to mount asses and mules and for want of saddles, sacks of hay'.[36] It might also be necessary to add oxen to the horses in order to pull carriages up steep inclines, as happened to Charles Abbot near Assisi in 1788. Francis recorded: 'dragged up to Pimperno by four buffalos'.[37]

The pleasantness of travel was closely associated with carriages proceeding at speed. This was not greatly impeded by other vehicles. Tourists rarely complained about traffic density. Instead, as Abbot noted in 1788, 'we were surprised at not meeting more than two or three carriages all the way from Mount Cenis into the very gates of Turin'.[38] Occasionally, travellers complained about the speed being too great, which will not surprise modern travellers in Italy. Brand referred, in 1793, to the 'alarming rapidity of Italian postilions', which led him to prefer riding himself.[39]

However, in general, complaints about speed related to slowness. This was frequently a matter of tired or 'bad' horses.[40] It led some tourists to make their own arrangements. In

Turin in 1787, *en route* for Venice, Garmston bought a carriage 'for I found from experience there was no travelling comfortably in Italy without a carriage of my own'. The alternative, in going post with *voituriers*, was, he claimed, 'to travel only 30 miles a day, from three o'clock in the morning'. This was not the limit to Garmston's concerns. He was worried about the care of the horses and their likely response:

> The horses in general are vicious in Italy, being seldom cut or broke properly. When you set off from an inn the staliere gets a large stick and lays it over the horses' rumps most violently, for two or three hundred yards, or they would not go at all. They broke my chaise twice, by kicking very high, and there is great danger of being overturned also.[41]

Whatever the region or means of transport, tourists faced several problems in common. Exposure to the elements made transport inconvenient and, in some circumstances, miserable. High winds and heavy rainfall were particular problems. In addition, many tourists had quarrels, over costs or delays, with postilions, drivers and postmasters. Some found them fraudulent; others simply troublesome. Lord John Pelham Clinton (1755–81) was glad when he reached Turin in 1776, 'as the voituriers had entirely exhausted my patience by their slow method of travelling'.[42]

The response by tourists to the problems posed by Italian routes and transport in part depended on their earlier experience. If they came via Germany then they were used to less reliable transport and worse roads than if their route had been through France, where, indeed, the diligence offered public transport by coach, which was not an option in Italy. Whatever its difficulties, however, transport in Italy was not so bad as to discourage tourism.

9.   Cost and Finance

Cost was one of the principal heads of the attack on tourism, and it was possibly the major topic of the printed criticism, especially in the latter half of the century when Jacobitism had largely ceased to be an issue and the sense of threat posed by Catholicism had receded. No official statistics of total cost were kept, and in assessing the cost it is necessary to consider the accounts of individual tourists.

Cost and finance were issues that played a major role in the correspondence of most tourists. Either they were young and dependent on relatives in Britain to arrange their finances and authorise their expenditure, or they were adult and concerned to arrange their financial affairs with British correspondents. Tourist correspondence and journals provide a mass of information, but it is often fragmentary. Although many tourists kept accounts at some stage, few kept complete sets of accounts for their whole trip or, rather, only a relatively small number have survived.

The cost structure of an eighteenth-century tour was very different to that of the typical modern one, if only because it generally lasted much longer. Allowances were frequently expressed in terms of so much per month, or even year, and when tourists arrived at cities where they intended to spend some time, such as Rome or Naples, they tended to strike a bargain for a period of weeks or months for their accommodation, and frequently, also, for their food as part of the same bargain. There was often a clear difference in price between accommodation and food over a long period and for shorter spans.

This was related to another difference, between prices agreed in advance, frequently by bargaining, and those which had not been. The latter were often substantially higher. Tourists who were travelling had less opportunity to strike bargains for a number of nights. Arriving late, especially if in small settlements, they were often obliged to pay whatever was demanded. At times, outrage led tourists to push on and travel by night, as William Drake (1747–95) MP, a member of the Buckinghamshire gentry following his father by visiting Italy, did at Gaeta in 1769,[1] but this was rarely comfortable or possible outside the summer, when it was indeed common for those who wished for speed through the malaria-infested Campagna.

Guidebooks provided the best predictions of costs and advised tourists on the need to bargain on arrival at inns. Those who tried generally found bargaining effective. An anonymous tourist, probably a member of the Riddell family, noted in his journal at Novalese, near the Mont Cenis pass:

> We have agreed with our landlady at this place for 3½ livres a head for our dinner, wood or firing, and wine, one livre a head for our coffee night and morning. The beds to be included. For the same fare yesterday we paid 23 livres owing to not having agreeing.[2]

Charging bills in French livres was not uncommon in areas like this near France.

Travelling at speed, or in areas where there was little choice of accommodation, meant that tourists' costs rose. Areas that were popular and where demand exceeded supply by a large amount, became more expensive. This was true, for example, of Naples in the winters of the early 1790s.[3] In addition, it was generally reckoned that tourists who spent most of their time in one or two cities, even expensive cities, would spend less than those who were constantly travelling.

Costs varied greatly by tourist. However much tourists might follow the same route, see the same sights, and often stay in the same hotels, they were not on a package trip. No two tourists did exactly the same thing. In particular, they stayed for differing lengths of time in the same places. They had to make their own arrangements, and provision was very varied in both accommodation and food. There was no standardised hotel accommodation. The sole sphere in which governmental regulation brought some degree of uniformity in pricing was transport. Most posting systems were governmental, essentially provided for couriers and others on state business, and the price of posting was fixed. However, as many tourists discovered, these prices bore little relation to what they were expected to pay, and disputes often arose over cost. Edward Thomas complained that the postmaster of Genoa gave him a false account of the posting costs to Milan, while Philip Francis had a very bad dispute in the Papal States in 1772.[4]

Irrespective of disputes, there were many complaints about the cost of posting. In 1787, Adam Walker claimed:

> Travelling in Italy is full dearer than in England, without a quarter the comfort, dispatch, or attendance. Our beds are on average, 2s 6d or 3s English, each per night; and nothing but a mattress laid on a full bag of straw, coarse sheets, and no posts or curtains, dinners 5s and 6s a head, and travelling full 1s per mile. At Milan our charge was so extravagant, we resolved to leave the place as soon as possible.[5]

As a proportion of their total expenditure, tourists probably spent less on food and accommodation and more on transport than their modern counterparts. The prices of food and meals could be cut either by purchasing food in the markets or by making an arrangement for meals to be supplied on a daily basis at a set price. Many tourists mentioned the price of food. Richard Pococke did not leave accounts, but he included details of particular meals in his letters to his mother. At San Marino, he

> demanded what I was to pay over night before I eat – they told me a penny my bed, I might have a pennyworth of soup, 1d of meat and salad, to which at supper they added a 1d of fricassee, and 1d cheese, and a large quart of wine 1d more; I had the best vermicelli soup I ever eat, all served very well, I paid 4d in the morning.

At Bologna, Pococke noted, 'the common price of wine on the road was 1d a quart and once I had it for ½, and good enough some of it; at Tolentino 4 pd of cherries for ½, and the common price everywhere is a half penny a pd the best sorts; we pay here 1sh 6d for dinner each, eat very well, five dishes and a dessert by ourselves, 6d each for beds'. Thomas Martyn (1735–1825), Professor of Botany at Cambridge, who toured Italy in 1779–80 and published a guidebook in 1787, claimed that a good dinner could be had in Venice for four Venetian livres (about 20d). When eating in their lodgings in Naples, Philip Francis and his friend Godfrey paid three carlins each for breakfast, and, including wine, ten each for dinner and five for supper, 57½ carlins then being worth a guinea.[6] Foreigners could not be sure that they paid the same as the locals. Walker certainly complained of being charged more in Rome.[7]

There are difficulties with assessing costs. There is no guide to the size of the portions: how ample was a good dessert? How much did a large eighteenth-century roast fowl weigh? Similar problems affect any discussion of the costs of accommodation. A 'large' or 'comfortable' room is difficult to compare with other such rooms, and rooms were far from standard in size or furnishings. Furthermore, there is often very little information available about accommodation for other members of a party: the bearleader and the servants. Best value was usually given if a guest ate where he stayed and many tourist costs were therefore expressed as board and lodging.

In 1734, Pococke stayed in Venice at 'Kennets a very good English public house, but more like a lodging' for 1s. 6d. a night, half the price of his dinner. At Milan, he stayed in 'an excellent' inn which cost him 2 shillings. Edward Thomas spent 4 shillings a day on lodging and food in a Genoese inn in 1750, claiming that it would have cost double had he not had local assistance in fixing the price. He spent 14d. a day for an 'excellent lodging' in Rome. Lucas Pepys (1742–1830), the medical son of a banker, spent £10 a month for good lodgings in Rome in 1768 and thought travel in Italy very reasonably priced. Francis and Godfrey together paid 15 carlins (about 5 shillings) a day for lodgings in Naples in 1772, less than the daily hire of their carriage (16 carlins) and less than they each paid for dining (20 carlins). In the Hôtel d'Angleterre in Turin in 1782, two bedchambers, 'one good, the other bad without a fire place', cost 7 shillings nightly. Martyn claimed that in Venice, 'which however is not the cheapest place in Italy to live in', a stranger might rent a good room for 5–10d. a day, 'or he may provide himself with a genteel apartment and dinner for 4–4s 7d a day'.[8]

There is much information about transport costs. In 1772, a carriage cost about £25 at Milan.[9] Posting charges varied by the number of people in, wheels on, and horses before, a carriage. It was less expensive to use public transport in France, but this diligence (public coach) system did not extend into Italy. Instead, tourists seeking to travel between Lyons and Turin often agreed with a *voiturier* to take them and their carriage (which had to be dismantled to cross the Mont Cenis pass) between the two cities for a price that included accommodation, food and posting. Walker paid 13 louis d'or for travelling in the opposite direction in 1787. Two years earlier, Sir Richard Hoare paid more, as he had a larger party. Hoare went on to pay for the *cambiatura*, the payment which ensured free posting in Piedmont:

> We paid the voiturier from Lyons to Turin for taking our two postchaises with four horses to each, a bidet [small horse] for my servant, all our baggage etc. over Mount Cenis, and for *our* eating and lodging, forty six louis d'ors, and we gave the drivers six louis. They undertook the job somewhat cheaper, as they belonged to Turin, and had brought some gentlemen from thence to Lyons. From Turin you must procure the cambiatura, which takes you near to Milan, viz to Buffalora; they made us pay in October 1785 21 livres for 8 chaise and one small saddle horses, besides the postillions.

Sarah Bentham noted the different costs of travelling from Venice to Naples in late 1793:

> In the evening Mr. Martin the banker called and endeavoured to persuade us to take horses from hence to go to Naples, the price fifty Louis, but we reckoned the post horses would not amount to more than 28 Louis and with fees to postillions would not exceed 43 Louis and therefore declined obliging our banker at both our own expense as well as inconvenience in respect to slowness of travelling.[10]

A separate transport cost prevailed within cities. There, it was usual to hire a carriage and this could be expensive. Francis and Godfrey hired a carriage and coachman for 18 carlins (about 7 shillings) a day in Naples in 1772.[11] At sea, it was necessary to make specific bargains. At attempt to ensure satisfaction was made on behalf of Charles Abbot and Hugh Leycester in September 1788 when they left Genoa in a felucca:

> Our agreement was to take us and our servant and carriage to Leghorn for five guineas, with liberty to reduce it to three, if we landed at Lerici, or four if at Viareggio. In case we were satisfied with our captain we agreed to increase the bargain one guinea on each stage. Our felucca was one of the largest and best. I believe the additional guinea was extorted by importunity but our banker made the bargain.

In the event, they landed at Viareggio, having made the passage in twenty-five hours.[12]

Food, accommodation and transport were the principal costs met by tourists. In addition, there was a rich miscellany of expenses. One major one was clothes, on which tourists tended to spend a lot of money. As they were abroad for a long period, they often needed to replace items of clothing. In addition, the social environment that many tourists frequented led to conspicuous consumption on clothes. To move freely in society, a gentleman was expected to dress well. Being a tourist did not alter this situation, although strangers were freed from some of the restrictions of European society. Joshua Pickersgill noted that strangers at the Turin carnival balls in 1761 were allowed to dance with whomsoever they wished while the local citizens were not permitted to dance with women of noble birth.[13] In Turin in 1750, Edward Thomas discovered the problem of social access: 'I have dined several times with Lord Rochford [the Ambassador, William, 4th Earl] in company of several of our English and Irish nobility and I have met with great civilities from them, but I was obliged to be at a little more expense in dress than I intended.' To dine with Horace Mann in Florence, Thomas went 'dressed in a light coloured rich silk, figured, and what they call a Lyons Drugget . . . with this my bag wig, Dresden ruffles and white silk stockings . . . I have also a suit of black silk for a change', and another of black velvet, made in Genoa, for the winter.[14]

To appear in court society, as at Turin and Naples, was expensive. John Holroyd commented in 1764 on the expenses of breeding 'fine gentlemen' at the Turin Academy, in which there were then five British students:

> They acquire a thorough knowledge of dress, and make the Academy life extremely expensive which in itself is surprisingly cheap. All but one keeps a fine equipage and running footmen and that one is followed by his chair wherever he goes, without going into it according to the fashion of the country.

It was not particularly expensive to attend the theatre or musical entertainments. It helped, as so often with prices, if one paid oneself. William Drake was overcharged at the Siena theatre in 1769 because he entrusted his purchase to his guide. Philip Francis paid sixpence to see a comedy in Florence in 1792 where the dancing was 'incomparable'.[15]

Guides were a source of expense. Sarah Bentham and her son were so impressed by their guide in Florence that they hired him to accompany them to Rome and Naples at 6 sequins a month.[16] It was usual to hire guides in large cities, just as it was common to hire an extra servant: often the two were the same man. Guides were notorious for attempting to defraud tourists. As they were paid little, guides sought to earn money by taking a commission from hoteliers, tailors and others whose services they secured for their temporary master. Hiring teachers could also be an expense.

Collectables, presents and souvenirs, either for oneself or for others, could be a major item of expense. Visiting Rome in 1726, Edward Southwell junior 'spent £150 on 5 marble tables, 2 landscapes of ruins, a little suite of brass medals, more for use than show, £50 worth of prints of modern and antique Rome and of the chief paintings, 2 or 3 fans, 2 or 3 cameos etc'. Richard Grenville (1711–79), later an MP and 2nd Earl Temple, bought his uncle, Richard, 1st Viscount Cobham, who had Stowe built, four Italian paintings costing £103 19s. 2d. in the early 1730s. Viscount Nuneham sent melon and broccoli seeds home from Florence in 1756. Norton Nicholls found that, for the time he was in Rome in 1772, James Byres cost 15 guineas as a guide, while he could get a half-length portrait by Batoni for twenty.[17]

Tips were a constant drain. So, less seriously, was expenditure on cosmetics and the barber – shaving soap, lavender water, powders, and tincture for the teeth – and on washing clothes.

The total costs of individual tourists were high, but, given the length of time they stayed abroad, the need to make independent arrangements and the distances many of them covered, they were not as high as might have been imagined, judging simply by press comment. The guardians of Montague Drake (1692–1728), who toured Italy in 1710–12 and was later an MP, asked the Lord Chancellor for a travel allowance of at least £800 to add to his annual income of £1,800. In 1717–20, Charles Compton (1698–1755), third son of the 4th Earl of Northampton, and later a diplomat and then an MP, had £250 in his first year abroad, and £200 thereafter, although he received an extra £50 in Rome. In contrast, Sir Carnaby Haggerston (*c.* 1700–56), a young baronet, his expenses increased by gambling losses, signed bills for £400 in a six-month period in Italy in 1718. John, Lord Brudenell spent £12,600 on his Grand Tour, but he was away from 1754 until 1760.[18]

It is impossible to state accurately the total cost to the nation of foreign travel. Frederick, Lord North (1732–92), the head of the government during the War of American Independence, wrote from Rome in 1753 that in the recent Holy Year British tourists had drawn over £70,000 from one banker alone. In 1785, William Bennett noted, 'If the calculation of the English who are settled or are travelling abroad as said to be delivered to Mr. Pitt can be depended upon, they amount to 40,000 and if each man spends only £100 per ann. drain each year £4,000,000 hard money from the nation.'[19] Like his father, William Pitt, 1st Earl of Chatham, William Pitt the Younger, First Lord of the Treasury, never visited Italy.

Several travellers were convinced that their compatriots were extravagant. Francis Drake, who toured Italy in 1750–2, complained:

> it is the fault and folly of the English to suffer themselves to be imposed upon, not to seem to lessen the national characters of wealth and generosity; our young travellers have generally so much money, and are so very lavish of it, that a man of moderate fortune, who would go abroad for improvement, and not for ostentation, cannot bear the expense.

Drake claimed that a tour that would have cost £500 thirty years earlier now cost £1,000, despite, he alleged, the fact that 'there is no country in the world where the provisions of all kinds are cheaper than in Italy and a stranger of any other nation may travel for a tenth part of the expense'. Similar complaints were not expressed by other tourists who made more than one tour.

Norton Nicholls (*c.* 1742–1809), a Suffolk rector, wrote to his mother from Naples in 1772 to blame his expenditure on his companion, James, 7th Earl of Findlater (1750–1811), underlining the social differences between tourists:

> I assure you in spite of what I spend I am economical and spend not above ½ as much as the people with whom I live . . . I find at present the great inconvenience of living with a Lord . . . because I suffer for the impositions he undergoes; he is used to be preyed on by his servants, by the inn keepers, by all the world, as we keep house together part of this falls on me, I scold eternally, and have changed some things for the better, but in general I find a considerable difference between living so and by myself.

Nicholls later wrote: 'there are but two methods of travelling, one being admitted everywhere as a gentleman and spending with the exactest economy a great deal, the other of living at coffee-houses and spending little'.[20] Findlater was not regarded as extravagant by other British tourists he met, but Nicholls's complaint, and his need to borrow money from Findlater and James Byres, are reminders of tourists' varied circumstances.

The presence of other tourists was held to drive up costs. In 1769, Dr Thomas Townson (1715–92), William Drake's bearleader, wrote from Florence:

> certainly neither Mr. Drake nor Mr. Maxwell has shown the least disposition to extravagance, or, as far as I can judge, been guilty of any; but the very expenses of travelling have been very great, and not the less so for our following the track of so many English as are now abroad.[21]

A mass of correspondence testifies to the efforts made to limit expenditure by parents, tutors and tourists. Extravagant tourists were severely reprimanded. Others were constantly aware of parental supervision, and felt obliged to account for their expenditure. Costs were pushed up by factors largely outside tourists' control. There was a certain amount of inflation, although, by modern standards, it was modest. There were also specific reasons for higher costs. Sir Francis Head (*c.* 1696–1768) reported from Rome in 1725 that the price of antique coins had risen as a result of foreign demand, and that because it was Holy Week, 'everything is excessively dear . . . lodgings, coaches are raised to more than double . . . what vast numbers of all nations are at present here'.[22]

When James Boswell (1740–95) planned a European tour in 1764, he wrote: 'I would by no means be extravagant; I would only travel genteelly'; he visited Italy in 1765.[23] The aspiration to travel genteelly was shared by most tourists and it inevitably involved expense. This expense invited emulation, aroused criticism, and defined for many the nature of tourism. Travel was a luxury because most tourists spent in accordance with their social status and their lifestyle at home. However, it was possible for men of medium incomes, such as Adam Walker, to travel, and, after the Peace of Paris (1763), such men travelled in increasing numbers. The nature of tourism was altering before the French Revolutionary War broke out in 1792.

Costs clearly led some tourists to change their plans. Edward Gibbon's shortage of money complicated his Italian tour. Most tourists, however, did not alter their plans for financial reasons. Those who travelled were on the whole those who could afford to travel, and their mode of living as tourists matched their situation.

Being able to afford the cost did not end the problems of finance. Most tourists, probably unwilling to risk robbery, did not travel with large quantities of any currency. Instead, they relied on paper instruments of credit. The usual arrangement was for a tourist to have an agreement by which he could draw on the foreign correspondents of his London banker for a certain sum. These correspondents were generally bankers themselves, though some were merchants. The tourist could also arrange to extend the geographical range of his borrowing by seeking credit from the correspondents of these correspondents. This system worked reasonably well, reflecting the degree to which most tourists spent much of their time in a small number of major towns.

James, Lord Compton (1687–1754), later 5th Earl of Northampton, drew on a Mr Knight in Venice in 1708. Ten years later, Sir Carnaby Haggerston from Northumberland profited from the connections of his Newcastle banker, Nicholas Fenwick. He drew £50 on him at Marseilles, £100 on his Livorno correspondent, George Jackson, and had a £200 credit at Rome arranged for him by Fenwick's Italian correspondents. In 1728, Edward Carteret sent advice to the Reverend Gaspar Wetstein, Lionel, 4th Earl of Dysart's Dutch bearleader: 'Mr. Boeheme tells me that the Freres Aubert will give you credit anywhere in Italy'. The following year, Stephen Fox was supplied with £500 by the Livorno agents of his banker Hoare. Before Villiers entered Italy in 1755, his bearleader William Whitehead drew up a list of bankers whose services could be used at Venice, Rome, Naples, Florence, Livorno, Genoa, Milan and Turin. Four were British, two of them, Joseph Smith in Venice and John Birtles in Genoa, consuls.[24]

During the century, the techniques and connections of banking houses improved and they were able to offer a more comprehensive service to tourists. In 1775, Robert Wharton (1751–1808) sought approval for an Italian trip and asked, if it was granted, for £100 more 'which you will desire Mr. Hoare to send me a letter of credit for on some banker at Lyons or Marseilles where I shall change my letters for others on the Italian banks'. At Livorno, he exchanged his French money for Italian *zecchini* with Monsignor Berte and obtained bills on the latter's correspondents. Planning a visit to Italy, Thomas Pelham asked his father for letters of credit from Hoare to his correspondents at Turin, Rome and Naples; 'in case of accidents, a letter to a banker at any great town would gain me credit at smaller ones, where I might have no letter'. Hoare instructed his correspondents at Lyons, Turin, Milan, Rome and Naples to supply him with up to £200 each and Pelham took advantage of the facility. Drake was less satisfied with Hoare's correspondents in 1768:

> My letter of credit from Mr. Hoare is upon the Tassins at Paris, who could give no other than on their correspondent at Lyons, Mr. Auriol; from whom I received one upon Mr. Debernardy at Turin, and from him another upon the Marquis Belloni at Rome, if these several bankers are to have each their profit upon the money I take up at Rome, as may possibly be the case, will it not be better to have a letter from Mr. Hoare immediately on his correspondent there?

Two months later, Drake's bearleader noted that the intermediary bankers were each charging 1 per cent commission.[25]

The principal alternative to an arrangement with the correspondents of a particular banker was to take bills of exchange that could be exchanged by any banker. However, many European merchants and bankers were hesitant about paying money to someone they knew nothing about, whose bill might subsequently prove to be worthless. It was not practical in Italy to wait until confirmation could be received that a bill had been honoured. In the second half of the eighteenth century, several London bankers, such as Sir Robert Herries (1730–1815) who visited Italy in 1794, offered bills accepted by a large number of foreign bankers. William Blackett (1759–1816), who succeeded to the family baronetcy and the Newby Hall estate, wrote to his father from Naples in 1785: 'with a letter of credit the bankers all over Italy and Germany take two per cent commission. If you have Morlands or Herries's bills you pay no commission at all'.[26]

In difficult circumstances, tourists could usually obtain money. Large or small sums could be borrowed from other tourists or from fellow-countrymen resident abroad. Lord Findlater lent Norton Nicholls 10 guineas at Naples and £30 at Venice in 1772. This was also a useful method for obtaining and disposing of small change. In Rome in 1777, Thomas Pelham took the Neapolitan money that John, Viscount Dalrymple (1749–1821), later a diplomat and 6th Earl of Stair, had not used. Wharton drew on the guide James Byres in Rome, while Byres arranged £50 credit for Nicholls. In 1788, having crossed the Mont Cenis pass, Charles Abbot recorded,

> our cash from Lyons was likely to fall short before we reached Turin, and Monsr. Le Notaire Rivet very civilly and very readily on my explaining matters lent us ten louis d'ors and took my acknowledgement in form, with my assurance that I would place that sum to his account with our banker at Turin.[27]

Tourists frequently complained about the commission charged by bankers for dealing with bills of exchange and other financial devices, and about the rates of exchange offered by them, which often differed from those in guidebooks. Bankers were largely unregulated and free to charge and offer what they chose. Yet they were the crucial linchpins for any tour. Bankers could also be of considerable use to tourists, in particular in arranging accommodation and introductions. Thomas Jenkins's windows were used by tourists keen to get a good view of Roman processions. Peter Beckford recommended prospective tourists in Sicily to ask their banker to arrange accommodation.

These possibilities did not compensate for the commissions charged. In 1771 Norton Nicholls had problems with the Milanese banker Leonardi, who 'endeavoured to practise a little dirty deceit on me of which an English banker would have been ashamed, it was to make a payment in zecchinis rating each beyond their value'.[28] In addition, if a tourist relied upon particular letters of credit from a London banker, then a change of route, or the non-arrival of these letters, could create problems. Bankers could also go bankrupt.

Bankers apart, difficulties could be encountered in the form of variable exchange rates, a shortage of coins, and the large numbers of currencies. James Hay (d. 1746), bearleader for James, Lord Compton (1687–1752), later an MP and 5th Earl of Northampton, complained in 1708 that the considerable number of Italian currencies made it difficult to do his accounts. Adam Walker noted in 1787:

> We find the exchange of money a troublesome business amongst these little states, they succeed one another so fast; for we have travelled the length of the Dukedom of Parma this day; and we came through part of the Pope's dominions, and the whole Dukedom of Modena yesterday . . . I can reckon ten potentates to whom we have been subjects in the course of two months.[29]

The availability of good coinage was also a problem. Martyn noted that Genoese money would not be taken in any other state and advised tourists 'not to have more of the current coin of any state, than you are likely to dispose of before you quit it', with the exception of the sequins of Florence, Rome and Venice, on which there was the least loss elsewhere. Sir Richard Hoare 'found great difficulty in getting sequins at Turin and Milan' and thought it best to take sufficient French louis d'or to reach Florence, where sequins were not scarce.[30]

Potential problems with finances were but one of the factors dissuading tourists from travelling outside the usual range of tourist activity. Financial facilities were well developed across most of Italy, although, as with so much else, in practice this meant the cities.

10. Hazards

British tourists were faced by a range of hazards from war to crime, accidents to ill health. Their impact varied greatly. For example, most tourists were not the victims of crime nor hit by serious ill health, while they were very differently affected by war. In the latter case, much depended on the position and attitudes of the individual traveller. For Horace Walpole (1715–97), son of the leading minister, Sir Robert Walpole (who never travelled abroad), or Henry, 9th Earl of Lincoln (1720–94), nephew and heir of Thomas, Duke of Newcastle, Secretary of State for the Southern Department (who never went on the Grand Tour), the situation was different to that for a tourist without powerful political connections. Both in Italy in early 1741, they were ordered home before they could be cut off by the Spanish forces which invaded that year.[1] Spain was then at war with Britain. This conflict, which broadened into the War of the Austrian Succession and lasted until 1748, did not, however, prevent other British tourists from visiting Italy.

Travel required permission, although the degree of stringency varied greatly. It was easy to leave Britain, although those holding posts and commissions were expected to stay in the country, particularly in times of war and international crisis. In Italy, tourists, in common with other travellers, were examined at numerous control points. Many towns were still walled, with gates at which travellers had to stop, identify themselves, and declare the purpose of their travel and often also where they were going to spend the night. The need for passports and for specific permission to enter a state varied. James Thoburn commented in the 1780s, 'It is necessary in Italy for the passport always to be with the carriage and not with the courier as in general he goes before. In every guarded town in Italy your passport is demanded at the entrance of the town where it is signed by an officer who is placed there on purpose. A little money is given.'

Some countries were strict. On arrival in the kingdom of Naples, it was necessary to show a passport that had been obtained from the Neapolitan envoy in Rome.[2] Difficulties were created over passports in the later years of the Walpole ministry, when Naples clearly supported the Jacobites. Charles Edward Stuart, the eldest son of the Stuart Pretender,

James III, accompanied the Spanish army that invaded Naples in 1734, and the British government was outraged by the public demonstration of support for him by its commander, Don Carlos, who became Charles IV of Naples. Anger at the courtesies extended to Charles Edward Stuart when he toured Italy in 1737 led to a breach in diplomatic relations with Venice that persisted until 1744. Relations with Parma were broken in the late 1720s due to Duke Antonio Farnese's support for the Jacobites. There is little sign that these breaches affected tourism, although Jacobitism played a role in some visits to Italy, for example that of Henry Hyde, Viscount Cornbury (1710–53), son of the 4th Earl of Clarendon and later an MP, to Rome to see the Pretender in 1730–1. John Bagshaw, the Consul at Genoa, reported in 1731 that at Rome there had arrived 'a vast number of English gentlemen most of them visited the Pretender for whom they had brought several remittances'.[3] More generally, the need for passports increased in wartime, whether Britain was a combatant or not.

As a variant on passport controls, quarantine regulations arose from the cordon sanitaire designed to restrict the spread of bubonic plague. Tourists who had visited North Africa or the Turkish empire had to undergo lengthy quarantines. In 1788, the antiquarian John Hawkins (1761–1841) had a thirty-day quarantine in Messina.[4]

The first major conflict of the century, the War of the Spanish Succession, involved hostilities in 1701–14. Britain took part in the conflict in 1702–13. There was serious fighting in northern Italy until 1706, when the French were defeated at Turin by Britain's Austrian and Piedmontese allies and driven back from Piedmont. The following year, Austrian forces successfully overran the kingdom of Naples. Prior to that, it had been ruled by the Bourbon claimant to the Spanish inheritance, whose claim was challenged by the Habsburg claimant. In 1704, William Kerr (*c.* 1681–1741), an army officer who was third son of the 3rd Earl of Roxburgh, and was later an MP, was granted a passport to visit Naples, the Spanish envoy distinguishing between the English, to whom he would not grant passports, and Scots. That year, Thomas, 8th Duke of Norfolk (1683–1732) was denied permission because he had visited both the English fleet and an Austrian diplomat.

Tourists who visited Italy during this war included Thomas Frankland, Samuel Tufnell, Edward Montagu, Uvedale Price, John Wallop and Sir Richard Grosvenor. Metcalfe Robinson, whose father was an MP, travelled to Italy in 1705, and British envoys helped him to obtain passports.[5] The war did, however, affect routes to Italy and, therefore, itineraries there. Rather than crossing France, tourists came via the Low Countries and Germany. Edward, Viscount Quarendon (1681–1713) and Edward Wortley Montagu (1678–1761), later an MP and ambassador, left Italy homewards in 1704 via Vienna, their last major stop in Italy being Venice. William Blathwayt (1688–1742), who was to inherit the Dyrham Park estate, and his brother John (1690–1742) travelled to Italy via the Rhineland and Geneva. Having reached Venice in 1707, they pressed on to Rome, leaving Lombardy and Turin until 1708, by which time the French had clearly been defeated. From Turin, the Blathwayts left for Geneva.

The tourists in Italy during the war frequently travelled together. Thus, Frankland (*c.* 1683–1747), later an MP, who was in Italy in 1704–5, met Charles, 1st Duke of Shrewsbury (1660–1718) in Rome in 1704 and in Venice in 1705, and William Kerr in Padua in 1705. Tufnell (1682–1758), again later an MP, and also in Italy in 1704–5, met Shrewsbury, Frankland and Robinson in Rome in 1704 and Kerr, Robinson and Frankland in Padua in 1705. Quarendon, in Italy in 1701–4, met Shrewsbury, and in 1704 travelled from Florence to Venice with Edward Wortley Montagu. Sir Richard Grosvenor (1689–1732), later an MP, was described as being one of a wild set in Italy in the mid-1700s with William Wyndham (*c.* 1688–1740), later Grosvenor's brother-in-law and the Tory leader in the House of Commons, and Simon Harcourt (1685–1720), later an MP. Lionel, 7th Earl of Dorset (1688–1765), later 1st Duke of Dorset, and the Hon. Richard Lumley (*c.* 1688–1740), later an MP, 2nd Earl of Scarborough, and a general, were in Venice and Padua together in 1706–7. Uvedale Price (1685–1764), also later an MP, was in Padua and Venice in 1711; and John Wallop (1690–1762), later an MP and eventually Earl of Portsmouth, was in Padua in 1709–10. Charles, 2nd Duke of Grafton (1683–1757), later Viceroy of Ireland, was also in Padua in the 1700s.

The war certainly affected more than tourist itineraries. Both the ships carrying back the books, statues, antiquities, music and paintings purchased in Italy in 1706–7 by Sir John Perceval (1683–1748) were captured by French privateers, and in 1707 he was forced to abandon a voyage from Livorno to Genoa, seek shelter at Lerici, and continue by mule when his ship was attacked by Neapolitan privateers. Damage inflicted during the war was noted by subsequent tourists, for example William Freeman in 1727, who found Asti much affected.[6]

Aside from a brief conflict with Spain in 1718–20, which did not involve conflict between the two powers in Italy, other than in the waters off Sicily, where the British fleet was victorious, Britain was not at war again until 1739, but international tension in the intervening period still affected tourists. In 1730, the threat of war in Italy arising from a possible attack on Austrian Italy by Britain, France and Spain, delayed William Mildmay (*c.* 1705–71) at Marseilles, although he was able to sail on to Genoa and then Livorno.[7]

The War of the Polish Succession (1733–5) involved sustained conflict in northern Italy in 1733–5, as well as the Spanish conquest of the kingdom of Naples in 1734. Most tourists were not directly affected, however, by the conflict, despite the widely held assumption that, under the treaty of 1731 with Austria, the Second Treaty of Vienna, Britain would enter the war on the Austrian side, which it did not in fact do. During the war, tourists found no difficulty in obtaining passports and touring the field of conflict. In 1734, Simon, 2nd Viscount Harcourt (1714–77), later Earl Harcourt, Ambassador to Paris, Viceroy of Ireland and a general, viewed the battle of Parma from the ramparts of the town, Sir Hugh Smithson (1715–86), later an MP and then Duke of Northumberland, and Sir Henry Liddell Bt. (1708–84), later an MP and then Lord Ravensworth, visited the French army near Mantua, and Richard Pococke (1704–65) was allowed by the French to visit the castle in Milan where new fortifications were being constructed. Andrew Mitchell was annoyed to find that, as a result of the war, the picture collections at Modena and Parma became inaccessible: the latter was moved to Genoa. Jeremiah Milles (1714–84), a cleric and antiquarian, found the ducal apartments in Modena inaccessible in 1734, because the contents were packed up in case of French occupation. Mitchell was shown the battlefield of Parma by a French officer, and also discussed that of Guastalla with participants. He found many of the churches and monasteries in Parma full of wounded and 'cart loads of wounded and sick sent in every day from the camp to the hospitals . . . miserable spectacle'. Nevertheless, apart from the removal of the paintings, Mitchell suffered no inconvenience from the hostilities.[8]

During the War of the Austrian Succession (1741–8 in Italy), tourism also continued, and there could be a somewhat facetious attitude towards the dangers posed by war. Nevertheless, although Britain was officially a neutral power as far as France was concerned until the spring of 1744, the Alps were a scene of hostilities prior to that, and northern Italy also thereafter. Furthermore, Britain had been at war with Spain since 1739: the War of Jenkins's Ear. Spain sought to gain the Italian possessions of Austria, and, to that end, Spanish forces, based in southern France, had invaded the dominions of Charles Emmanuel III, an ally of Austria who blocked the route to the Duchy of Milan. In December 1742, a Spanish army, under the Marquis de Las Minas, occupied the Duchy of Savoy, pushing Charles Emmanuel back to Piedmont, and conflict continued in the region until the end of the war. In 1745, a French army advanced along the Genoese Riviera, crossed the Ligurian Alps and defeated Charles Emmanuel at Bassignano, going on to capture Asti and Milan. Both cities were recaptured the following year and the Bourbons were defeated by Austro-Sardinian forces at Piacenza. An invasion of Provence by the latter, supported by the British navy, was initially successful in late 1746, but the French successfully counterattacked in January 1747. The previous month, the Austrians had been expelled from captured Genoa by a popular revolt, and their efforts to regain the city were thwarted. There was also conflict in central Italy between Austrian and Neapolitan forces, while Britain came close to war with Naples in 1742.

Both the international situation and the war affected tourists. In April 1743, Viscount Beauchamp wrote to his mother about a Yorkshire gentleman named Boswell and his wife, then at Lyons, who wished to push on to Italy: 'God knows how they will get there unless they go to Marseille and from thence to Genoa by sea and so to Turin, for the Spaniards in Italy are like the dog in the manger for they will neither put into Italy themselves or let anybody else'.[9] An alternative and longer route from France into Italy existed: via neutral Geneva. It was one that Beauchamp himself was to follow in 1744, and Richard Neville Aldworth (1717–93), later an MP, entered Italy that way the same year with Sir Thomas Sebright Bt. (1723–61), Horatio Walpole (1723–1809; cousin of the famous writer and later MP and Lord Walpole) and the latter's bearleader, George Turnbull (*c.* 1703–48), a cleric and antiquarian. However, in early 1743, this route was threatened by the Spanish army in Savoy. Lady Hertford wrote to Beauchamp from London:

> We talk here of a design to besiege Geneva. If it is true what reason have we to be thankful to Providence and Mr. Sturrock's [his bearleader William Sturrock] determination not to carry you there; however the Spanish army lying so near it is a sufficient inconvenience if nothing worse was to happen.[10]

Possibly the international situation was responsible for Beauchamp's decision in June 1743 to push on south into southern France, rather than east towards the Alpine passes. The following month, Sturrock reported his fears about the outbreak of plague in Messina and his suggestion that, if it spread to Calabria, plans for an Italian trip should be abandoned.[11] That autumn, Sturrock looked ahead towards a winter at Geneva as 'we cannot think of crossing the mountains till we see how things are likely to turn out in Italy'.[12] In the event, Beauchamp did enter Italy in 1744, only to die of smallpox at Bologna that September.

Other tourists also had their travels affected. Henry Oxenden (1721–1803) and his younger brother George were able in 1745 to get a pass from Louis XV to travel to Italy via France, but they were forced that winter 'in order to avoid the Spaniards . . . to traverse the Alps and the Grisons, for 18 days' *en route* from Novara to Bergamo, 'a most terrible journey'. In addition, their letters of introduction were intercepted by the Spaniards. Travelling in 1750, Edward Thomas noted war damage at Coni and near Genoa.[13]

Britain was at war with France during the Seven Years' War (1756–63), but not with France's ally Austria. This alliance kept Italy peaceful, not least by restraining Sardinian expansionism. Deteriorating Anglo-French relations led to the end of the Italian tour of William, 18th Earl of Sutherland (1735–66), and his bearleader, James Grant (1720–1806), both officers in the Royal Scots, who were ordered to rejoin their regiment in Ireland in 1755. However, John Murray, the Resident, was able to write from Venice in 1759, 'We are here in as perfect a state of tranquillity, as if there was a profound peace all over Italy.'[14]

As a result, there were many British tourists there, their number increased by conflict in Germany and war with France. Sir Wyndham Knatchbull-Wyndham (1737–63), later an MP, visited Italy in 1758–9. The war ensured that he entered and left Italy via Venice. Adam Fergusson (1733–1813), later a baronet and an MP, visited Italy in 1757, travelling to Turin via Germany, and returning the same way, as he could not go back through France; so also did Neil, 3rd Earl of Rosebery (1729–1814), whose enjoyment of Italy had been enhanced by a mistress. James Grant (1738–1811), the heir to a baronetcy and later an MP, arrived in Italy from Geneva in late 1759 with Thomas Wynn (1736–1807), another heir to a baronetcy, and later an MP and 1st Lord Newborough. Grant left in 1760 from Venice for Munich and home, while Wynn set off later in the year from Verona for Munich. Similarly, George, Viscount Mandeville (1737–88), later an MP and then 4th Duke of Manchester, had set off back in 1758

25. *Sir Wyndham Knatchbull-Wyndham*, by Pompeo Batoni, 1758. Knatchbull-Wyndham (1737–63), a member of a wealthy Kent landed family, who had already succeeded to the family baronetcy, visited Italy in 1758–9, travelling from Venice via Padua and Florence to Rome, where he sat for Batoni, leading to what Winckelmann claimed was one of the best portraits in the world. Knatchbull-Wyndham left Italy via Venice. He was to be elected unopposed as MP for Kent in 1760, being re-elected unopposed at the general election of 1761, but dying suddenly in 1763. His bearleader had been Louis Devisme (1720–77), a Huguenot clergyman.

from Verona. Sir Humphry Morice MP (1723–85) went to Italy for his health in 1760, returning for the autumn session of Parliament in 1762. George, Lord Grey (1737–1819), later an MP and then 5th Earl of Stamford, toured Italy in 1760. Francis Russell, Marquess of Tavistock (1739–67) was in Italy in 1761–2. While in Rome in 1762, he met Augustus, 3rd Duke of Grafton (1735–1811), John Crewe (1742–1829) and Dr John Hinchliffe (1731–94), his tutor, later Master of Trinity and Bishop of Peterborough. Hinchliffe was to marry Crewe's sister, while Grafton became his patron after meeting him on the Continent and was responsible for his being appointed Chaplain in Ordinary to George III. Crewe, later an MP and then Lord Crewe, entered Italy over the Brenner pass in 1761, and, in 1762, left Italy from Turin via Lausanne. George, 3rd Earl of Lichfield (1718–72) went to Italy for a second visit in 1760–1.

He met Anthony, 11th Viscount Gormanston (1736–86), who travelled with the Catholic intellectual John Needham (1713–81) as his tutor, and Edmund Rolfe (1738–1817), who entered Italy via Geneva.

Thus, there were a number of British tourists in Italy during the war and, as in other periods, they enjoyed each other's company. The letters of James Stuart Mackenzie, envoy in Turin, to his brother, include references to many British tourists passing through Turin, and in March 1761 he reported that passports for travel via France could be obtained.[15]

Similarly, the correspondence of John, Viscount Mountstuart, envoy at Turin from 1779 until 1783, makes it clear that many British tourists passed through the city during the War of American Independence,[16] which broadened in 1778–83 to include war with France, and, from 1779, Spain. However, the war prevented Philip Yorke (1757–1834), later 3rd Earl of Hardwicke, from shipping home the artistic purchases he had made in Italy,[17] while those treasures that were shipped home on the *Westmorland* were captured and ended up in Spain.[18] Due to the war, Yorke travelled to Italy via Holland and Germany, arriving at Venice in 1778. The apparent proximity of a new war with France in the autumn of 1787 worried tourists in Italy,[19] but the crisis speedily subsided.

Personal disputes were more of a problem than war. Tourists were involved in many disputes, most involving money. As noted earlier, there were no set prices for accommodation and food. Guidebooks and published travel accounts frequently warned against fraud, and noted a variety of types. It is unclear how far these warnings affected the presuppositions of tourists. Adam Walker, who encountered difficulties with his postilions, wrote of the Italians, 'As to the lower orders of men, they seem what we call blackguards, in the most savage sense of the word . . . ever on the watch to cheat or impose upon strangers'.[20] Warning about a very different type of fraud was provided by Northall who wrote of young aristocrats being deceived by antiquarian guides in Rome into buying paintings that were copies, thinking they were original works by Raphael, Titian or Michelangelo.[21]

Frontiers provided opportunities for quarrels over passports and customs regulations. Both were best settled by bribes. In 1788, Charles Abbot recorded in Novalese, 'our courier having satisfied the custom house officer with about three shillings our baggage was not disturbed'. Five years later, his mother, Sarah Bentham complained about exactions on the boat journey from Fusina to Venice:

> during the short passage we were stopped three times by customs house officers, who came in a boat alongside us and with long hooks grappled our boat and demanded money . . . upon being stopped by a third we would no longer be duped; but absolutely refused giving more.[22]

Tourist conduct varied. Some allegedly urinated on the Senate of Lucca from a balcony or excreted in Italian churches,[23] but most behaved in an acceptable fashion. Tourists did not seek trouble and most of the disputes they became involved in related to difficulties over alleged frauds. In 1725, Francis Colman, envoy in Florence, had a tailor and an attorney who had quarrelled with two tourists imprisoned. Edward Thomas complained in 1750 about 'the fraud and bad disposition' of the Genoese: 'they are not even ashamed to be detested in cheating you even in trifles . . . If they go to reckon any money or cast up a sum, they are sure to make a mistake to their own advantage.'[24]

In March 1765, George Damer (1746–1808), later an MP and 2nd Earl of Dorchester, and Sir Thomas Gascoigne Bt. (1745–1810), later an MP and a colonel, were involved in a drunken brawl in Rome in which a coachman died. The crisis was lessened by the distribution of money and the friendly intervention of the Governor of Rome, but the tourists had to flee. Travelling from Rome to the Tuscan frontier in 1772, Philip Francis was

cheated regularly at every post, in the very teeth of the tariff. There is no remedy, for if you refuse to pay, they take away the horses. At last we are clear of the Romans, and here I most devoutly pray that both they and their neighbours the Neapolitans may be everlastingly cursed. Sooner than live with such villains, I would renounce society.[25]

Francis's views of the Italians were echoed by Robert Manners in 1779 – 'I cannot mention a single face that I have met with here [Florence] or in any other town in Italy that I wish to see again. I think even to the very beggars I see falsity wrote on their countenances' – and Richard Garmston:

I do not approve of the people in the Venetian state, they impose upon strangers, more than any other people I ever met with, and you pay more for going, upon *very bad roads*, than in any other part of Italy, for the postilions and ostlers are never satisfied. The post horses are very indifferent, and the Master of the Post too proud to be spoken to, but he leaves all to the conduct of an impertinent staliere, who always takes part with the postilioni.

Thoburn complained in 1788 that the postilions were 'in general a set of rascals never content give what you will'. He added a specific warning about those 'on each side of Terracina. It is said the master of the inn gives to the postilions a little money for every carriage they can break, on the account they must stay at his house till such times as the carriage is repaired or otherways buy one off him, as he jobs much in second hand carriages'.[26]

In an attempt at extortion, Sir James Hall was falsely accused in Venice in 1784 of stealing a diamond when he visited the diamond polishers. He observed that Italy was the only country where rascals were not ashamed to have their rascality discovered. The following year, his geological interests led to his being stopped as a thief, because his carrying hammers excited suspicion.[27] An anonymous memorandum on touring recommended, 'everywhere in Italy agree for your bed, eating and everything else at the first coming to any places to avoid disputes'.[28]

Faced with problems, tourists could have little hope of redress by local judicial institutions. Legal action was slow and expensive, and there were serious language difficulties. Many tourists encountered problems with customs officers. The ability to appeal to British envoys, however, ensured that, in the event of serious difficulties, assistance could be obtained. Diplomats, such as Colman and Mann, complained often of the cost and time involved in entertaining tourists. They were expected to entertain them, present them at court, introduce them into local society, fulfil a number of miscellaneous requests and protect them from brushes with the law. At the same time, diplomats could greatly enjoy the social dimension of visits by tourists. The protection provided by the diplomatic service was an indication of the relatively small-scale nature of tourism and the role of personal connections in what was still essentially an aristocratic milieu.

Crime was a threat tourists had to face, although, despite thinking the police dishonest and many of them criminal, Francis Drake claimed that it was 'much safer travelling all over Italy than in many parts of England' and argued that danger was confined to frontier zones. In the mountains south-east of Viterbo in 1756, Villiers found 'a few soldiers placed by way of escort to strangers to defend them from robbers'. Henry Nassau and a friend were robbed in Venice, which he visited in 1732.[29] James, 4th Viscount Charlemont (1728–99), later Earl of Charlemont, chased a sham German baron who had stolen the money of a compatriot and got it back. Stevens was threatened near Bolsena, an area in which military escorts were necessary in 1766. Brand was robbed at Viterbo.[30]

Tourists showed an understandable interest in the quality of the police. However, the majority encountered no difficulties. In 1787, Adam Walker thought 'it is a compliment . . . to Italy, that we neither were robbed, attempted to be robbed, or heard of a robbery, the time we travelled through it, and we travelled early and late'.[31] Mountainous regions were more frightening, especially near frontiers. Travelling from Lugano to Bellinzona in 1791, Bruce and Brand

> crossed the famous Monti Cenera a place celebrated for ancient chestnut trees of wonderful beauty in whose hollows the proscribed villains of the Piedmontese, Milanese and Venetian states used to lurk to the great annoyance of unwary travellers. As we were a strong party and well armed I was under very little apprehension knowing the antipathy of your Italian to a pistol but the sight of frequent skulls some bleached with age and others so fresh enclosed in iron cages on the top of high posts stuck about the forest in terrorem convinced me it was necessary to keep a good look out.[32]

Accidents were another threat. Carriages were very susceptible, unsurprisingly so given the poor and often uneven nature of road surfaces. Many tourists were halted as a result of such accidents, usually broken axletrees. Anne, Lady Exeter's broke near Loreto in 1699. The carriage of George Lucy (*c.* 1714–86) became stuck on a hill *en route* from Rome to Florence in May 1758, and he was forced to turn to a flea-infested and 'filthy place'. At Vercelli in 1772, Philip Francis found 'the axletree has again given way: a cursed plague and the loss of five hours'. Hester Piozzi's coach broke down at Spoleto in 1786, and she and her Italian second husband Gabriel had to travel on to Bologna with Leonard Chappelow and Charles Shard, who came to their assistance. In 1792, Brand's axletree broke on the way from Livorno to Rome, although fortunately, 'it was within a mile of the only place in a whole day's journey where it could have been well mended and we slept in an excellent inn instead of the far fam'd and detested Radicofani'.[33]

Overturning was frequent and could be unpleasant. Even with drag chains, there were particular problems when carriages went downhill. In 1787, Garmston was nearly overturned passing another carriage on the Padua–Ferrara road which was too narrow for two to pass without great difficulty.[34] Horses could also be a problem, difficult to control and prone to accidents or ill health. Stevens had to stay two days at Viterbo in 1739 because of lame horses.[35] On the way from Bologna to Florence in July 1755, Sneyd 'travelled all night by the light of the moon: 2 miles from the second post we were overturned by the postilion falling asleep'.[36] For many coach accidents, no details were given, but their number suggests that travel was more hazardous than has usually been appreciated. Thus, the coach of Mary, Dowager Duchess of Ancaster (d. 1793) broke down near Florence in 1785, leading her to abandon her first attempt to reach Rome.

Aside from vehicle breakdown, travellers faced a variety of hazards. Trunks could be lost, litters break, and coaches almost fall in the river when postilions lost their way. The miscellaneous, yet frequent, nature of accidents and mishaps is striking. It reflected a society where technology was limited, safety standards were perfunctory, regulatory procedures absent in many spheres, and the general rate of accidents high.

Accidents also occurred when not travelling. The painter and antiquarian James Russel reported from Rome in 1752:

> I had the satisfaction to attend most of the gentlemen travellers at Rome, and amongst others the Lords [George and Frederick] Cavendish; but unfortunately for me, as I was breakfasting with those Lords, Mr. Lowth unluckily let fall a boiling tea-kettle of water upon one of my legs; which accident laid me up for six weeks; whereby I was rendered incapable of serving those gentlemen.

Robert Lowth (1710–87), the Cavendishes' bearleader, was an Oxford academic who eventually became Bishop of London. Another painter, James Irvine, was 'laid up' in Parma in 1788, 'with a strained foot got at blindman's bluff'.[37]

Getting lost was a hazard, although less so in Italy than in Germany. The weather was a particular problem. Rain made roads difficult, and snow melt due to thaw made them impassable. Storms prevented sea and lake travel, high winds river travel, and floods ferry passages. For example, snow on the Apennines in January 1725 blocked the routes for carriages. Even without these hazards, many roads seemed risky to tourists. This was not only true of precipitous passes, but also of some roads close to, and even overhanging, rivers. Crossing the Po in 1793, *en route* from Padua to Ferrara, Sarah Bentham had to use a road along a high, narrow bank close to a river. From Ferrara to Cento, the road also ran on high banks, which struck her as dangerous.[38]

More generally, travel was not easy, and it was rarely pleasant to spend days on end in coaches, another reason for the zeal with which tourists raced from town to town. However, tourists' experience of travel in Britain was not trouble-free. Coaches overturned and travellers were killed, horses fell because of bad roads, and accidents were common.

The hazards of travel have to be placed in perspective. Coach accidents were frequent, but usually not serious. Most of those who died from illnesses were already poorly when they left Britain. A tourist was more likely to suffer from food-poisoning than a stiletto. Nevertheless, the hazards are too readily forgotten. Although they proved serious or fatal in only a few cases, that was scant consolation to travellers wondering whether they would be robbed, involved in a major accident, or afflicted by a serious illness.

Ill Health

Ill health while travelling could be a serious problem. To fall ill in the major towns at least ensured the mixed blessing of medical attention, but outside the towns it was difficult to obtain. Sir Henry Liddell (1708–84) became 'exceedingly ill' in Savoy in 1733, and his bearleader, Shallett Turner (1692–1762), a fellow of Peterhouse, Cambridge, had to ask the British envoy in Turin, William, 3rd Earl of Essex, to persuade his doctor to attend or to send advice.[39] Liddell survived and became an MP, while Turner became Regius Professor of Modern History at Cambridge. Travellers who had accidents crossing the Mont Cenis pass generally had to send to Turin for assistance.

Yet even in the towns, the situation was far from perfect and tourists had little confidence in the attention they could expect. They tended to rely on local doctors, although there was a general preference for British ones. This was not always a wise choice. In February 1784, Brand wrote from Naples that Sir James Graham Bt. (1761–1824), later an MP, had had

> a very violent fever . . . His partiality to everything English made him consult a Physician [Metcalfe] whose skill I hold in sovereign contempt for I found he had no confidence in himself and would have prescribed anything that I proposed. He would have given him Madeira and roast veal when his pulse beat 120 in a minute. [Frances] Lady Warrens' maid died under his care.

Fortunately, Metcalfe fell ill and Brand was able to persuade Graham to consult the well-regarded Neapolitan doctor Cyrillo, who had studied in London, and who cured him.[40] The following October, Thomas, 7th Viscount Bulkeley became ill with 'a bilious fever' because of the heat and fatigue of a journey from Vienna to Venice. At Trieste, the British consul recommended 'an excellent physician',[41] and Bulkeley had no lasting ill-effects.

Much of the ill health suffered was intestinal, due to bad water and poorly prepared food. Pococke found the water at Ferrara to be very bad, the writer Mariana Starke (*c.* 1762–1838) warned of the quality of the water there, as well as at Naples and Venice, and Peter Beckford of that at Cremona and Venice.[42] William, Duke of Gloucester (1743–1805), a brother of George III, had the flux in Tuscany in 1771.

Coughs and colds were another problem. At Naples in 1787, Garmston suffered as a result of watching an eruption of Vesuvius from his balcony for three hours.[43] The volcano had a more serious effect on Frederick, 4th Earl of Bristol and Bishop of Derry (1730–1803), who was seriously injured by a falling stone in 1766 while visiting the crater when the volcano was near erupting. Malaria was a fear in the Campagna,[44] while, in 1775, Alexander, Lord Balgonie (1749–1820), later 9th Earl of Leven, was nearly stung by a scorpion which had crept into his bed at Padua, and also nearly drowned twice in Venice. Most tourists, however, were simply reported as ill, as was George Heneage (1768–1833), a member of a landed Catholic Lincolnshire family, in Venice in 1787. There was no indication what they were suffering from.

Illness affected travel plans. William, 2nd Earl Cowper (1709–64) fell seriously ill at Venice in early 1730. His return home was strongly pressed by John Hollings, a doctor consulted by post, who advised the taking of '40 grains of a viper in powder every morning and evening at any hour he likes best, either in two or three spoonfuls of chicken broth, or wine or water, whichever he pleases, asses milk twice daily and cassia pulp dissolved in a glass of warm barley water twice weekly'. Thanks probably to his youth, Cowper recovered. The previous year, when Stephen Fox (1704–76), an MP and later Earl of Ilchester, suffered ill health, including 'palpitation', in Naples, he received medical advice by post, including 'the opinion of all the physicians that staying in Italy the hot months will be very prejudicial to you'. His companion, John, Lord Hervey, MP (1696–1743), was also very ill.[45]

Although death is not commonly seen as part of the Grand Tour, a number of tourists died. Others were frequently reminded of the risk of mortality. In 1787, Adam Walker saw the gravestone of James Six (*c.* 1758–86), a Fellow of Trinity College, Cambridge, who had died in Rome the previous December, allegedly as a consequence of an over-prescription of laudanum to counter a fever he had contracted following exposure to smoke in ascending Vesuvius. Garmston's passage along the dangerous road between Tolentino and Foligno, where, as with most roads, there was no barrier between the road and its neighbouring precipice, was not eased by the knowledge that several years earlier a British traveller had been killed and his carriage dashed to pieces by the carelessness of the driver.[46]

Most references to deaths, for example that of Henry Hoare (1730–52), the eldest son of the banker, at Naples, gave few, if any, details. It is usually impossible to ascertain whether the traveller was ill before leaving Britain, or whether he or she died as a result of an accident or an illness. Most accounts, especially the brief items in newspapers, do not distinguish between those travelling for pleasure, those who travelled for health, and those who resided abroad.

To travel abroad for health represented a fusion of two of the most important developments in upper-class activities during the century: tourism and travelling for health. On his second European tour, George Berkeley acted as companion and tutor to St George Ashe (*c.* 1698–1721), the son of the Bishop of Clogher, who travelled for health and education. Ashe visited Italy, including Apulia and, in early 1718, Sicily, before dying in Brussels in 1721. In 1739, Spark Molesworth died at Naples, whither he had gone for his health, but Sir Erasmus Philipps MP (1699–1743) survived a similar trip, although his health did not improve. In 1741, Hugh Bethel (*c.* 1691–1752) went to Naples for his asthma, his second trip to Italy, although health had not been the cause of his travel there in 1711–14, when, indeed, he had enrolled at Padua university. Bethel travelled in 1741 with Colonel James Moyser (*c.* 1688–1751), a soldier with an interest in architecture, who also had poor health. Moyser was swiftly cured, but Bethel did not recover until late 1742 and then only when he visited Venice.

Despite these travellers, in the first half of the century far more of those who travelled in search of health went to Spa in the Low Countries. This resort benefited from its proximity to London and from the town's reputation for a good social life in the summer season.

In the second half of the century, however, Naples and the south of France became increasingly popular for invalids: their warm air was seen as beneficial, as indeed was the idea of a change of air, and ideas about what Stevens termed 'the betwitching beauties of the climate'[47] were spread in the travel literature. George Lucy (*c.* 1714–86) spent the winters of 1756–7 and 1757–8 in Naples as part of a tour to Italy intended to help him with health that had been affected by youthful excess. He found the weather bad and the Neapolitans unsociable, but stayed the intervening summer in nearby Gruno. Wills, 1st Earl of Hillsborough (1718–93) took Margaretta, his first wife, to Naples in 1765, but she died there in January 1766, eight weeks after arriving. Dr John Armstrong (1709–79) went to Italy for his health in 1770, and William, Duke of Gloucester went there in 1771–2, in large part in order to find relief for his asthma, although an ancillary reason was his interest in Madame Grovestein, whom he met by arrangement in Italy. He went to Italy again in 1775–7, but this time with his wife Maria and daughter Sophia, and again in 1786–7, on this last occasion with his family and his mistress, the beautiful Lady Almeria Carpenter (d. 1809), who was officially his wife's lady-in-waiting.

The last decade before the French Revolution saw even more Britons travelling to Italy for health. In 1785–6, Augustus, Viscount Keppel (1725–86), a celebrated admiral, who had found his trip to Spa useless, spent the winter in Naples, sailing there directly. In 1788, Dr Philip Lloyd (*c.* 1729–90), Dean of Norwich, was 'much advised to try the heat of an Italian summer' for his health. Three years later, John Carr (1764–1817) took his sister Harriet (1771–1848) to Italy in the hope of curing her consumption. Sir William Forbes Bt. (1739–1806), a prominent banker, went to Italy in 1792–3 with one of his daughters and his wife Elizabeth for the sake of the latter's health. They spent the winter in Naples. Sarah Bentham, her son, John Farr Abbot (*c.* 1756–94), and her ailing daughter-in-law, Mary Pearce (*c.* 1762–93), went as speedily as possible to Naples in 1793, but Mary died within five weeks. That November, Brand wrote from Naples, 'The annual flight of English, men, women and children, is prodigious and all winter round this gulph'.[48] Henry Penton (1736–1812), MP for Winchester, had better luck when, suffering from gout, he went to Naples and Rome in 1793–4 on his second trip to Italy. It is sometimes uncertain that travel was for health reasons, but nevertheless likely. Arthur, Viscount Sudley (1734–1809), later 2nd Earl of Arran, probably went to Italy in 1767–70 for the sake of his first wife, Catherine, who died soon after their return.

Deaths from illness, as opposed to accident, were frequent. Victims included Charles Perrott (*c.* 1677–1706), a member of a wealthy landed Oxfordshire family, of a very violent fever in Venice, Edmond, 2nd Duke of Buckingham (1716–35) of consumption in Rome, and George, Viscount Beauchamp (1725–44) of smallpox in Bologna. Sir James Macdonald of Sleat (1743–66) was ill for much of his time in Italy in 1765–6, particularly, but not only, of 'an universal rheumatism'. This did not prevent him from seeing Herculaneum and Pompeii and climbing Vesuvius, but he died in Rome. In 1785, Sir Humphry Morice (*c.* 1723–85) died at Naples where he had spent most of the last ten years of his life. Mary, Dowager Duchess of Ancaster died in Naples in 1793. Ill health and death must not be forgotten when one sees the self-confident poses of tourists in their portraits.

11.   Activities

> If Italy don't spoil his chastity and Germany his sobriety I flatter myself he will
> preserve the character he sets out with of an honest worthy young man.
>
> Sir George Oxenden of his eldest son, Henry (1721–1803), 1746[1] (Henry, in fact, had a
> relationship with Madame Bulgarini, his *cicisbea*)

Sex

Alongside the stress on the pursuit of education and gentlemanly style in much of the
exemplary literature about tourism, many tourists devoted energy to sex, gambling and
drinking. Travel abroad provided major opportunities for sexual adventure. Tourists were
generally young, healthy and wealthy, and were poorly, if at all, supervised. A large number
made a beeline for the high-class courtesans and also took full advantage of the relaxed
sexual habits of married women. In 1751, Lady Mary Wortley Montagu claimed that 'the boys
only remember where they met with the best wine or the prettyest women'.

Many tourists enjoyed sexual relations while abroad, but, to a great extent, it was the well-
behaved, such as Thomas Pelham, and scholars, such as Richard Pococke, who wrote lengthy
letters. There is very little personal correspondence, other than demands for money, from
those whose conduct was castigated by their contemporaries. The vast majority of the
journals that have been preserved relate to blameless or apparently blameless tourists, but
the latter reflects a process of selection. In his lengthy account of his travels published in
1726–38, John Breval (*c.* 1680–1738), who was in Italy in 1721 as bearleader to George
Cholmondeley (1703–70), later an MP and 3rd Earl of Cholmondeley, made no mention of
the Milanese nun with whom he allegedly had a relationship. As Breval had earlier lost his
Cambridge fellowship after assaulting his then mistress's husband, it is unclear what moral
guidance he offered.

Philip Francis might speculate on whether he would prefer relations with the Venus de'Medici (a reference point and source of erotic impulses for other tourists as well) or Titian's Venus,[2] but such daydreaming was banished from the accounts of his more respectable contemporaries, although Kenelm Digby (1754–1812) sought to find in Verona in 1790 'beauteous females' similar to those painted by Veronese. Alban Butler (1710–73), bearleader to James (*c.* 1728–90) and Thomas (b. *c.* 1728) Talbot in 1746, would not allow them to see the Venus de'Medici as its 'softness and grace of life' made it 'too dangerous an object for any one to look upon'. He was a Jesuit and his charges both became Catholic priests, an untypical fate for those on the Grand Tour.

In several cases, there is evidence that journals and correspondence have been tampered with subsequently, presumably by descendants; and this may well have been widespread. Some of the obliterations in the manuscript narrative of James, 4th Viscount Charlemont (1728–99), who was in Italy from 1747 until 1754, are opposite passages describing matters of sexual interest.[3] A letter of 1764 from Francis, Marquess of Tavistock to John, 2nd Earl of Upper Ossory (1745–1818) included a reference to Topham Beauclerk (1739–80), the latter's travelling companion in 1763–4: 'I am amused at your account of Beauclerk but wish rather to see him gaming and setting up in England than engaged with so dangerous a woman as the Cornara', the phrase 'engaged with' being added in a different hand above another that has been obscured.[4] Obliterations in a journal of a visit to Italy in 1784, possibly by Marmaduke William Constable (d. 1819), a member of a Yorkshire Catholic landed family, may have removed sexual references.[5] Some obscure references in journals may be sexual. Sneyd referred to being 'introduced to 2B' in July 1754, while, a year later, he 'took Lena'.[6]

It is not known in some cases whether tourists who were noted for sexual exploits acquired that reputation in Italy. In 1769, William, 2nd Earl of Harrington (1717–79) may have been the 'Lord Herington' reported in Florence. Four years later, Henry Conway (1719–95) wrote about his planned tour: 'I shall not run, or rather limp after whores and opera girls like poor Lord Harrington in pink and green'.[7] Other tourists noted for sexual exploits in France, such as Evelyn, 2nd Duke of Kingston (1711–73) and William Dalrymple (d. 1807), also visited Italy, in 1730–2 and 1785–6 respectively, presumably with similar interests.

The public attitude to sexual adventure abroad was generally unfavourable. Encapsulating the sense of threat that foreign travel aroused, it was heavily influenced by the prevalence of venereal disease, the ravages of which substantially defied contemporary medicine, and the consequences of which could be serious, not only from the point of view of individual health and morale, but also because it harmed the chances of securing heirs to an estate.

Venereal disease was indeed a serious problem. Charles Howard, Viscount Morpeth (1719–41), an MP and son of Henry, 4th Earl of Carlisle (1694–1758), with whom he toured

Italy in 1738–9, died of venereal disease contracted in Italy, precipitating a by-election in Yorkshire. In 1754, Sir Charles Hotham Bt. (1735–67), who had been sent abroad due to poor health, wrote from Naples, 'Sir James Gray [the British envoy] carried me to the Princess Francavillas who my Lord Rockingham has still I fear some reason to remember. If she was no handsomer when he had to do with her than she is now, he in my opinion deserved what he got, the p-x, for his pains. Such a parcel of ugly women as is in this town, I think I never saw in any one place in my life'.[8] Charles, 2nd Marquess of Rockingham (1730–82), who toured Italy in 1748–50 when Earl of Malton, was twice later First Lord of the Treasury and therefore head of the ministry: in 1765–6 and 1782. Hotham noted that he had been spoilt at Siena where he had met a very beautiful woman. Lewis Monson (1728–95), the second son of Lord Monson, and later an MP, caught venereal disease in Florence in 1750. Henry Pelham Clinton (1750–78), eldest son of Henry, 9th Earl of Lincoln, and later an MP, contracted venereal disease in Florence in 1771 from the Venetian dancer Maria Lamberti, who supplemented her income by prostitution, although the relationship between presents, protection and prostitution was far from clear-cut, particularly to tourists. An anonymous writer suggested that 'a great many of our gentlemen travellers have reason enough to be cross on account of some modish distemper the Italian ladies may have bestowed on them with the rest of their favours'.[9] A long series of distinguished tourists remembered their travels for years afterwards for reasons that bore little relation to the restrained portraits by Batoni that decorated their libraries.

The language used by some of the tourists to describe their affairs was noteworthy as a clear contrast to Addisonian restraint and the discourse of politeness that has received so much scholarly attention. This politeness was not so much descriptive as a strategy to cope with a very different culture by inculcating particular aspirations and norms. The contrast remains today. It is instructive to consider entries in John Ingamells's superb *Dictionary of British and Irish Travellers in Italy 1701–1800* in the light of surviving papers. The entry for Thomas Steavens (*c*. 1728–?1759), the son of a prominent London timber merchant, refers to his blaming women for illness in 1753 and to his having been, in 1755, in 'the good graces of the prettiest lady' in Rome, and a marchioness to boot, but, although there is reference in a footnote to letters from Steavens in the correspondence of his friend Sir Charles Hanbury Williams, the following are not quoted. In 1752, Steavens described his visit to Italy in 1749–50:

about half a mile from Leghorn I met the Ancilla who had heard of my being there . . . [meeting] began on mine [side] by an entire loss of sense of motion. As soon as I could move, I got into her chaise, and as soon as I could speak I began to reproach, though I had no sort of reason to be angry, but, though we were but half a mile from Leghorn, I had questioned, argued, reproached, quarrelled, and made everything up before we reached

the gates of the town. We stayed there that night, and I promised to see her back to Florence
. . . We lay the next night at Lucca and the night after at Florence, I was there three days,
without once thinking of the Venus of Medicis; as for our parting, – if you can form to
yourself all the wilderness of misery and grief, all the agonys, tremblings and torments that
can enter into the heart of man, you will have an idea of my condition; I had never known
till then what happiness and misery were, and I must take this opportunity of saying that,
if all the foolish and all the malicious devils that infest this world were to tell me that the
Ancilla did not love me at that time, I would not believe them. I know Italian nature well
enough, but I know human nature too well to think that the latter can be so far disguised
by the former. Vice may wear an appearance to virtue, there may be policy in that, but I
have proofs of this girl's sincerity and generosity too. I left Florence about three in the
morning, when I came to Lucca began a letter to the Ancilla, but was too miserable to end
it, sent on my baggage to Lerici, and returned to Florence. I stayed there two days more,
and then set out again.

Back at home, Steavens caught venereal disease from a Drury Lane orange-seller. Having
had the painful recourse of a mercury cure in Paris, he recuperated at Angers where his
thoughts returned to Italy and the Ancilla:

we wrote constantly to one another, but, however pressing her letters might be, I always
declined giving her any hopes of seeing me again. Notwithstanding this, I was miserable
beyond measure when I heard, about three months afterwards, that a Mr. Lethieullier was
excessively in love with her. She informed me herself of this, and desired to know whether
she should let him visit her; her motive was want of money for, though she was strong in
gowns, lace, snuffboxes etc. she had not much of the ready. My motive for not forbidding
her Lethieullier's company was the fear of laying myself under an obligation to return to
her, thus was I divided between love and prudence. I wrote her however most violent
letters for doing what I had tacitly consented to, that is letting Lethieullier frequent her
house. I reproached her with it when we met, but her behaviour at that time, as well as
what I had learnt at Naples, from English who were come from Florence, and at Leghorn,
where she had danced at the Carnival, convinced me that I was the amant du coeur, and
the other merely an affair of convenience – this then is the subject of my ode which was
made at Genoa.

Steavens included a poem of love and sexual jealousy. Benjamin Lethieullier (1729–97), who
was in Italy in 1750–2 with his half-brother Lascelles Iremonger, was later an MP. His entry
in the *Dictionary* makes no mention of this relationship, and this leads to the possibility that
many other entries are similarly limited. In 1753–6, Steavens returned to Italy where he was
in the good graces of the marchioness.[10]

Philip Francis observed: 'In England the commerce between the sexes is either passion or pleasure; in France it is gallantry, sentiment or intrigue; in Italy it is a dull insipid *business*.'[11] Many tourists found their time far from dull. Italy was notorious for prostitution, especially Venice, whose courtesans were reputed for their skill: 'the most insinuating, and have the most alluring arts of any in all Christendom', according to Stevens. Some tourists became heavily involved. Pococke wrote from Venice in June 1734, 'Mr. Wynn . . . has been 2 or 3 years at Venice, enchanted with a mistress', a reference to Richard Wynne (b. *c.* 1704), who had been in Italy since 1729. Three years later, Henry, 3rd Earl of Radnor's dominance by a Venetian mistress attracted comment. Radnor (*c.* 1695–1741) spent much of his life after 1726 in Italy, living with a singer he met in Naples that March. One of the brothers of the 4th Earl of Chesterfield 'spent a great deal of money on a Venetian woman, whom he thought in love with him'. In 1763, Francis, Marquess of Tavistock warned John, Earl of Upper Ossory that 'Venice [which he had visited the previous year] is the most calculated for luxurious idleness of any place I know and therefore very dangerous to you'.[12]

Two years earlier, John Hinchliffe, with all the disapprobation of a clerical bearleader, remarked, 'If licentiousness is the same thing as liberty, no nation upon earth enjoy an equal freedom with the Venetians.' In contrast, Algernon, Earl of Hertford (1684–1750), later an MP, a general and 7th Duke of Somerset, and the father of George, Viscount Beauchamp, found Venice fun in 1706 and captured the *frisson* and excitement: 'beauties without number who are so good natured as to take all occasions to pull off their masks, and not let us, sighing over the case, be long without seeing the treasure it guards'. He spent at least a fortnight in Venice. John Stackhouse (1742–1819), a former fellow of Exeter College, Oxford, who toured Italy in 1772, reported dark designs at work:

> The turn for gallantry in Venice is supposed to be as strong if not stronger than in other parts of Italy. The *casinos*, a sort of private house which are often used for these sort of engagements, are in so general vogue that hardly any man of considerable fashion is without one. It is supposed that the state out of policy not only suffers this turn for debauchery but even encourages it, to prevent its citizens from being too busy in affairs of government.[13]

Venice was not the sole cockpit of sexual adventure. In Rome in late 1729, John, Viscount Hinton (1708–64), later 2nd Earl Poulett, broke the windows of the house of a woman of 'mauvaise vie'. He left the city with his twin, Peregrine Poulett (1708–52), later an MP, having lived a life that brought him scarcely any honour, according to Baron Philip Stosch (1691–1757), who sent the government reports on tourists judged suspect. In 1739, Thomas, 2nd Lord Mansell (1719–44) was provided with a list of villas, palaces and churches to see in Italy. These were marked as the journey progressed in 1739–40, but he was also notorious for his whoring.[14]

Women indeed provided part of the education of travel. In 1760, Charles Boothby Skrymsher (*c.* 1740–1800) was in Turin where 'he attached himself . . . to a very clever woman, who was of great service to him; she brushed him up greatly'. The far older Madame de St Gilles (the Contessa di San Gillio) also aroused the passion of Lord Charles Spencer (1740–1820), second son of the 3rd Duke of Marlbourough, later an MP. The following year, Boothby's departure from Florence left the Countess Marianna Acciaioli in tears.

A decade earlier, Philip Stanhope (1732–68), later an MP and a diplomat, met Eugenia Peters (d. 1783) in Rome, subsequently secretly marrying her in a union of two illegitimate children. His father, Philip, 4th Earl of Chesterfield, who never visited Italy, was strongly opposed to the match. Chesterfield's correspondence reveals that his son was not only smitten by love in Italy: 'The Princess Borghese was so kind as to put him a little upon his haunches, by putting him frequently upon her own. Nothing dresses a young fellow more than having been between such pillars, with an experienced mistress of that kind of manége.'[15]

The Princess, Agnese Colonna (1702–80), was indeed popular with tourists. According to Edward Thomas in 1750, she had 'an assembly every evening of the top people of Rome'. In December 1740, Horace Walpole wrote to Henry, 9th Earl of Lincoln (1720–94), later also 2nd Duke of Newcastle:

> I did not give you so strong an idea of the Princess Borghese, as you seem to have contracted. I did not imagine *she would even surpass what you could have the assurance to hope for*. I knew your merit, and thought on some occasions you would not want assurance; and her benevolence and penetration have been known. I only hope that the presence of the Prince did not confine her good nature to under the pharaoh table.[16]

The idea of sex with a woman of position clearly excited some tourists, and rumours of their conquests spread. Thomas Coke recorded being told by the poet David Mallet (*c.* 1705–65), who had served as bearleader to James Newsham in 1735–7, 'that he had lain with a Sovereign Princess in Italy'. Brand reported from Pisa in 1791 that an Irish peer was there with his wife and his mistress, an Italian countess.[17] Others were less exalted in their preferences. Sir Bourchier Wrey (*c.* 1714–84), later an MP, allegedly had sex with his landlady in Rome in 1740 with the encouragement of her husband.[18]

Lincoln had a varied Grand Tour from the emotional point of view, falling in love with Lady Sophia Fermor (1721–45), whom he met in Florence in late 1740[19] and also saw in Rome and Venice, and making himself unhappy on her account. Sophia was travelling with her father, Thomas, 1st Earl of Pomfret, mother Henrietta and sister Charlotte. Lincoln was also noted for his energy as a lover. Walpole, with whom Lincoln may have had a sexual relationship, sought to lure him from Turin to Genoa by telling him of the 'millions of pretty women' there,[20] while Sir Charles Hanbury Williams wrote him an ode including the lines

> . . . when I say that you fuck more
> Than ever mortal did before
> You know it is but truth.[21]

George Lyttelton (1709–73) set off for Italy in 1729 with a warning from his father against 'grapes, new wine, and pretty women'. The engagement of George's son Thomas (1744–79), later an MP, was broken off in late 1764 because he was 'detained by circes and syrens of the coast about Genoa'. Taking with a lock of his fiancé's hair had served little good. Thomas had been thoroughly warned by his father of the 'danger from Italian amours', as well as 'of the other danger', presumably homosexual relations. His father thought religion the sole safeguard 'against the circes of Italy' but, as Thomas was not devout, feared he had no protection 'against a handsome countenance'. In 1769–71, Lyttelton made a second trip with a mistress claiming to be his wife, by whom he had a son.[22]

Francis Whithed (1719–51) visited Italy in 1740–6 with his elder cousin John Chute (1701–76). They spent 1741–5 in Florence where Whithed had a mistress, Angiola Lucchi, by whom he had a daughter, Sophia, to whom he eventually left £6,000. Francis, Marquess of Tavistock (1739–67), and his close friend Thomas Robinson, MP (1738–86), later 2nd Lord Grantham, were both tempted by married Italian women. In April 1762, Tavistock wrote to Robinson from Bologna: 'I got your letter two days before I left Rome. I tried 2 or 3 times to see the Contesstabilessa but was always unfortunate, and as her husband is said to be very watchful at present, I was afraid to send it her by a note as I thought it might produce disgrazzias in the family.' That December, he wrote again from Genoa:

> whether my constancy is as frail in vertue as in love, I cannot tell – at Turin I saw the D—s, who was very civil to me as well as her husband, yet in spite of her beauty vertue (not virtue) conquered love . . . As to the D. I lived a good deal in their house and I found it very agreable as his Grace is in great spirits and good humour, but I kept clear of all thoughts of love. Indeed I hope to do the same all through Italy for if once that gets hold of me, I can no longer answer for myself. The Princess Gilles and I were very well together for our short acquaintance. She charged me with a 1,000 humorous messages for Lord Charles Spencer through you on the subject of the Gabrieli. Tell him if ever he hopes again for her good graces to write to her and renounce the Gabrieli, who carries his picture round her arm and his heart on her neck.[23]

Caterina Gabrielli was an opera singer whose favours were enjoyed by more than one tourist. In 1785, the envoy in Turin had to intervene in the case of 'a silly young countryman of ours, Mr Fox Lane, a man of fashion and great fortune having, from an infatuated complaisance to the lady he was in love with, changed his religion, or rather for the first time adopted one, which unluckily for him, is the Roman Catholic . . . all I could do was to get him away from hence as soon as possible – he is gone to England . . . I cannot but look upon this step as an act of infatuation and childishness.'[24]

Horace Mann commented on how 'an English traveller frequently deranges the whole harmony of "cicisbeship"', by which a married woman had a male companion who accompanied her to social gatherings, and was sometimes her lover. The system provided opportunities for a relationship that was in accordance with local customs. In the spring of 1791, Brand took his charge, Charles, Lord Bruce (1773–1856), to Siena 'to see an old lady to whom Lord Ailesbury [Thomas, 4th Earl, 1729–1814] was cavalier servente *thirty nine* years ago! . . . She gave us many anecdotes of Lord Ailesbury's Siena life which perhaps had better been concealed.' The lady urged Bruce to live like his father, 'the very reflexion' Brand had wished to avoid.[25] Thomas Pelham of Stanmer (1728–1805), later Lord Pelham and eventually 1st Earl of Chichester, had a long affair in Florence in 1750 with the married Countess Acciaioli, who then took another British lover. Pelham's wife Anne, whom he married in 1754, warned their son Thomas (1756–1826), who visited Italy in 1777, about the moral snares of tourism: 'the trials and temptations of all sorts to which in a world of vice, dissipation, and luxury, you will be exposed, how much you will be invited to depart from the paths of virtue and religion in which you have hitherto walked'.[26]

The Countess Acciaioli's married friend Maria Serristori had a relationship with Rockingham in 1748–9. Florence was clearly a city where many tourists had an active sex life. In 1739–40, Thomas Worsley (1710–78), later an MP, was the *cicisbeo* of the Countess Maria Anna Suares. In 1755, Francis, 10th Earl of Huntingdon (1729–89) was reputed to be the lover of Marchesa Capponi, 'the flower of Florentine nobility and, as I've heard, lewdness'.[27] In 1760, in the same city, George, Viscount Fordwich, MP (1738–89), later 3rd Earl Cowper, spent 'his whole time by acting the *cicisbeo* to the Marchesa [Corsi]'.

This practice did not please some female tourists. In 1788, Nancy Flaxman (*c.* 1760–1820), the wife of the sculptor John Flaxman, condemned it as an 'odious custom'. However, not all British were critical. Anne Miller suggested that

if the Bolognese ladies are censured for gallantry, some allowance should be made for their education in convents, and their being led to the altar as victims, for sacrifice to any disagreable wretch their parents think proper to bestow them upon.

She also provided guidance as to costs, at least in Florence:

This city is in high favour with young Englishmen; who are perfectly at their ease during their residence here. The ladies in general of easy virtue, and their expenses light, as a genteel present is from two to five sequins; it is true, these ladies are apt to borrow to supply their play-purses, but the sums are but small.[28]

Francis Drake offered clerical admonition about 'cicisbeship', although he also saw at least one advantage:

> There is one great inconvenience that attends most of my countrymen, from the vast civility of the softer sex, whose endearing behaviour detains them too long, while by some tender attachment to a favourite cicesbeia, they lose too much of their time. It is always observed, that those who have stayed the longest at Siena are the most perfect in the language, since a few lessons from a female instructor, make a stronger impression on the mind, than all the learned lectures of a male tutor.

Siena was allegedly the best place to learn Italian, as it was apparently spoken there with the greatest of elegance and purity.[29]

'Cicisbeship' contributed to the idea that Italian women were highly sexed, which was the counterpart to the idea, expressed by George Carpenter in 1717, that Italian men, including the better sort, 'are much given to pimping'. Richard Creed noted in Livorno in May 1700: 'Here it is the fashion when a man has a miss; he must go to her window in the daytime and court her, that all the town may see him make his addresses; and this the women pride themselves in mightily; the men must ask and beg to be let in; although they are sure to the contrary; but at night, when nobody sees, the women are not so hardhearted as to keep the men in the cold.'[30]

Reporting that two prominent Genoese women had obtained divorce on the grounds of impotence, and that a third was to follow, Swinton wrote:

> In short the Genoese ladies, if not belied, have larger expectations and higher notions of the pleasures of matrimony than they ought to have; insomuch that divorces are very frequent amongst them, and a man must be of determined courage, mettle, and resolution to venture upon some of them. They are the proudest creatures in the universe, and most intolerably and insufferably insolent, especially to their husbands.

Although Stevens praised the beauty of the women in Rome (albeit writing that they applied too much paint), and Pococke those of Padua, some male tourists were less than impressed by the looks of the women they met. In Genoa, Swinton noted:

> the generality of women here are the most ugly hags in the universe. Their heads are of a monstrous size, their complexion swarthy and olive-coloured, their features large and their mouths exceeding wide . . . I imagine myself in the land of Gorgons. What few beauties we have here are chiefly of the nobility, who are pretty much confined, as in most other foreign countries . . . This is my opinion, what sort of beauty is suited to the Italian taste I know not, but I'm certain an Englishman would be shocked at the sight of them.

Francis, 10th Earl of Huntingdon was unimpressed by the women in Turin who had affairs with British tourists. William, Marquess of Kildare (1749–1804), later 2nd Duke of Leinster, found the society ladies of Naples 'hideous' in 1766, and thought there was an 'astonishing' number of 'ugly women' in Florence the following year, although, in 1788, Charles Abbot recorded that the common observation that Florentine women were very beautiful was true. In 1772, Philip Francis claimed:

> In general the women have bad features, and worse complexions, particularly the Neapolitans, who, I think, are the most unhealthy looking people I ever saw. Yet I do not deny that there is beauty in Italy. The women rub their faces and necks with powder and leave it on. This I fancy, besides looking nasty, spoils the skin.[31]

Brand was more scathing about Sicilian women.[32] The frequency of comment on the looks of Italian women suggests not only that tourists were interested in them, but also that it was believed to be an appropriate subject for comment.

Foreign travel also provided an opportunity for couples to live together unconstrained by the pressures of British life. In 1744, George, Earl of Euston (1715–47), MP, the heir to the Duke of Grafton, who had already toured Italy in 1734–5, and was now a widower, eloped there with a Miss Neville 'of a very ancient family in Lincolnshire, with eleven thousand pounds for her fortune; and celebrated beauty', giving her a promise of marriage that he never fulfilled. Lovers who did not elope still found it convenient to leave the country. Free from prying eyes, Henry Fox, 1st Lord Holland (1705–74), later a prominent politician, could live with his older protector and Dorset neighbour, Susanna Strangways-Horner (1689–1758), who left her husband and travelled with Fox and her daughter Elizabeth, partly in Italy, in 1732–4. Widows also benefited from the opportunities of foreign travel. Frances, Countess of Salisbury (1670–1713), widow of the 4th Earl of Salisbury, visited Italy in 1700–1, Colonel Josselyn following 'at a modest lover's distance'.[33]

Italy was a haven for wives who did not get on with their husbands, irrespective of whether they had other relationships. Margaret, Countess of Orford (1709–81), daughter-in-law of Sir Robert Walpole, pleaded ill health as her reason to stay in Italy from 1733, where she had a number of lovers, including the Reverend Samuel Sturgis (*c.* 1701–43), her lover from 1736 until she dispensed with him in 1741, moving on, in 1741–2, to Pietro Barbarigo, son of the Governor of Verona, and then, in 1742–5, to Count Richecourt, chief minister of Tuscany. Horace Mann informed Horace Walpole in 1743 that 'the reputation of our female travellers is very low'. Margaret returned to Italy in 1755. By then her first husband, the 2nd Earl of Orford, had died (in 1751) and she was separated from her second, the Hon. Sewallis Shirley (1709–65), an MP who had visited Italy in 1731–2. From 1755, she was linked to Giulio Mozzi (1730–1813), a Florentine poet. Having returned to Britain in 1770, she lived in Italy from 1771 until her death in Pisa in 1781. Elizabeth, Lady Craven (1750–1828) travelled abroad after separating from her husband in 1781, visiting Italy in 1785 and 1789–90, on the latter occasion with Christian, Margrave of Brandenburg-Ansbach, whom she was to marry in 1791.

Men also found it convenient to carry on relationships abroad. After being acquitted of rape in 1768, Frederick, 6th Lord Baltimore (1731–71) left England. In Venice in 1771, he had a 'seraglio [harem] of Italians, Greeks, Blacks etc.', and he died in Naples that year leaving a seven-strong 'seraglio'.

Living with another's spouse was also easier abroad. Jane, Countess of Lanesborough (1737–1828), daughter of the Earl of Belvidere and widow of Brinsley, 2nd Earl of Lanesborough, lived in Livorno with John King (*c.* 1753–1823), a Jewish moneylender and political pamphleteer, until King's wife and children arrived in 1785, whereupon King divorced his wife. He and Lady Lanesborough stayed in Italy, the *Town and Country Magazine* referring in 1787 to 'the degenerate Countess'; they died in Florence in 1823 and 1828 respectively.

Without any comparable breach of social and religious divides, Elizabeth, Lady Webster (1771–1840) separated from her older husband Sir Godfrey Webster Bt. (1748–1800) to travel with Henry, 3rd Lord Holland (1773–1840) in 1795. They married in 1797, and Sir Godfrey killed himself in 1800. In the same milieu, William Amherst (1773–1857), later a diplomat, Governor-General of Bengal, and Earl Amherst, who toured Italy in 1794–6, had, from 1795, a relationship with Sarah, Countess of Plymouth (1762–1838), who was in Italy with her husband Other, 5th Earl of Plymouth (1751–99) and two children in 1791–6. After the Earl died, the Countess married Amherst in 1800. Lady Knight was scandalised:

> They talk and act as their convenience directs. I am told laws civil and divine are not any guide to their words or actions . . . our present travelling ladies out-Herod Herod, or to speak more modernly, live with more effrontery than even their teachers, the French ladies.[34]

Although they did not live together, Henrietta, Countess of Bessborough (1761–1821) attracted Lord Granville Leveson-Gower (1773–1846) when they met in Italy in 1794: her husband, Frederick, the 3rd Earl (1758–1844), had returned to deal with problems in his inheritance. She bore a child by Leveson-Gower in 1800, while Sarah Plymouth's second daughter, born in 1797, was reputedly the child of Amherst. Henrietta's mother, Margaret, Viscountess Spencer (1737–1814), who travelled to Italy with her husband and one of her daughters in 1763, had to put up with the assumption that she would take part in Italian social customs. George, Viscount Villiers wrote to her:

> You have hitherto scarcely stopped long enough at any town in Italy to make acquaintances with the people of the country, but at Rome you may possibly, and certainly at Naples. And that you will have a cavalier servente is as certain. Do not therefore be so reserved as not to let us know who it is; whether it is a Don Tito or a Don Antonio, il Signor Marchese, or only an humble Abbate, let us but have his name. It will come round from others whether you tell it or no . . . You might as well think of going to a conversationi in an English riding dress as without a cecisbeo.[35]

26. *Henry, 3rd Lord Holland,* by François Xavier Fabre, 1795, one of his six portraits of Holland. Holland (1773–1840) had succeeded his father in 1774 and been educated at Eton and Christ Church. After Oxford, he travelled abroad in 1791, arriving in Italy in 1793, and finally leaving, via Trieste and Vienna, in 1796. In the meanwhile, Holland travelled widely and began a relationship with Elizabeth, Lady Webster, who was to divorce her husband and to marry Holland in 1797.

Villiers's letter captures the goldfish-bowl quality that the Tour gave rise to in aristocratic circles, with the activities of friends, relations and acquaintances being widely reported, as Italy and London were linked by letter. At times, there is a novelistic quality to the resulting descriptions of events and settings, with a comparable conflation of picaresque detail and epistolary structure.

While it was possible to conduct an affair more openly than in London, that did not mean that all were so conducted; and local society could be disapproving if proprieties and conventions were breached. Sir Brook Bridges Bt. (1733–91), later an MP, withdrew completely from Florentine society while carrying on a torrid affair with 'a dancing girl' in 1760. In 1778, Ferdinand IV of Naples and his wife Maria Carolina refused to receive at court Anne 'Nancy' Parsons (*c.* 1735–1814), then travelling with her younger husband, Charles, 2nd Viscount Maynard (1752–1824), because she had a 'past' as a result of a visit to Naples in 1770 as the mistress of John, 3rd Duke of Dorset (1745–99). John, Lord Boringdon, who was to meet her in Turin in 1793, described her as 'a woman of strong sense, but not very feminine manners'.[36]

Homosexuality was regarded in Britain as a foreign vice of Mediterranean origins, as indeed was sodomy. Homosexuality had long been particularly associated with Italy, was indeed sometimes called 'the Italian vice', and in some writings was linked to Catholicism. There was also a widespread conviction that Italy was, in the words of Adam Walker, an 'effeminate country'. In 1716, Henry Davenant, the envoy in Genoa, wrote:

> Mr. [Richard] Cresswell was arrested by an order of a Deputation of the Senate, which has the inspection in cases of sodomy . . . He was immediately carried to the prison . . . with a young Genoese boy he had lately dressed up . . . He has been so public in his discourse and actions that they can fix on him the fact above 38 times, in his own house, the streets, in porches of churches and palaces, in short I never heard of so flagrant a delinquent . . .[37]

Cresswell (1688–1743) had been an MP (1710–15) and was married.

In the second half of the eighteenth century, a period of repression in Britain replaced the relative tolerance of the first half, when the laws were not enforced. As no such equivalent hardening of attitudes took place in Italy (or France), it seemed apparent that travel abroad offered the best opportunities for practising homosexuality. George, 8th Earl of Huntingdon (1677–1705) procured partners in Venice in 1703. William Beckford had a homosexual crush in Venice in 1780. A sense of rejection by society led him to leave England for Naples in 1782. John, 2nd Earl Tylney (1712–84) died in Naples: he had lived from 1752 in Italy.

Seeking sex in Italy was widely accepted, but problems were created when impressionable young men fell in love. Venereal disease was bad, but so was a *mésalliance*. Male tourists could fall in love with either female tourists or other women. This entailed the risk that the careful matrimonial economy of dowries and connections would be upset, and represented a more serious threat to aristocratic prestige and parental supervision than other forms of tourist activity. In Rome in 1793, Charles, Lord Bruce (1773–1856) fell for Henrietta Hill, a slightly older tourist who had arrived in Italy the previous autumn with her mother, Anna, Lady Berwick, a widow, and her two sisters. They married outside Florence in May 1793, but with the blessing of Bruce's father, Thomas, 1st Earl of Ailesbury. Later that year, Henrietta attracted the interest of Edward, Viscount Coleshill (1773–1856), but 'only coquets with him'. Lady Berwick failed in her attempts to marry off her other two daughters, Anne and Emily. In general, marriage was not the issue. Douglas, 8th Duke of Hamilton (1756–99) became involved with 'Lady A–n' in Naples in 1776, transferring his desire when he visited Florence later that year to Louise, Countess of Albany, the wife of the Young Pretender.[38]

Foreign women were also the targets for British men, leading to much heartache and helping to underline to British relatives the degree of volatility and social uncertainty that the Grand Tour could give rise to. Forceful intervention was necessary in some cases. The involvement of George, Viscount Parker (c. 1697–1764) with a Venetian woman, and his failure to heed the instructions of his father, Thomas, 1st Earl of Macclesfield, the Lord

Chancellor, led Macclesfield to mobilise diplomatic support to regain his son in 1722. Parker became an MP and was married that year, and he later succeeded his father as 2nd Earl of Macclesfield. Parker's bearleader, the antiquarian Edward Wright, described their travels in *Some Observations Made in Travelling through France, Italy, etc.* (1730), but his charge's sex life was not considered a fit subject for mention.

In 1743, James Stuart Mackenzie (1719–1800), the second son of the 2nd Earl of Bute, and later an MP and envoy to Turin, eloped to Venice with Barberina Campanini, a famous dancer he had met in London, only for the British envoy in Berlin to have her be forced to fulfil her contract to perform in Berlin, from where Mackenzie was banned. Nothing so dramatic had occurred on his earlier trip to Italy in 1739–41. Barberina had earlier engaged the attention of Samuel Dashwood (1717–94), when he visited Italy in 1740–1. The painter James Irvine (1757–1831) wrote a letter in 1788 that revealed much heartache, although, in the event, he did not return to Britain:

> I said I would go and make love at Parma and so get turned out of doors and finish the business completely. There is little danger of that happening, but my present sensations make one wish to disengage myself as soon as possible of every object which can detain me in Italy where I am likely to enjoy little happiness either real or lasting, and to return to England where by an active life I may dispel all gloomy and disagreable ideas.[39]

It is not surprising that impressionable young men, poorly, if at all, supervised, sometimes fell for local women. Very few married them. Older tourists could consult their own convenience. In 1705, Charles, 1st Duke of Shrewsbury (1660–1718), a prominent politician, married Countess Adelhida Paleotti, a widow whom he met in Rome in 1701. She first converted to Protestantism.

Such unions were unusual. Brief affairs or visits to brothels were far more common, although it is impossible to assess the extent to which tourists took advantage of the possibilities. Prostitution was open and readily available. To judge from correspondence and journals, 'the low vices of our countrymen in Italy', of which Walter Bowman (1699–1782), bearleader in 1732–4 to Simon, 2nd Viscount Harcourt, complained,[40] were of less interest than accommodation and food, painting and statuary. Contemporary printed criticism would suggest otherwise. There was no common response to the opportunities of travel, and no reason why there should have been one.

Gambling

The same was true of gambling, which played a major role in polite society. As in Britain, where gambling was seen as a way to show sporting character and a gentlemanly disdain for conventional caution, many tourists gambled heavily. They were happy to wager on most things. In 1767, Charles James Fox won a bet with his cousin William, Marquess of Kildare in Florence on how many sheets of paper the latter had with him. Most tourists, however, gambled on cards, often with each other. On 13 February 1704, the Duke of Shrewsbury played whist all day in Rome with George, 3rd Earl of Cardigan (1685–1732), George, 8th Earl of Huntingdon (1677–1705), and Edward, Viscount Quarendon (1681–1713), cards serving as a common link for men of different ages. Charles Stanhope gambled heavily in Venice in 1732. The Duke of Gloucester 'played at cards with a few English gentlemen' at the masked ball held in his honour in Livorno in 1771. Tavistock wrote of Turin in 1762:

> I played almost every night for want of something to do and generally lost about 10 or 20 pistoles but the last night but one I had an immense run of luck and won about 80 which brought me near exactly home. I should be sorry to be thought to game deep amongst such thieves as these are.[41]

Losses could be serious. The Jacobite Catholic Sir Carnaby Haggerston (*c.* 1700–56), who visited Italy in 1718, showed a great facility for losing money that made his frequent requests for funds less acceptable.[42] John, 2nd Lord Boringdon lost about £165 on his tour of 1793–4, out of the tour's total cost of £1,350. Gambling losses, like venereal disease, represented the threats posed by whim and passion to the attempt to safeguard order and stability in the fortunes of Georgian families. Tourism accentuated the risks in both cases.

Drinking

Many tourists drank heavily. Alcohol was inexpensive and easy to obtain. There were few barriers to alcoholic consumption and little condemnation of heavy social drinking. In 1743, Horace Walpole directed his acid at the pretensions of 'the Dilettanti, a club, for which the nominal qualification is having been in Italy, and the real one, being drunk: the two chiefs are Lord Middlesex and Sir Francis Dashwood, who were seldom sober the whole time they were in Italy'.[43] Charles, Earl of Middlesex (1711–69), later 2nd Duke of Dorset, had toured Italy in 1731–3 and 1736–8, while Dashwood (1708–81), a baronet who became an MP, Chancellor of the Exchequer, and Lord le Despenser, was there in 1730–1 and 1739–40. The Society of Dilettanti, founded in 1732 by young men who had toured Italy, testified to the conviviality of tourism, but also to the varied pleasures it offered. The Society recreated the experience back in London, by being at once an amiable dining club, where drink flowed liberally, and a body that sponsored the arts, encouraging archaeological, artistic and operatic links with Italy.

Many tourists commented on the propensity of compatriots to enjoy drink. The architect George Dance (1741–1825), who was in Italy in 1759–64, subsequently produced a caricature

27. *British Gentlemen at Sir Horace Mann's Home in Florence*, by Thomas Patch, 1763–5. One of Patch's successful caricature groups, this depicted one of the entertainments that Sir Horace Mann was noted for and that contributed greatly to the pleasure of British tourists in Florence.

28. *A Punch Party*, by Thomas Patch, 1760. A satirical account of the exuberance of tourists, specifically the importance of alcohol to their socialising. Patch's paintings are a valuable counterpoint to the portraits more commonly depicted.

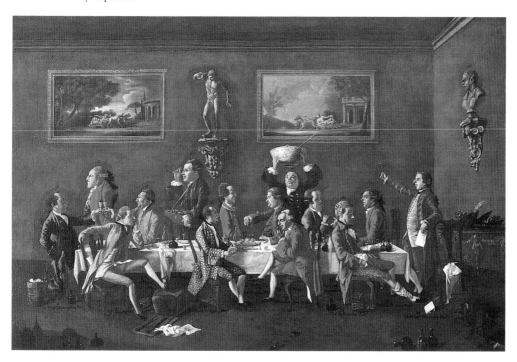

entitled 'Morning amusements previous to a jaunt to Tivoli' that showed two men in their beds drinking punch, while another, already dressed and standing, declared 'Come its time to sett off for Tivoli'. In 1787, Walker spent a sleepless night at Milan because of the antics of a group of drunken English: 'last night a party of them, about a dozen, drank thirty-six bottles of burgundy, claret, and champaign (as our landlord showed us in his book) and made such a noise till six in the morning we could not sleep'.[44]

The Range of Activities

There were other tourist activities besides those that invited criticism. Taking part in the social round was a major activity, although its character varied depending on the political nature of the state being visited. Republics lacked a court and therefore the classic court activities, particularly being presented and hunting. In 1791, John Carr wrote home about his and his sister's visit to Turin:

> both the King and his son's wife, the Duchess of Aosta, spoke to Harriet as she had hold of Mr. Trevor's [the envoy's] arm. It is a sight worth seeing but going hunting in a carriage does not answer to our idea of the Chase. At the death all the court is assembled by sound of trumpet, and Harriet had the compliment paid her of being presented with a foot of the stag.[45]

Three years earlier, Buller, who lacked the Carrs' connections, had not been presented, but an important aspect of his brief trip to Turin involved visiting the palaces there and nearby, and seeing the royal family at dinner.[46] Those who enjoyed hunting were interested to see how it was done in Italy and benefited from their entrée to court society. Some tourists were painted in hunting garb or poses. Peter Beckford (*c.* 1739–1811) hunted with Charles Emmanuel III in late 1765.

The appeal of courts varied greatly. In 1728, Freeman found Parma 'a very handsome large court it being at a time when there was acting the completest opera in Italy. The town was full of strangers, the streets are large and well kept, the richness of the Duke's coaches and accoutrements are remarkable et merite bien a voir.'[47] George, Viscount Sunbury arrived in Turin in 1737:

> The Court is polite indeed, and strangers are well received as it, but I can't help thinking it is dull enough, fusty with old forms and ceremonies, and destitute of the pleasures that generally attend on Princes. I had an audience of the King, as he insists upon all English noblemen's having, by way of paying them a compliment. He is a well bred civil man . . .[48]

29. *Peter Beckford of Steepleton* by
Pompeo Batoni, 1766. After
succeeding his father in 1764,
Beckford (?1739–1811), who had
been educated at Westminster
and New College, Oxford,
travelled to Italy via France and
Switzerland. He visited Turin,
Milan, Genoa, Bologna, Florence,
Perugia, Parma, Rome and
Naples, and was keen on hunting,
a hobby noted here by Batoni.
Beckford, now Lord Rivers,
returned to Italy in 1783, with his
wife Louisa and their two
children. Louisa died in Florence
in 1791, but Beckford and his
children stayed until 1799.
Beckford wrote *Familiar Letters
from Italy to a Friend in England*
(1805).

– a view of Charles Emmanuel III (1701–73, r. from 1730) that John Holroyd, later 1st Earl of
Sheffield, did not share in 1764. He found the Turin court pro-British, but 'the King is a
miserable, sneaking, creeping, soreyed little fellow and is considered as a dismal bigot
notwithstanding [he] was once the most renowned prince in Europe'. Holroyd was also
unimpressed by court activities:

There is as much parade about the royal family at Turin as is at any court in Europe at
present. Their principal amusements are prayers and going every evening to a public place
in state attended by half a dozen coaches and guards . . . All persons of distinction creep
about in carriages there during a part of the evening where they bow to everybody they
meet and every time they meet them.[49]

William, Marquess of Kildare was unimpressed by Ferdinand IV of Naples when he met him in 1766. He attended Ferdinand's coming-of-age celebrations the following year, as did Dodwell Tracy (1747–68), who saw 'the celebrated Gabrieli covered with diamonds' sing at a concert in the opera house. In Italy, Kildare also played cards, studied Italian, fenced and rode.

The appeal of courts was related to the attraction of particular occasions. In addition to court activities, these could be provided by the reception of prominent British tourists. Thus, in 1764, Holroyd 'hastened' from Turin to Genoa 'to take advantage of whatever public entertainments might be made for the Duke of York': Edward (1739–67), the younger brother of George III, visited Italy in 1763–4. He spent ten weeks in Genoa, in part because he was attracted by Angela Serra (Madame Durazzo), an amateur painter, with whom he appeared hand in hand at a reception at the Palazzo Ducale.[50] Ten years later, Thomas, 7th Viscount Bulkeley and George Grenville, later Lord-Lieutenant of Ireland and 1st Marquess of Buckingham (1753–1813), rushed from Naples to Rome in order to see the cupola of St Peter's illuminated for the visit of Henry, Duke of Cumberland (1745–90), another of George III's brothers.

Other activities bore no relation to courts and potentates. Tourists revelled in visiting sights in the cities in which they were based and making trips into the countryside. Urban gardens were a variant. In Genoa, Freeman was impressed by the palace 'gardens which abound in statues, waterworks, and orange trees of which they form bowers and grottoes'.[51] In cities, the sights were ticked off. Visiting Turin in 1734, Richard Pococke met Robert Bristow (1712–76), the son of a leading London merchant and later an MP, and John Delmé, the son of another leading merchant:

> we walked together in fine walks planted with trees near the Citadel, went to the coffee house . . . We saw the Citadel, went into the underground works, there are four passages. They say it exceeds any fortification in the world. We went up to the Capuchins on the other side the Po, to see the town . . . we went to the cathedral. Saw the King and his eldest son, the Duke of Savoy, at Mass.

Pococke, who was to be an indefatigable traveller, also had scientific interests, and was keen to observe anything different. Leaving Turin on 26 June 1734:

> being a little in the night we saw the fiery or glowing flies. They are about a quarter of an inch long, the tip of the head black next part yellow, the rest of the body on the back black, has wings like chafers, the belly black except near the tail which is yellow; this yellow part when they make any motion shoots out light and appears pellucid; when they fly it appears as they move their wings and is like a small flash. We saw hundreds of them appearing and disappearing in flashes . . . as they make motions they flash continually, as

30. *Edward, Duke of York,* by Pompeo Batoni. Younger brother of George III, York (1739–67) visited Italy in 1763–4, the first member of the Royal family to go there as a tourist. Sailing from Plymouth to Genoa, York pressed on to visit Turin, Milan, Florence, Siena, Rome – where he sat to Batoni – Bologna, Parma, Venice and Padua, returning to Genoa via Milan and Turin and sailing back to Dover. York was particularly keen on the company of attractive women, but also took part in a round of activities befitting his status, including hunts and receptions. He also heard the castrato Giovanni Manzuoli sing, played the violin and witnessed scientific experiments. York died in Monaco in 1767 *en route* for a second visit to Italy.

they crawl every step or progression causes a flash, and though the light be from the belly, yet when you do not see the belly you see the flash, which extends about a quarter of an inch round. In the dark it appears like the fire, with a candle the light is like a gloworm.

In the absence of photography, prose had to be the record.[52] Natural curiosities and scientific investigations interested many tourists. Dodwell Tracy recorded in Naples:

The Prince of San Severo who is a great chemist hath a great many curiosities of art that he himself hath performed all which he showed to us and explained with great politeness and gave us a book of the curious effects of his art.[53]

Remains from the prince's anatomical work can still be seen in the wonderful Museo Cappella Sansevero. Visiting Naples for his health in the winter of 1777–8, with his wife Lady Elizabeth, James Stuart Mackenzie devoted much attention to Vesuvius, and also bought three views of the volcano, two by Pietro Antoniani and one by Pietro Fabris.

In the major cities, it was less often necessary to rely on courts for social activities. Edward Southwell reported from Naples in 1726:

> I dined about 16 successive days abroad at Naples, with Irish officers, with the Factory [British merchants] and other English gentlemen, and the evenings were taken up in assemblies, balls, operas, comedies etc., and the mornings in seeing churches and curiosities.[54]

Critics were correct to claim that some tourists were more interested in sex, gambling and drink than in improving themselves. However, many would probably have acted in the same fashion at home. Tourism let them sow their wild oats abroad. Their experience was also moulded by the opportunities offered by Italians. In his drawing of *The Arrival of a Young Traveller and his Suite during the Carnival in Piazza di Spagna, Rome*, David Allan (1744–96), who pursued his career as a painter in Italy in 1767–77, depicted dancers (one woman showing her legs), singers, vendors and beggars, who approached the travellers' coach. The drawing also showed a picture dealer offering a pornographic picture, as well as another trying to sell a painting of the Virgin and Child, which may well have been a fake.

Several critics suggested that many tourists were too young. The most perceptive and best-informed travellers' accounts written by those who toured for pleasure tend to have been by older tourists, such as Mitchell and Walker. The correspondence of young tourists, and of their bearleaders, was frequently about debts, gambling and the purchase of clothes. However, some young tourists, such as Thomas Pelham, sent informed and intelligent letters. There was no equivalent from John Damer (1744–76) and George Damer (1746–1808) who visited the Uffizi with a Captain Howe in 1764: they 'submitted quietly to be shown a few of the pictures. But seeing the gallery so immensely long, their impatience burst forth, and they tried for a bett who should hop first to the end of it.'[55]

Young men frequently encountered schoolmates and other connections on their travels and this helped provide a social life that was more accessible and familiar than that of Italian society and less tedious than that of exemplary sightseeing at the behest of a bearleader. In July 1768, Kildare wrote to his mother that he had met over forty old Etonian acquaintances since arriving in Italy in November 1766. Whatever the number of school friends, the growing size of the tourist population provided many opportunities for company as Viscount Bulkeley and his wife Elizabeth discovered when they found fifty to sixty British tourists in Naples in January–February 1786. Already, at the end of the previous century, Richard Creed had listed thirty-nine English visitors as being present on

THE ARRIVAL OF A YOUNG TRAVELLER AND HIS SUITE
DURING THE CARNIVAL
in Piazza De' Spagna Rome

31. *The Arrival of a Young Traveller and his Suite during the Carnival in Piazza de'Spagna, Rome,* by David Allan, who arrived in Rome in 1767, finally leaving the city in 1776. He probably stayed near the Piazza di Spagna in 1773. Aside from portraits and history paintings, Allan made copies, as well as topographical drawings, and produced numerous sketches. In 1773, he was the first British artist to win the Concorso Balestra, a competition held by the Accademia di S. Luca. That was for the *Departure of Hector,* a very different work to the *Arrival* which depicts the Piazza, including the Caffe degli Inglesi and the hotel Ville de Londres on the right from which a servant descends to drive away those accosting the newly-arrived tourist.

24 December 1699 to witness the opening of the Holy Door at St Peter's in Rome for the forthcoming Holy Year.

Given the length of time that a major tour lasted, it was understandable that most tourists were young. Older men had their careers to pursue and their estates to manage, and those who made foreign trips tended to make short ones to Paris. Older men who travelled for a long time usually had a specific reason. Health was a factor for some. Lieutenant-General Sir Richard Lyttelton (1718–70) and his wife, Rachel, Dowager Duchess of Bridgewater, visited Italy in 1760–2 to seek relief for the gout which had hit his military career. The death of their

32. *Hester Lynch Piozzi*, by unknown artist, 1785. Recently married to Gabriel Piozzi, her daughters' music master, Hester Piozzi (1741–1821) visited Italy in 1784–6 with the particular perspective provided by her husband's background. She greatly liked Venice, but found Rome, where she sat for her portrait, squalid. Problems included illness in Florence, insects in Lucca, a coach breaking down in Spoleto and the heat of a Venetian June.

wives led Andrew Mitchell to Italy in 1732–4 and (alongside poor health) David, Viscount Stormont (1727–96) in 1767–8. David Ker (1742–1811) spent 1792–4 in Italy with his three young daughters and their governess. His wife, who had died in 1785, had been a Venetian singer, Maddalena Guardi. Thomas Barrett-Lennard (1717–86) went to Italy in 1750 with his wife, Anne, following the death of their child.

A need, financial or political, to be out of Britain could also be important. Some older men took long trips for pleasure, including Joseph Leeson, later 1st Earl of Milltown (1701–83), who visited Italy in 1744–5 and 1750–1, Sir Matthew Fetherstonhaugh Bt. (1714–74) and his wife Lady Sarah (1722–88) in 1750–1, and James Alexander, MP (1730–1802), a very wealthy Ulster landowner, who had made a fortune in the East India Company, with his wife, Anne, in 1777. She died later that year in childbirth in Ireland, having become pregnant on her tour.

Families also travelled, although the composition of family groups varied greatly. Thomas, 9th Viscount Kilmorey (1703–68) was in Florence in 1751 with his wife, Lady Mary (1712–84), her brother-in-law, Joseph Nightingale (1695–1752), and the latter's son,

Washington, and daughter, Elizabeth. They all travelled on to Rome together. In 1787, Henry, 3rd Duke of Buccleuch (1746–1812) visited Italy with his wife, Elizabeth, and two of their four daughters. Daughters were kept close to their parents when travelling in Italy; sons far less so if both they and their parents were in Italy at the same time. Fewer women than men travelled, and, although their tours have left a good record in correspondence and travel literature, this was less so in portraiture. Batoni, for example, painted only seventeen British women.

Elderly parents were frequently accompanied by children. In 1785, Mary, Dowager Duchess of Ancaster arrived in Florence with her second daughter, Lady Georgiana Bertie (1764–1838). In the winter of 1792–3 they were again together, but this time with Lady Georgiana's new husband, George, 4th Earl of Cholmondeley (1749–1827), then on his fourth trip. In 1785–6, Viscount Keppel was accompanied to Italy by his illegitimate daughter, Elizabeth. Some tourists who had travelled first to Italy when alone or with male companions returned later with spouse and sometimes children. Generally this reflected the fact that the tourist had got married in the intervening period. Thomas, 2nd Lord Leominster (1698–1753) visited Italy in 1718, with Martin Benson as his bearleader. In 1739–41, now Earl of Pomfret, he returned with his wife, Henrietta, and two daughters, Sophia and Charlotte. Sometimes, however, both trips, without and with spouse, were made when the tourists were married. Thus, Thomas, Lord Grey de Wilton (1749–1814), later Earl of Wilton, got married in 1769, but went to Italy in 1785 with a male companion, Vincent Foxley, before returning in 1788 with two Eleanors, his wife and daughter.

These were exceptions. Most older men could not spare several years for foreign travel and the Grand Tour tended to remain the prerogative of youth. As such, it fulfilled a major social need. Young men who were not obliged to work were given something to do after school. University could only be a temporary stopgap, as few scions of the aristocracy stayed for three years. Foreign travel kept the young out of trouble at home. A certain amount of drinking, gaming and wenching was accepted as a cost of the system.

12.   Social and Political Reflections

Lord Cholm—y's intended departure for the Continent, is not, it seems to revive the languid flame of love in a personal visit to Miss Dal-ble, that affair having been long at an end and the lady perfectly happy in the arms of a new *inamorato*: his Lordship's tour however is not to be of a very solitary nature, as one of the most accomplished women of this island has actually consented to accompany!

Readers of the *Morning Herald* of 11 April 1781 would not have been surprised by such an item of fashionable gossip. Indeed, George, 4th Earl of Cholmondeley (1749–1827), who had travelled extensively in Italy in the early 1770s, went to Italy in 1781–2 with Elizabeth Armitstead (1750–1842), a leading London courtesan, who was subsequently to travel to Italy with Charles James Fox in 1788, to marry him in 1795, and to go to Italy with him again in 1802. The notion of tourism as a means for the pursuit of pleasure was well established and any focus on the didactic goal of travel was constantly undercut by a very different reality of pleasure: the discourse of social benefit clashing, as so often, with the dictates of individual pleasure, although, in this case, the pleasure was not restricted to socialising and sex. Elizabeth Armitstead also appreciated the paintings she saw, especially the Correggios in Parma and the Guercinos in Cento.

Travel to Italy in the eighteenth century can be seen as representing the summation of both processes – benefit and pleasure, and much of the interest in reading the accounts of contemporary tourists reflects the presence there of differing aspirations. Italy was at once the focus of artistic and, more generally, cultural education, and a peninsula of pleasure, whether the delights in question were, for example, those of opera or the more sensual joys for which Venice was noted.

Yet the attraction of Italy for some was being undercut by the degree to which it seemed to represent the past, not simply the past of Classical splendour and culture, but also the past of the present. For the British, modern Italy appeared a land in the grip of reaction. Its

33. *Dr James Hay as Bearleader*, by Pier Leone Ghezzi, *c.* 1725. Hay, who died in 1746, was a Scottish doctor who acted as a bearleader on at least eight occasions between 1704, when he accompanied Nicholas Bacon to Italy, and 1730, when he was in Rome with Richard and William Wynne. Hay was fairly dour, critical of sloth and concerned about costs. He was keen to ensure the education of his charges, and favoured Padua for Lord James Compton in 1707 as a safer place than Venice to learn Italian.

reputation as a haunt of superstition was exacerbated by Italy's connection with Jacobitism, specifically as the place where the last Stuarts took refuge and ended their days. James Stuart (1688–1766), 'James III' from 1701, lived in Italy for most of his life from 1717. He spent much of his time in Rome, although he also lived in Urbino, Bologna and Albano. His son, Charles Edward (1720–88), 'Bonnie Prince Charlie', lived in Italy until 1744, returning in 1766. Charles's brother, Henry, Cardinal Duke of York (1725–1807), 'Henry IX' from 1788, lived in Italy for most of his life, although he was in France in 1745–7. He presided over the Papal conclaves of 1758, 1774–5 and 1799, an apt symbol of the link between Jacobitism and the Catholic Church. Papal support for the Jacobite claim ensured that no British diplomat could be accredited to the Papal States. Difficulties could be created by Italian states over the passports of British travellers, while inconvenience was created for tourists by the travels of the Jacobite princes. Britain broke off diplomatic relations with the Duke of Parma in 1728 due to the latter's reception of 'James III'. Similar tension over the reception of Charles Edward in Venice in 1737 led to a breach in diplomatic relations that lasted until 1744. While the Jacobite court was at Bologna or Avignon, it was easy for British tourists to avoid it, but this was not the case with Rome.

Before the defeat at Culloden in 1746, Jacobite visitors to Rome excited the suspicion of the British government and the criticism of some commentators. Several visitors made little effort to hide their views. Henry, 3rd Duke of Beaufort (1707–45) visited 'James III' in Rome in 1726 on numerous occasions and held a grand entertainment to mark the anniversary of the Stuart Restoration in 1660. John Bagshaw, the consul in Genoa, reported in 1731 that at Rome there had arrived 'a vast number of English gentlemen most of them visited the Pretender for whom they had brought several remittances'.

Other tourists felt under pressure from the Jacobites. In 1730, William Mildmay wrote from Rome that they were 'diligent in intruding themselves into the company of all travellers'. Four years earlier, John Mills was 'determined' not to go near Bologna 'as long as the Pretender is there'.[1]

More generally, Italy appeared to be dominated by autocratic rulers and Catholic super-stition. Tourists were frequently presented to the Pope, the Kings of Naples and Sardinia, the Grand Duke of Tuscany, the Dukes of Modena and Parma, and the Governor of Milan, but these meetings did not generally provide occasions for any positive evaluation of Italian politics or government. George, Earl of Euston (1715–47), the heir to Charles, 2nd Duke of Grafton and later an MP, was received by Charles Emmanuel III at Turin in 1734, and the king discussed international relations with him, leading a British diplomat to send a report, but most tourists had little positive to say about government in the Italian states.

There was a longstanding negative portrayal of Italian rulers and courts. A mixture of Jacobean 'blood-drama' and a belief that the politics of these rulers and courts was motivated by Machiavellian cynicism remained potent, and it was repeated in popular histories and other sources. This affected John, 5th Earl of Cork's *Letters from Italy* (1775), which he had written in Florence in 1754. In this book, the later Medici were presented as treacherous, debauched and evil. William Mildmay had certainly been less than impressed in 1731 by Giovanni Gastone de' Medici, Grand Duke of Tuscany from 1723 until 1737. He presented him as enjoying seeing carried out the sexual acts, particularly sodomy, which his drunkenness had rendered him unfit to perform.

Most tourists left less lurid accounts, but there was still an impression of control and coer-cion that suggested a government very different to that of Britain. In December 1699, Richard Creed presented Francesco Maria Farnese, ruler of Parma and Piacenza from 1694 until 1727, as a harsh figure: 'the Duke is the great landlord and all his subjects are his slaves and pay him what he demands'. The Duke of Mantua was more lurid, although also tyrannical:

Ferdinando Carlo Gonzagia the second [r. 1665–1706]; he is a very plain man to look on, just like an English farmer, and every day drives himself all the town over in a little calash with one footman; he has four pistols in it; he is about 50 years old, but he is a man of pleasure. He has at least eighty misses in his keeping, and he keeps them handsomely; and they perform his operas; for they are all handsome and all sing or dance; he has about 70 children in town; but none by his Duchess [Anna Isabella]; he is very absolute, imprisons who he pleases; he hangs and raises money at his pleasure; he spends all, for he has no heirs.

Creed, however, was also sufficiently perceptive to appreciate the tension and divisions beneath the commanding appearance of absolutist states with their suggestion of a unity of purpose. In Milan, he noted that the Governor of the citadel was not under the control of the Governor of the town and suggested that he was intended as a check on the latter.

The use of the language of tyranny was increasingly uncommon, but a critical account of the extent and ambition of government authority was still offered. Visiting Turin in 1726, John Mills wrote that Victor Amadeus II, ruler of Savoy-Piedmont from 1675 until 1730, was 'very well beloved' by his subjects. However:

whether it is out of politics or natural curiosity he knows everything that is done in every house in Turin, and if there is any irregularity or debauch committed, he is sure to punish or reprimand accordingly . . . The subjects here are forbid conversing with or going to the house of any foreign minister. I am told this piece of policy prevails in all states through Italy.

Mills noted a different form of control in Lombardy, which had been conquered by Austrian forces in the War of the Spanish Succession and gained by the Emperor Charles VI (r. 1711–40), the Habsburg ruler, under the Peace of Utrecht of 1713:

In Milan there are two factions one for and the other against the Emperor. On enquiry I learned that the latter is much the strongest, besides having the common people on their side. Never was government more hated and more feared than is the German [Austrian] in the Milanese on account of the oppressions the people lie under, which are more than they are able to bear, and more burthensome than under any of their former masters. They would be glad of an opportunity of getting rid of it had they anything to help them, but the Emperor has 30,000 men to keep them in awe and makes the people pay for the maintenance of a great many more. He is adding new fortifications to all the towns I passed through in the Milanese.[2]

Austrian control of Naples from 1707 until 1734, which was indeed unpopular, did not impress Edward Southwell in 1726:

And indeed the Neapolitans suffer so many additional taxes and impositions under the present government, that the least spark would kindle them into a flame, and induce them to recall the Spaniards. All the gabelles are not only high, but mortgaged out to pay the interest of the public debts, and every fresh tax is immediately sold off for ever, to create a present plenty, so that there is no country, wherein the public are more harassed and whence the prince draws less advantage. The Emperor has had thoughts of borrowing money at 3 per cent from the Genoese or of raising a bank wherewith to pay off these public debts, and to take the taxes into his own hands, but that would ruin the state creditors who perhaps draw 8 or 10 per cent for the original sums they have advanced; and perhaps the Emperor will let the debt continue or rather raise them out of the same policy as King William [III, r. 1689–1702] used with us, because where a title is precarious, the more money the natives lend to the Prince, the deeper must they be engaged to support *him* in his possession, from whom alone they must depend for interest and principal.

Again, the princes and nobles have no further power over their vassals, nor any present share in the state, but the magistrates are men of low families and hard study, who have fortunes to make ... Then the Spaniards spent part of their gains in the country, and though the Viceroy commonly made an immense estate, yet the King was not rapacious; but the Germans [Austrians] fleece the country, all is sent to Vienna. Nay the 70,000 licensed whores at Naples are discontented, and cry out that they owe their rags and misery to the Germans, who are good economists, and most of them married; whereas the Spaniards were rich and vicious, and left the Neapolitans money enough to be good customers also.

As to the 60,000 persons who live there by the law, frequent revolutions produce new quarrels, new titles and new business, and they will flourish, as long as the pride, envy and malice of mankind.[3]

Such references to current politics were uncommon, and became far more so in 1749–91 when Italy was at peace and Britain played scant role in its politics. Instead, the political references became less specific, while timeless reflections on the rhythms of history and its relationship with culture became more common.

While Britain was playing an active role in Italian politics in the first half of the eighteenth century, tourist comments in part reflected the nature of British foreign policy. Thus, in 1725–31, when British relations with Charles VI were poor and he was seen as a supporter of Jacobitism and of a Catholic league, it was unsurprising that Southwell had a negative impression of Austrian-ruled Naples and Mills of Austrian-ruled Lombardy.

Later in the century, more sympathetic remarks were made. Robert Gray (1762–1834), a cleric who toured Italy in 1791–2, praised Grand Duke Leopold's legislation and legal reforms in Tuscany (1765–90), and Charles Abbot also noted them, not least the raising of the age at which girls could enter convents, although he wrote that Leopold's economical approach to expenditure made him unpopular. Edward, Duke of York (1739–67), a brother of George III, was interested in the copy of Beccaria's *Dei Delitti e Delle Pene*, a call for the end of capital punishment, which he was given when he visited Milan in 1764. Arriving there seven years later, Shelburne remarked that the Inquisition was now weak – 'only the name remains' – and that there had been a major shift in the culture:

> Found in the room of the chief inquisitor Mirabeau's book in favour of atheism . . . The Literati, by all accounts new in Italy – at present you may be recommended from town to town from one set of literati to the other, as formerly from convent to convent . . . Beccaria just taken into the new Council of Trade.

Shelburne, nevertheless, added that the government was 'afraid to trust the people of the country'.[4] More generally, however, there was a marked failure among tourists to realise the degree to which there was an Enlightenment in Italy and, more specifically, to understand the extent to which, particularly in Lombardy, Parma and Tuscany, there were attempts to 'reform' and 'modernise' government and society as understood by contemporary standards.

Instead, a shift in the attitude towards Italian republicanism during the century had a major impact on the response to Italy. In the seventeenth century, Venice had appeared not only as a seat of pleasure but also as a model of civic virtue. Genoa had never enjoyed the same renown, but it had benefited from the favourable interest displayed in Italian republics. They could be seen to resonate with Classical values which were closely associated with republicanism. In *The Jacobite's Journal* of 12 March (os) 1748, the Whig novelist-magistrate Henry Fielding (who never visited Italy) wrote of 'Greek and Latin authors which have been the bane of the Jacobite cause, and inspired men with the love of Athenian liberty and old Rome, and taught them to hate tyrants and arbitrary governments'. Virtue was held to be a republican characteristic, the product of states with a 'balanced' constitution such as republican Rome, and British tourists displayed sympathy for republican relics such as Lucca and San Marino. Thanks to the traditional positive impression of republicanism, it was possible to differentiate between the degenerate modern and the noble ancient inhabitants of towns such as Florence, Pisa and Siena. The medieval republicanism of these towns was praised and their decline associated with their subsequent loss of independence.

By the eighteenth century, the perception of Italian republics was less positive. As yet there was no widespread aesthetic of splendid decay to lend romantic appeal to Venice. Although the city's attraction was still strong as a centre of culture and, even more, pleasure, politically it was seen as an increasingly inconsequential state, a model only of rigidity. Francis, Marquess of Tavistock advised John, Earl of Upper Ossory in 1763 'to study a little the constitution of the Republic of Venice, in order to inspire you with a proper dread of aristocracy – I am sure it is very useful for an Englishman'. The following year, Henry, Viscount Palmerston criticised the power of the Council of Ten to seize and kill without trial, and wrote of the government, 'under the form of an oligarchy it seems to be a perfect tyranny'. However, he added:

> These powers though enormously great yet often changing hands and those who exercise them one moment being subject to them the next are not often abused and they are agreable to the common people who are in general below any apprehension of them for themselves and who find in them their best defence against the nobles whose tyranny would be very great over their inferiors were it not for this check. The people in general are attached to this government and live happy under it: the taxes are not heavy, they have generally plenty and it is the policy of the state to encourage every pursuit of pleasure in all ranks of people.[5]

In 1755, George, Viscount Villiers provided a very different social echo when he visited the Doge's Palace: 'The entrance is open to everybody, and the stairs are in a most beastly condition from what is called the Liberty of the People.' He preferred access to be limited. Seven years later, John Hinchliffe used his visit to Venice in order to denounce Italian government as a whole, and, as with denunciations by others, to treat this as part of a denunciation of an entire culture:

> If states like men have their different ages in which they in a manner naturally flourish and decay, this of Italy surely is near its grave. Not only the blessing itself is gone, but the very love and idea of Liberty, and a low sneaking politique is substituted in the place of manly generous sentiments. The case is much the same with morality; we exclaim in our part of the world against the passions, as the corrupters of men, but here men seem to me to have corrupted the passions – The conveniences and sometimes the very necessaries of life are sacrificed to a vain appearance of magnificence . . . A very extraordinary affair that happened here some weeks ago will give your Grace [Augustus, 3rd Duke of Grafton] a sketch of that liberty so much boasted of in this republic. An Avagador (somewhat like a tribune of the people) lodged a complaint before the Grand Council against the inquisitors of state; the charge gave occasion to a debate whether or no that office should not be entirely abolished; the majority were for its continuance; and the city testified its satisfaction in the determination by illuminations and every other demonstration of joy, as if it was an acquisition to be pleased with, that three despotic governors were continued, who have the power to hang, drown or perpetually imprison them; a few days after, the Avagador was imprisoned at Verona where it is generally thought he will spend the remainder of his life. The common people I am informed by an ingenious Abbé . . . are not so extravagant in their sentiments of the affair, as at first sight one would naturally imagine. Among the fifteen hundred nobles there are at least a third said he reduced to a state of absolute beggary, whose circumstances would tempt them to oppression were it

not for the sword which is held over their heads by an invisible thread . . . in my opinion liberty is at best but very precarious when it depends upon absolute power for its support. The Sardinian monarch [Charles Emmanuel III] seems to be a snowball from mountains gathering as it goes. It is the only power I believe that your Grace has observed which is at all in a rising state.[6]

Indeed Italy was to be united around the Piedmontese state the following century.

Genoa's reputation was damaged by the rebellions of its Corsican colony, and it also seemed inconsequential and rigid. According to Edward Thomas, 'the people are ruled by many tyrants who use them as slaves. Their being so fond of having the crown [of Corsica] up everywhere, I think, is a tacit approbation of monarchy, but I could not but smile to see the motto they put under it, Libertas. This is fit only for the crown of England.' Shelburne, who visited Genoa in 1771, and who had contacts with enlightened European opinion-makers, was dismayed by the state:

all corruption . . . no public spirit – everything jobbed – no Liberty of the Press – that and all personal liberty at the mercy of Inquisitors of State . . . No military knowledge or spirit. Fortifications ruinous . . . Several raw materials allowed to be exported – upon the solicitation of particular merchants, who obtain laws to pass by bribery to answer the purpose of their particular trade.[7]

Genoa had also suffered physical damage during the Austrian siege of 1747–8. In 1730, William Mildmay condemned the distortion of the Genoese constitution by the nobles who sought to avoid burdens. In contrast, the small republic of Lucca was essentially a pleasant curiosity, a lovely backwater. Mildmay thought that the frequent ministerial changes in Lucca decreed by the constitution were bad for the constancy of government policy. Palmerston used Lucca and Tuscany to counterpoint liberty and despotism: 'The condition of its people is happy compared with that of the Grand Duke's subjects and by a natural consequence its small territory is extremely full of inhabitants.'[8]

Francis Drake (1721–95) extended his denunciation of modern Italy to include the republics. An Anglican cleric, Drake was in no doubt that Catholicism had contributed greatly to Italy's fall. From 1746, he was a fellow of Magdalen College, Oxford, where Gibbon spent 'fourteen months the most idle and unprofitable of my whole life', and Drake's remarks indicate the reflections that could be passed on to the next generation:

It is impossible to make any parallel between the customs, fashions, religion, or policy, of the Italians with those of our own country, because the contrast is too apparent, to admit of any resemblance. The difference is this, that those who are subject to an hierarchy, or a despotick prince, are not even allowed to act, or think for themselves, but submit their persons and consciences to the guidance, and power of the prince, or the priest . . .

An happy Englishman, who has never been beyond the narrow confines of his own Country, can have no idea, that a nation, whose situation on the face of the globe, allows them all the blessings, and advantages of life, and who once were masters of the then known world, are now become for these two reasons, the poorest and meanest of mankind. The whole riches of the country are in the hands of the priests, or the princes of the different states, or amongst very few of the nobles, while the bulk of the people languish and labour under the greatest wants, and necessities. The present Greeks, and modern Italians are striking instances, how nature can degenerate in mankind, by tyranny and oppression. To consider the Italians, under what government we please, whether under an hierarchy, republic or monarchy, there appears the same abject spirit and degeneracy of soul . . . contrary to the known policy of all well regulated governments, the poverty, and ignorance of the subject, is esteemed the security of the state, and instead of encouraging arts, and sciences, trade, or manufactures, they rather discourage all useful industry, and knowledge, least the people should grow too rich to be slaves, or too knowing to be bigots. Whoever has seen the immense repositories of riches, in the chapel at Loreto, the sacristy of San Genaro, at Naples, of San Ambrosio and Carlo, at Milan, San Marco at Venice, the Jesuit churches at Rome, and in all their convents, and monasteries, will not then be surprised at the disette [shortages] and penury of the lower class. Here are almost all the riches of the country amassed together, in holy lumber, which are of no use, but to enrich a shrine, or make a figure at a procession, where the infatuated people revere and even adore the very causes of their own ruin . . . Where commerce . . . is thus despised and left to the lower people . . . Italy must still continue poor.

Aside from this unremittingly hostile account, Drake had more specific criticisms of Genoa's republican constitution that, in part, reflected the conservatism of Tory Oxford:

A power to do mischief in one person, is much easier controlled, than where it is lodged in many; a large body of men in authority, may, by their influence on their dependents, and unanimity amongst themselves, continue their tyranny, in defiance of all opposition. In a monarchy, the distributive, and executive justice is better ministered, than in an aristocracy, where the wheels of government are so clogged by so many jarring interests, and so many parties of equal authority, in the administration.[9]

Enthusiastic about Classical Athens and Rome, from which they claimed to derive their mores and culture, British tourists were, on the whole, ambivalent, if not hostile, in their reaction to the achievements, both medieval and Baroque, of Catholic Italy. The great triumphs of this culture that were most readily accessible were its architectural and artistic achievements, but, for Protestant tourists, their continued association with Catholic religious practices provided an unwelcome context.

If the current political interest of Italy was in decline, the peninsula was also of scant or declining interest in other fields. The numerous tourists interested in military activities – in viewing manoeuvres or attending military academies – aimed essentially for Prussia for the former and France for the latter. The prestige of Italy as a land of the present was in decline. It was still important in spheres such as science, medicine and music, but even in these it was in apparently relative decline, especially by the second half of the century. A musical world that looked to Vienna, Mannheim and Paris had less time for Italy. Furthermore, transalpine Europe was now more advanced in science.

For British tourists, this tendency was accentuated by the particular development of Britain in this period. Tourists from the social élite of a burgeoning economy and an apparently successful political system, from a great and powerful world empire, were less inclined to feel a sense of inferiority than in the seventeenth century; at that time, to its own people, Britain had seemed superior in little besides its Protestantism. By the eighteenth century, in spite of the popularity of Batoni, Mengs, Piranesi and other Rome-based artists, it appeared that the country of Newton and Sloane, Reynolds and Watt, had little to learn from modern Italy. One of the more successful books by an Italian author read in Britain was the 1739 English edition of Francesco Algarotti's *Il Newtonianismo per le Dame* (1737), in which the theories of light and gravitation were explained in a series of dialogues: an Italian serving to reflect back British greatness. Algarotti (1712–64) spent much of the late 1730s in London, becoming a fellow of the Royal Society. In a similar fashion, Giovanni Canaletto (1697–1768), with his splendid canvases, used talents developed to depict Venice to show the glories of modern London which he visited in 1746–50 and 1755–6. A neo-imperial, modern pride in London was expressed in his views. They reflected an abrupt shift in national self-confidence. Victory over France and Spain in the Seven Years War and growing economic strength led to a degree of national complacency.

The London on show had modern buildings, such as the Greenwich Observatory, Somerset House and Westminster Bridge, as well as the rebuilt Westminster Abbey. There was no contemporary equivalent in Venice, and this offers an important clue to shifting views about Italy. In Rome, Pope Sixtus V (r. 1585–90) had had a major impact in helping dramatise the city with a Baroque reshaping. The arterial roads of the period provided triumphant views, and the Baroque left impressive churches. What was lacking, from the British perspective, was an equivalent secular architecture. Despite the Palazzo della Consulta, there was no Bank of Rome to match those in Amsterdam or London.

Tourists concentrated on cities in the eighteenth century: they spent most of their time there and, until the end of the century, there was no cult of mountains or seaside to detract from this metropolitan focus. British tourists saw no modern townscape in Italy to match that of London, although there was a smaller modern townscape in Turin. In addition, although individual tastes varied, in general, British commentators showed a marked preference for modern over old architecture: for the Classical (seen as a reborn modern style that looked back to the qualities of the ancient world) over the Gothic. This was true both of individual buildings and of townscapes.

Much of Italy was a bad disappointment from this perspective. George Berkeley (1685–1753), the philosopher, praised the regularity of Catania, rebuilt in Baroque style after the devastating earthquake of 1693, but few tourists penetrated as far as Sicily, which he visited in 1717–18. Those who did were more interested in Greek remains and they were more likely to visit Palermo or Messina than Catania. Turin, with its rectilinear street pattern and squares, met with approval: in 1750, Edward Thomas found 'the city the most regular and beautiful for its size in the world'.[10]

Most Italian cities, however, seemed cramped, their close-packed medieval centres and narrow, twisting streets associated with dirt, disease and poverty. Villiers disliked towns with narrow streets, such as Lucca and Genoa.[11] As in the countryside, moral order was apparently reflected by images of the city, and, moreover, this replicated and reinforced ideologies and the socio-cultural order. This tied into the wider metaphor of the city/*urbs* as a reflection of society; of the shifting meanings that urban landscape accumulates and loses. Italy was found wanting from this perspective. The dominant buildings across much of Italy were generally ecclesiastical in purpose and that did not commend them to most British tourists. Cathedrals such as Padua, Pisa and Verona ('a heavy lumpish building', according to Robson)[12] were medieval and gloomy, as were Lucca's churches. There were new palaces, particularly the Bourbon creations of Caserta and Colorno, but they were outside Naples and Parma respectively and did not become great sights. Visiting Turin in 1788, Charles Abbot claimed 'The Castello del Re deserves to be admitted for its beautiful front and that only – behind it are two old lofty Gothic towers.'[13] For him, they could not match the work of Filippo Juvara (1678–1736), who was responsible for a number of important works in and around Turin in the early eighteenth century.

There was no combination of recent buildings in Italy to compare with those constructed in London since the Great Fire of 1666. This period has been seen as one of the great rebuilding of British cities. Brick buildings with large windows were erected in a regular 'Classical' style along and around new boulevards, squares and circles. Parks, theatres, assembly rooms, subscription libraries, racecourses and other leisure facilities were opened in many towns. The total stock of public buildings in the West Riding of Yorkshire alone rose from about ninety in 1700 to over 500 by 1840. This was also the period of the creation of Georgian Bath, Liverpool and Dublin, the New Town of Edinburgh, and the West End of London. Urban building and rebuilding in Britain, especially in London, was seen as rational, measured and modern, and as representing the wider health and progress of Britain. Aside from Turin, which lacked the commercial dynamism of British cities, there was no major equivalent in Italy. The nearest was the free port of Livorno, which was presented as a dynamic city where commerce brought people and prosperity. Freeman found it in 1727 'entirely filled with merchants of all countrys, very populous, streets handsome and straight, with a good Palazzo in the middle of the town a playhouse . . .', but most Italian cities seemed very different to British tourists.

A similar contrast also appeared to exist in the countryside, although tourists devoted far less attention to it. Much of Italy seemed poorly cultivated or barren, not least (but not only) compared to the new-model agriculture of enclosing England. This was the age of Agricultural Revolution in Britain, particularly lowland England and Scotland.

Italy seemed backward and its social politics were presented as regressive, which fuelled notions of the British as an 'elect' nation. In 1728, Freeman travelled between Bologna and Milan 'through the finest country which can be seen full of corn, wine and oil all of which would be exceeding cheap' were it not for the policies of the 'little Dukes' and the Emperor, the ruler of Lombardy. He commented on the way in which peasants were taxed even on eggs, butter and herbs.[14] Villiers linked the unpopularity of the governments of Naples and Milan to high taxes, while he claimed that the trade of Venice and Rome was in decline. Shelburne claimed that in Milan the 'nobility and best people' were 'taken up with little schemes to throw the weight of taxes on the lower sort'.[15]

Although parts of Italy, especially Lombardy, impressed tourists as well cultivated, it was a different rural landscape to that of Britain. In 1788, Abbot noted:

> Having crossed the Tiber in going out of Borghetto we were suddenly surprised with the appearance of pasture ground, enclosures and hedges, with a winding road through them, which made both of us at once agree that we had seen nothing so much like England since we left it.

The Campagna near Rome swiftly disillusioned him and he explicitly compared it to earlier accounts of its productivity: 'The total reverse of Milton's Description and of Claudian's in the Journey of Honorius upon the approaches to the world's great metropolis'.[16] The habit of judging Italy by past descriptions was well established.

In Italy, there was no series of new stately homes open to respectable tourists as in Britain, no Castle Howard or Blenheim. The same was true of landscape gardens. Some were spectacular, most obviously Vanvitteli's at Caserta, but the British did not find anything to challenge the quantity and range provided by William Kent, 'Capability' Brown and others. This was an important indication of what appeared to be an Italian failure to create a benign and harmonious man-made landscape to match the splendours of nature.

Tourists paid great attention to Palladianism and, particularly in the first half of the century, a visit to see the buildings near Vicenza designed by Andrea Palladio (1508–80) was considered an essential part of the Italian section of the Grand Tour, but they were appreciating the works of a long-dead architect. Furthermore, Palladianism marked a key cultural shift: English Palladians, the architect, collector and patron Richard, 3rd Earl of Burlington (1694–1753) and the painter and architect William Kent (1685–1748), who visited Italy in 1714–15 and 1719, and 1709–19 respectively, abandoned Baroque Rome for Vicenza and presented the Baroque as Catholic, 'absolutist' and architecturally impure. In his *Vitruvius Britannicus* (1715), the Scottish Palladian architect Colen Campbell (1676– 1729), a protégé of Burlington, criticised the Baroque on moral as well as cultural grounds:

> How affected and licentious are the works of Bernini and Fontana. How wildly extravagant are the designs of Borromini, who has endeavoured to debauch mankind with his old and chimerical beauties, where the parts are without proportion, solids without their true bearing, heaps of materials without strength, excessive ornaments without grace, and the whole without symmetry.

In contrast, the conception of a Palladian landscape permitted a fusing of urban and rural into one holistic and encompassing vision of order, which could be appreciated and appropriated by British tourists.[17] Most of rural Italy, however, did not offer Palladian gems. More mundanely, the pleasure of travelling through Italy compared to Britain deteriorated during the century, because the Italian road system did not improve anywhere near as much as that of Britain (or France). There was nothing to match the major turnpiking of English routes from mid-century.

John, Lord Hervey (1696–1743), touring Italy with Stephen Fox (1704–76), versified his comments in 1729:

Throughout all Italy beside,
What does one find, but Want and Pride?
Farces of Superstitious folly,
Decay, Distress, and Melancholy:
The Havock of Despotick Power,
A Country rich, its owners poor;
Unpeopled towns, and Lands untilled,
Bodys uncloathed, and mouths unfilled.
The nobles miserably great,
In painted Domes, and empty state,
Too proud to work, too poor to eat,
No arts the meaner sort employ,
They nought improve, nor ought enjoy.
Each blown from misery grows a Saint,
He prays from Idleness, and fasts from Want.[18]

These impressions were of varied importance for individual tourists, but, in combination, they helped to mark the degree to which Italy increasingly appeared a country of the past; and that became, for many, its glory, especially in the way Giovanni Piranesi (1720–78) and other artists immortalised that past. This shift can be considered in a number of lights. The degree to which Italy's past was embraced, while its present was shunned, reflected a changing perception of both past and present and of the interplay of the two. There was a sense of double atrophy in the contrast between the present and both the Classical past *and* the Renaissance past. As already mentioned, contemporary Italy appeared less attractive, and certainly no model, both because of changes in Britain and because the reasons why Italy had been criticised the previous century – Catholicism, Papacy, autocratic government and rigid social practices – were no longer matched by the same degree of compensatory respect for Italian republics and praise of her culture and intellectual life.

The links between contemporary Italy and her past glories appeared more tenuous in the eighteenth century. This was particularly a consequence of the declining reputation of modern Venice. The republican liberty and energy of Classical Rome could be presented through the refracting example of Venice in the seventeenth century, but such an association appeared less credible in the eighteenth. Alan Brodrick (1702–47), later 2nd Viscount Midleton, was disabused of his notion 'of the grandeur of the noble Venetians' when he visited the Senate in 1724.[19] Instead, there was greater interest in republicans and republics outside Italy, especially, in the second half of the century, in Corsica, Geneva and the United States of America, each of which appeared more dynamic and more of a model than Venice, let alone Genoa.

It is also important to note the great increase in interest in Classical Italy among tourists in the eighteenth century, and the impact that this had on the perception of modern Italy. Richard Creed, who visited Rome in 1699–1700, made only one mention of Roman remains: his was very much an account of Baroque Rome. Such an emphasis would have been unthinkable sixty years later, and indeed, in 1705, Metcalfe Robinson (*c.* 1683–1736) wrote to his father, Sir William Robinson of Newby Park, from what he termed

> the famousest place in the world and the first motive that induced me to become a traveller: for indeed ever since I knew the name of Rome, and much more as I got an insight into its greatness and the stupendous effects of it in buildings, aqueducts, ways, sculpture etc. which yet are to be admired in these glorious remains of antiquity; I found always my desire increase of having a better knowledge of them, than is to be found in descriptions, and rather to admire the things themselves.[20]

The excavations at Herculaneum and Pompeii played a major role in the development of European taste, in part thanks to the relative inaccessibility of Classical remains in Turkish-ruled Greece and Asia Minor. Neo-classical excitement and enthusiasm, not to say hype, in

34. *British Connoisseurs in Rome*, attributed to James Russel, *c.* 1751. The group in front of the Coliseum and the Arch of Constantine includes James, 4th Viscount Charlemont, Sir Thomas Kennedy, and, possibly, Joseph Leeson and Sir Charles Turner. Russel acted as an antiquary for tourists, as well as an art dealer. Charlemont played an active role in the tourist community in Rome from the summer of 1750 until May 1751, returning that autumn and staying until October 1752 and again in the winter of 1753–4. Kennedy, who was in Rome for much of 1751–2, was in Charlemont's circle.

the 1770s and 1780s about the discoveries was very influential. There were also important excavations in and around Rome. The Neo-classical painter and archaeologist Gavin Hamilton (1723–98) excavated Hadrian's villa at Tivoli in 1769, and did his utmost to make this a major site on the tourist itinerary. The sculptures and other remains that were discovered in such excavations helped to bring an important aesthetic appeal to interest in the Classical world.

British tourists had a strong grounding in the Classics and many compared the sites with descriptions by Horace, Lucan, Pliny, Strabo and Virgil. The sculptures themselves, however, and, more generally, the entire Neo-classical aesthetic, for example Johann Winckelmann's ecstatic description of the Apollo Belvedere, helped to give the Classical world greater appeal. The British sought to appropriate Classical Italy and to make it a part of their cultural heritage that was defined on British terms.

Thus tourists became more engaged with Italy's past. This affected their response to what they saw, and also their itinerary. For example, the Greek Doric temples at Paestum near Naples attracted increased tourist attention from mid-century. They played a major role in the controversy of the late 1760s over the respective merits of Greek and Roman styles and in the revival of the use of the Doric order. The Greek remains of Agrigento in Sicily also excited interest. Thus, to a certain extent, the Grand Tour moved southwards geographically as well as further back in time, as the roots of the Classical, and thus modern, world appeared to be within the grasp of tourists. The moves south and back in time were linked, and had a common impact.

Such sites were a world away from the Italy that modern reformers were striving to create. Indeed they gained much of their appeal from the degree to which past glory contrasted with a setting of present insignificance, poverty and backwardness. The remains thus served to demonstrate the cyclical nature of history: Italy, particularly Rome, was a *memento mori* of civilisation. James Thoburn claimed that Rome was no more than a third of the size it had been. Edward Southwell wrote from Rome in 1726,

> I have spent 3 months with great pleasure and some profit among the ancient and modern curiosities of this famous city, which have cost me daily reading and application and filled 140 pages in my journal, and I must own these heaps of magnificent ruins, and the view of so many places not only renowned for the actions and fate of so many heroes, but by the pens of so many famous writers do fill the mind with great ideas of the Roman grandeur as also with various reflections upon the vicissitudes of all human things.[21]

Edward Gibbon wrote that the Capitoline Hill 'gave ample scope for moralising on the vicissitudes of fortune, which spares neither man nor the proudest of his works, which buries empires and cities in a common grave'.[22]

Such reflections were a standard cultural trope. Italy was now a stage depicting their validity. The replacement in Classical Rome of republicanism by the autocracy of imperial rule was blamed on the enervating consequences of the spread of luxury produced by the wealth brought by conquest, a warning to the great modern empire, Britain. In Italy, it seemed possible to witness the decline both of Classical Rome and of post-Classical European civilisation. A stereotypical perception of Italy and the Italians as a country and a people both elevated and humiliated by the past had emerged. The very countryside seemed ruined. In the winter of 1699–1700, Creed wrote in Rome:

> The country or Campania of Rome turns to very little account; there not being people to manage it, it is naturally low, but for want of care is all boggy; and so produces a very ill

unwholesome air; the Roman government depopulates and ruins all the country; here it ruins the soil as well as the body.

In the *London Journal* of 4 November 1727, 'Philopatris' claimed 'All our travellers observe . . . Italy is almost quite dispeopled, and the people in it are reduced to a misery that scarce can be imagined by those that have not seen it'. This criticism was even extended to Britain's ally, Charles Emmanuel III of Sardinia, ruler of Savoy-Piedmont. Edward Thomas wrote in 1750, 'All the people here from the first to the last notwithstanding the goodness of their King are slaves, not one daring to go out of the Kingdom without His Majesty's special licence, and they are all obliged to take up arms when he commands them. British Liberty how invaluable a treasure art thou?' In 1764, Holroyd criticised Charles Emmanuel's treatment of his Savoyard subjects: 'he and his father though great and much commended princes have always racked their subjects very much'.

The results could be seen in the living standards of the people and in their environment. In 1788, James Buller thought 'the villages in Piedmont better built than in France and the streets of the towns much wider – But the want of glass in the windows which are not always supplied with paper and the iron bars look very bad'.[23] Turin, however, aroused a more favourable response, not least by Richard Pococke in 1734. He linked the appeal of some active Italian cities to those of Classical Rome, noting of Turin, 'at the ends of many streets you see the hills and mountains, which makes it look like *urbs in rure*, and this place pleases me much'.[24] This *urbs in rure* quality was also seen in Florence, Genoa and Naples, although not in Venice. It looked towards the *urbs* in ruins appeal of Classical Rome. Aside from the powerful aesthetic appeal of both *urbs in rure* and *urbs* in ruins, there was also a striking juxtaposition of sights, as well as a remembered vivid contrast with the bustling mercantile metropolis of London which filled the eye with action. The latter suggested success and progress.

The kingdom of Naples came in for particular criticism from tourists. Visiting in 1794, John, 2nd Lord Boringdon (1772–1840) wrote: 'Nothing could exceed the infatuation and bad government of the court of Naples . . . acts of the greatest tyranny and injustice. The Duc d'Arpini was exiled, merely from the police having discovered in his apartments some numbers of the French journal the *Moniteur*, which I had lent him.'[25] Naples was already acquiring the reputation for autocracy and conservatism that was to help garner support for Italian unification around the kingdom of Piedmont in the 1850s and 1860s. Tyranny, however, was not discerned only in Naples. In Florence in 1788, Charles Abbot noted: 'At the door of the theatre we saw a man masked observing everybody who entered. It is usual here, and at all the theatres in Italy, for government to station such a person there.' This sense of surveillance was also found elsewhere, George, Viscount Villiers writing 'the Gondoliers are in the secret of all the intrigues but are obliged to tell everything to the Inquisitors of State and are generally employed as spies by them'.[26]

Eighteenth-century Britain was an example of the process by which modern, progressive nations frequently resorted to Rome in two ways: first to claim Rome's mantle of civilisation and, second, to observe the spectre of empires-fallen, both to reflect their present potency, by contrast, and also, on occasion, as an admonishment against complacency. The remembrance of the Classical past was linked to the process by which impressions of Britain were reconstituted in, and by, Italy.[27] Similarly, in the 1920s and 1930s, at a time of relentless modernising, Italian Fascism turned to the Classical past in order to lay claim to Rome's historical legitimacy, but also as a counterpoint to such modernism.

The popularity of Gibbon's *Decline and Fall* (1776–88) helped further to focus the sense of the vicissitudes of the past and the related morality of history on the decline of Rome. That Rome was now the centre of Catholicism only emphasised this sense of flux and decline in the perception of Protestant Britons. For those who wished to make comparisons with modern Britain as a warning about possible decline, Rome had great potency. The imaginative map and idiom of such comparisons was to be widened, as Britain acquired an Indian-based Oriental empire from the 1750s on. This encouraged comparison with imperial Rome because, unlike Britain's North American empire, but like that of imperial Rome, the new British empire in India had no ethnic underpinning and was clearly imperial. Writers in the tradition of civic humanism, and, later, Romantic writers, such as Byron, Shelley and De Quincey, searched for points of reference around which to discuss and resonate their anxieties about the effects of empire upon metropolitan culture.[28] Imperial Rome was the obvious parallel.

In 1792, Thomas Brand wrote from Palermo to his friend, longstanding correspondent and fellow Anglican divine, the Reverend Robert Wharton, who had not visited Sicily when he toured Italy in 1775–6:

> We have had a little specimen of Sicilian travelling in a three days excursion to Segesta where is the finest remain of Doric Architecture in the Island. – It is in excellent preservation and commands a country which once I suppose was unequalled over the whole surface of the globe – What a country would this be with spirit of commerce and industry with well educated nobles and with a government regulated by Wisdom and Equity. And what a desert it is at present. For about 16 miles from Palermo the road is excellent, thanks to a bishop of great wealth and public spirit – beyond it is rugged and precipice or mud. There is not a wheel in the whole country, the roads are mere paths for a single mule and the few huts scattered round are as bad as Hottentot Kraals – we slept at Alcamo – Climate and Nature will do a great deal cramp them as you will: hence the vast population of the little towns – but they have the air of savages and it is still prudent tho' not absolutely necessary to go armed and attended by what is called a Campieri.

Brand continued by comparing England and Sicily: 'the two countries which are the extremes of Civilisation and negligence'.[29] In short, Italians were unfit to inherit their Classical past, and it was reasonable, indeed necessary, for it to be appropriated by the 'civilised' British. Similarly, the Tribuna, the big octagonal room that was central to the experience of visiting the Galleria (or Uffizi Gallery) in Florence, the ultimate 'art gallery' of eighteenth-century tourism, was seen as an important context for aesthetic display on the part of tourists, as in the posing *milordi* of Johan Zoffany's painting of the *Tribuna* commissioned by Queen Charlotte in 1772 and largely finished by the close of 1773.[30]

In 1764, Palmerston expressed the view not only that the modern Italians, or at least Romans, were unworthy of their past, but also that they were actively opposing its appreciation: 'It is grievous to think what treasures of sculpture are still concealed in the earth . . . Every discouragement is thrown in the way of those who would search.' Palmerston's perception of oppression extended to individual works of Classical splendour: Trajan's Arch in Benevento, Italy's best-preserved triumphal arch, was 'oppressed by buildings that are joined to it on each side and are even continued over the top of it'.[31] Aside from the commonplace that modern Italy was not worthy of its Classical past, came the view that it was not even worthy of its subsequent culture. In 1788, Charles Abbot wrote:

> It seems in some degree ridiculous that the Genoese should abound in pictures and statues commemorating their former heroes and victories in the Great Council Chamber of the Ducal Palace, at a time when their navy is reduced to a few galleys – Corsica lost – and their very existence at the mercy of the Court of Sardinia.[32]

An impression of neglect was also captured by many visitors. Mitchell complained about spoiled frescos in Bologna 'sadly mangled either by ignorant or invidious people'. Villiers noted that the neglected Palazzo Trevisano on Murano was falling into ruin, and claimed, 'The paintings in general at Venice are lost for want of care.' John Stackhouse wrote of Mantua: 'The different works of Giulio Romano in and near this town are the chief objects of a traveller's curiosity. This great master has distinguished himself no-where more than at the Palazzo de Te . . . but I was sorry to find his works both within and out of doors both falling into ruin, owing to the negligence and poverty of the present owner.'[33]

Although less common, it was also possible to argue that tourism was helping to corrupt Italy. Philip Francis claimed in 1772:

> The English have contributed to corrupt the morals of the Italians. Besides our disregard of money, we are too honest and too generous a people, to deal upon equal terms with such dirty knaves . . . upon the whole it is a disadvantage to the country, that they have so many curiosities to show strangers. It is inconceivable how many people are diverted by this idle occupation from labouring to get their bread. Every blackguard is a cicerone.[34]

Appreciation of the wonders of Classical, Renaissance and/or Baroque civilisation did not therefore lead to a positive appraisal of modern Italy. The opposite was the case: Italy was seen as 'decivilised'. In contrast, the 'South Seas' of the Pacific Ocean that were being explored by the western Europeans from the 1760s, and were making a powerful impact on fashionable opinion, were seen as at once uncivilised by European standards and yet as offering a glimpse of primitive virtue in the form of a true society populated by communal 'noble savages'. The same was sometimes argued of Native Americans.

There was no sense in these cases of the fall from civilised grace that Italy seemed to provide. Indeed much of Italy seemed decadent, fallen as a consequence of cultural, social and psychological faults from Classical splendour, and, as such, part not of the reforming Europe of apparently Enlightened progress, but an extension of the Orient. This was a period of growing Orientalism, seen not only in interest in India, but also, in a different form, in the response to the Classical remains in the Near East. Greek remains in Italy, such as Paestum and Agrigento, invited reflections similar to Palmyra and other stages in the imaginative East. Robert Wood (?1717–71), who spent much time in Italy between at least 1738 and 1755, published *The Ruins of Palmyra* in 1753 and *The Ruins of Baalbec* in 1757; he was later an MP. The excitement aroused by Wood's works helped to increase interest in Greek remains in Italy and also affected the perception of them.

A perception of decline was not simply an impression derived from deserted ruins such as Paestum. A sense of decay was also felt by many tourists visiting the cities, for example Francis Drake at Pisa and Siena. John Mitford wrote in 1776 of reaching

> the decayed town of Pisa . . . The buildings erected as receptacles for the victorious galleys of the republic, are now made the stables of the prince. The loss of liberty has reduced this once flourishing town from one hundred and sixty thousand inhabitants to about fifteen thousand.

Earlier, William Freeman had found Pisa 'a large handsome town but entirely dispeopled'. Abbot thought the quays 'not disfigured by dirt or business'.[35] The *Flying-Post: or The Post Master*, a London newspaper, in its issue of 2 October 1718 printed a long letter describing Messina allegedly written by a gentleman on his travels. This was a bleak picture of decline, of uninhabited and decaying houses, narrow and poorly paved streets with few people in them, and those with a melancholy air, very poorly turned out soldiers, and many robbers; but also with numerous, well-dressed, privileged clerics who involved themselves in worldly affairs. The implication was that these two aspects were linked: clerical influence was cause and consequence of decline.

Rome was more populous and active than Messina, but the contrast between Classical and modern Rome was still one that emphasised present decay, while the city's earlier role as a focus of Spanish Habsburg and Counter-Reformation interests and power did not excite sympathy. Henry Carr (born after 1694), a member of a Durham landed family, wrote thence to his brother-in-law in 1739,

> As to the appearance of the town itself considering the very great numbers of palaces that are in it I believe most people are disappointed, for setting aside the churches, pillars and obelisks which are of themselves a great ornament the rest does not answer one's expectation, the lower part of fine palaces being frequently let off and divided into little shops and greatness and meanness are so jumbled together (as we often see them in life in the same person) that the appearance they make upon the whole is but very indifferent, and even where the palaces are not so disguised, the contiguous houses being often ill built there is not any of them which strikes the eye at once like Grosvenor or St. James's Square, or several other squares and streets we have in London.[36]

This contrast was a commonplace. The elegance and extent of the new townscape in west London impressed contemporaries. Aside from the contrast between Rome and London, that between Classical and modern Rome was also frequent. In 1760, George Keate (1729–97), who toured Italy in 1754–5, published his *Ancient and Modern Rome, a Poem written in Rome in the Year 1755*. Piranesi's etchings of contemporary Rome, *Vedute di Roma*, which appeared from the late 1740s, led to tourists being disappointed when they saw the reality, some of which they found squalid.

The tourists tell us as much about Britain and the British as about Italy and the Italians. Modern Britain was held to define civilisation, a view not common in earlier times, and one that reflected the greater self-confidence and wealth of the British in this period. This was a fusion of Protestantism, economic growth, international success and the Whig myth, a fusion that was particularly successful from mid-century. The Whig myth was more successful and lasting in creating standards by which Britain appeared superior to foreign countries than in sustaining a coherent and united viewpoint on domestic politics. British self-regard and condescension towards foreign countries, not least Italy, was not dependent on contemporary foreign praise for Britain,[37] although, in so far as British commentators and tourists were aware of it, it could not but have contributed.

As well as in images and metaphors of decline and decadence, it was also possible to present Italy as picturesque and sublime. This theme drew on the representation of the Italian landscape by the influential Neapolitan painter Salvator Rosa (1615–73), particularly what commentators such as Sir Joshua Reynolds (1723–92), who visited Italy in 1750–2, saw as his depiction of it as wild and savage. The response by tourists and painters to dramatic natural sights, especially the drama of rocky coastlines, was affected by such art, although the depiction of the Campagna by Claude Lorraine did not prevent tourists from noting the flat, ill-cultivated reality. Yet, like mountains, volcanoes, waterfalls and the remains of Classical civilisation, this representation seemed divorced from contemporary Italian

35. *Caprice with Ruins of the Roman Forum*, by Claude Lorrain, *c.* 1634. Claude Lorraine (1600–82) helped to set the visual image of Italy, particularly with the juxtaposition of luminosity and ruins in order to create an effect at once dramatic and poetic. The impact of the light in this picture is accentuated by the use of shadow, which also has the effect of making present-day human activity appear far less important than the grandeur of the past represented by the illuminated ruins.

society: indeed Rosa both subordinated figures to landscape and peopled his countryside scenes with bandits and other marginals. This served as a further comment on Italian civilisation and led to a tradition of depicting *banditti* in landscapes.[38]

Modern Italy could be rushed through as Classical and natural sights were ticked off. George, Viscount Villiers's account of Rimini, which he visited *en route* from Bologna to Loreto and Rome in December 1755, authenticating what the locals could not be relied upon to get correct, made this explicit:

As I entered the town I passed over the marble bridge built by Augustus and Tiberius. It is plain but elegant and well preserved. In the town they showed me what they called the Suggestum, from which Caesar is supposed to have harangued his army, but it seems rather like the pedestal of a pillar. The remains of the amphitheatre, if ever it was one, are not worth looking at. The front of the Church of St. Francis built by the Malatesta, whose tombs are on the outside, appears grand at first sight, but, on examining it, the faults in the taste and architecture are very obvious. The gate of the town through which you go out is a triumphal arch built by Augustus and a very noble one indeed . . . As this arch and the bridge are the only things worth seeing at Rimini, there is no occasion to stop, but only to get out of the chaise on coming in and going out of the town.

Similarly, 'there is no occasion to stop at all at Spoleto, for one may see everything by getting out of the chaise for the temple before one enters the town and for the aqueduct just on going out of it'.[39]

Thus Italy in this period was increasingly seen as a country slipping into the past, one whose present inhabitants were of limited consequence. The tourist experience became one in which awe and interest was focused upon Italy past, and not upon developments in contemporary Italy. Edward Gibbon stressed this appeal: 'the footsteps of heroes, the relics, not of superstition, but of empire, are devoutly visited by a new race of pilgrims from the remote, and once savage, countries of the North'.[40] In its lack of interest in contemporary developments, this tourism prefigured the obsession with sand, sea and sun in later tourism to the Mediterranean. The net result was the same. As more tourists travelled to Italy, they knew and cared less about its current culture and society and, instead, saw the Italians as foreign to their concerns. This led to contempt, indifference or neglect; and, particularly, to a widespread ignorance about the country they were visiting. In addition, in so far as the 'authentic' cultural experience of travel was represented, as it increasingly was in the nineteenth century, as being in the secret precincts off the 'beaten track', where it could be discovered only by the sensitive, true traveller and not by the vulgar tourist,[41] this authenticity, like the democratising and institutionalising tourism that developed in the nineteenth century,[42] rested on an appreciation of historical Italy and of Italy as history. Venice was to have an especially powerful and aesthetic appeal,[43] but it was seen and presented as a city of past splendours, a rich spectre of past glory.

The extent to which the developing eighteenth-century perception so far discussed was linked with modern clichés about Italy is unclear. The nineteenth-century *Risorgimento* perhaps reawakened interest in Italy as a 'proper' country among British politicians and intellectuals, with the theme of the nation striving for freedom and, to an extent, breaking the claims of the past. Not only did George, 6th Lord Byron (1788–1824) obviously enjoy living in Italy, but, with his links with the Carbonari, he had strong sympathies with Italy's aspirations towards political freedom, such as they were, and he might easily have died in Italy instead of as part of the modern crusade for Greek freedom. William Wordsworth was greatly influenced by 'the *idea*' of Italy, a fusion of Classical civilisation and landscape and hopes of modern regeneration, and engaged with Italian poets, moralists and historians.[44] However, Italy's reputation in Britain may have suffered in the early nineteenth century from being the place of refuge chosen by dangerous radicals with dubious lifestyles such as Byron and the free-living radical poet Percy Shelley (1792–1822), who lived there from 1818. In turn, Byron absolutely loathed most of the English travellers he met in Italy, except for other bohemians such as Lady Blessington.

Yet, later in the nineteenth century, the cause of Italy became more popular, not least because revolution no longer seemed a serious prospect in Britain. Writers such as the Brownings and, especially, historians such as Trevelyan were very interested in Italy-present, while Charles Dickens, a keen supporter of the *Risorgimento*, devoted much space in the journals he edited to Continental topics.[45] The local newspaper in William Bell Scott's painting *The Nineteenth Century, Iron and Coal*, finished in 1861, carries an advertisement for a 'Grand Panorama!!! Garibaldi in Italy. Struggles for Freedom . . .', a show which ran in Newcastle that March.[46] The manner in which Giuseppe Garibaldi (1807–82), who had played a crucial role in Italian unification by driving the Bourbons from Sicily and Naples in 1860, was applauded by working-class crowds when he visited England in 1864 testified to the way in which Victorians of all social classes were able to relate many of the events taking place on the Continent to their own struggles and aspirations.

Yet such enthusiasm proved short-lived: once united, Italy ceased to arouse sympathetic interest, and, even during the *Risorgimento*, there had been an important element of condescension. A lack of interest in modern Italy was very apparent at the turn of the nineteenth and twentieth century, for example in E.M. Forster's novel *A Room with a View* (1908). The reconceptualisation of Italy into a less impressive society, if not a land of the past, that was such a powerful feature of its imaginative treatment by eighteenth-century British travellers, has remained potent and dominant ever since. Apart from the republicanism of Garibaldi and the *Risorgimento*, and, to an extent, the *apparent* 'order and backbone' that the Fascist dictator Benito Mussolini produced and that aroused contemporary interest in the 1920s and 1930s, Italy has since been regarded in such a fashion, as less civilised or developed. Although postwar Italian achievements in design, fashion, film and food enhanced Italy's status substantially, this approach can be readily seen in current attitudes, although it is less overt than in the past. Nevertheless, modern discussion of Italian politics and crime, and the sizeable publishing industry based on guides, travel books and reminiscences of Italy, both manifest this tendency to see Italy as in some way less developed than other major western countries.

13.   Religion

Of all the places I have seen I know none so fit to convince a man of the absurdity of Popery as Rome itself.

Charles Hotham (1693–1738), 1712[1]

Religion, as much as language, food and currency, helped make Italy foreign. Symbols such as crucifixes and shrines were everywhere; as were members of the regular and secular clergy. Processions were encountered frequently in the streets and religious buildings dominated towns. That tourists commented so often upon religious matters did not reflect an obsession, but was simply a response to the situation they encountered. Many were very hostile to Catholicism; others simply critical. Most discussed Catholicism without mentioning the situation in Britain. The lack of sympathy with, and understanding for, Catholicism affected the appreciation of other aspects of Continental society and culture. This was not a feature of tourism that contemporary critics condemned. Instead, they drew attention to what they regarded as the ideological and religious dangers presented by travel to Catholic Italy. Given the nature of British religious education and ideology, it is not surprising that most tourists were hostile to Italian Catholicism.

Anti-Catholicism was the prime ideological stance in eighteenth-century Britain. The methods, practices and aspirations of the Catholic Church appear to have appalled many. Newspapers, sermons, parliamentary speeches and much correspondence reflected a reiterated theme: that Catholicism was equated with autocracy, drew on credulity and superstition, and led to misery, poverty, clerical rule and oppression. Conyers Middleton, who was in Italy in 1723–4, published a *Letter from Rome* (1729) in which he dissected pagan elements in Catholic practice, a theme subsequently taken up by Sir William Hamilton.[2] The association of Jacobitism with Catholicism strengthened the antagonism, which was not greatly shaken by alliances with Catholic powers.

Catholicism excited fear and unease, although the response of George Hutchinson was extreme. An Irish Presbyterian weaver, he visited Rome 'by God's command' in 1742 to try to convert Pope Benedict XIV and 'preached mightily against statues, pictures, umbrellas, bag-wigs, and hoop-petticoats'. Interest and, at times, humour and ridicule were other responses. This was particularly the case with relics which symbolised the inversion of reason held to characterise Catholicism. Credulity and superstition were seen both as the essential supports of a Catholic ascendancy and as the products of it. By means of a tight control over education and the propagation of religious practices that ensnared reason and deluded the senses, the Church wove a web that entrapped the people. Visiting Rome in 1700, Richard Creed noted evidence of popular credulity. In March he reported that in the church of Nicolas of Tolentino:

> the fathers make little cakes as big as a farthing; and stick seven of them together; and so call them the seven loaves; they bless the flour and make them with holy water and so give them to the people; to eat when they are sick; and if they recover they say the cakes cured them; if they die they say the cakes saved their souls.

He also described the blessing of the animals on 15 January, as well as a lay religious fraternity involved in burial customs, the lying in state of a cardinal, the opening of the Holy Door at St Peter's, and Christmas displays in the churches. On Good Friday, Creed noted, 'It is customary for the Pope at this time to curse all people in the world that are not papists; but he being ill we escaped.'[3]

Popular devotion and clerical entrapment were also seen as winning the Church money and power. Tourists frequently commented critically on the lavishness of the shrine of the house of the Virgin at Loreto and on the gifts displayed there. Palmerston commented in 1764 on 'the Treasury or the absurdities of Loreto which are both very extravagant. I think Addison observes justly that to repeat the follies of the Roman Catholic religion is about as wise and as entertaining as telling one's dreams'.[4]

Nunneries were another great source of interest. It was very common for tourists to visit them, and several tourists, for example Robert Wharton in Naples in 1776, attended ceremonies in which women renounced the world to enter nunneries. Monasticism was also condemned. Monks were widely held to be idle in all but their greed. Catholic religious observances were usually treated either as credulous superstition or as empty and formal, the invention of 'priestcraft'. Pilgrimages, Mariolatry and scourging were all condemned. The Italians were seen as both devout and hypocritical. Nancy Flaxman noted in 1788, 'The devotion of the people is very exterior for they will murder with their rosary in their arms.' In Milan in 1771, Shelburne suggested that gender played a role in popular attitudes: 'a general conviction having taken place of government laying hands on them [riches of the Church] – none but women have any prejudice on that head'.[5]

36. *A View of Loreto,* by John 'Warwick' Smith, 1785. Smith (1749–1831) spent from 1776 until 1781 in Italy where he had been sent by George, 2nd Earl of Warwick. He travelled widely in Italy and once returned produced more paintings. An accomplished topographical watercolourist, many of Smith's works were engraved in *Select Views in Italy* (1792–9).

There was considerable ambiguity among tourists about religious art. Andrew Mitchell admired the paintings he saw in Italy in 1732, but noted,

One cannot help regretting (after seeing the vast profusion of paintings in these churches, by the ablest masters), the bestowing so much industry and art upon so silly subjects as the life and actions of one enthusiast and the fabulous martyrdom of a bigot. Corporal and ridiculous representation of the Deity serve to corrupt and debauch our ideas of him.[6]

Swinton, who was a chaplain, thought the depiction of the Virgin's conception and the Incarnation in a Genoese church 'very shocking'.[7] Thomas Brand was surprised in 1784 by the presentation of God on stage:

We spent two days very pleasantly at Bologna in looking at the best of the pictures in the mornings and in Madame de Bianchi's box in the evening. Here we saw the tragedy of the universal deluge, melancholy subject in which the perdition of the whole human race makes the catastrophe. In the first act Noah preaches, 2. the Birds fly into the ark. 3. the Beasts assemble. 4. The incredulous laugh at them but in the fifth the clouds fall from heaven the abyss opens below and there is a rare confusion of elements till the curtain drops. All this was ridiculous enough and amusing. One part made me shudder: it was a conversation between Noah and the Supreme Being represented by the mysterious luminous triangle with the Hebrew characters within and rays of glory round the circumscribed circle. This was surrounded by pasteboard [word obscured by tear] and illuminated by lanthorns behind: it was let half way down over the stage and a fellow behind the scenes bawled in the vilest voice words supposed to be divine. I am far from superstitious but this hurt me: it made me shudder with a kind of venerable horror. Had they brought Punch into the ark I should not have minded indeed I laughed very much at all the animals especially the wild ducks and swans who I think might as well have stayed where they were but this was too bad.[8]

More generally, the sensual appeal of Catholicism to tourists, who believed the religion to be irrational, evil and spiritually corrupt, posed a difficult problem of balance. Some tourists encountered hostility to Protestantism. Swinton met criticism in Genoa of the treatment of English Catholics, and claimed that the population of Livorno hated the English on account of their Protestantism. He saw his travel as providing a warning of the Catholic hope of benefiting from divisions within England in order to reimpose Catholicism. Swinton also thought that the Genoese were 'absolutely and wholly led by the nose' by the clergy.[9] Visiting the Vatican in 1721, George, Viscount Parker noted the wall painting of the murder of Admiral Coligny, the leader of the French Protestants, in 1572. Lady Harcourt was keen that her son, George, Viscount Nuneham, who visited Rome in 1755–6, should not have an audience with the Pope.[10] In 1750, Edward Thomas would not fall on his knees like other spectators when the Host was taken through the streets in Turin on Corpus Christi Day. He was sceptical about the Holy Shroud, noting that it was also supposed to be in three other places. Similarly, William Theed thought the blessing of the animals on St Antony's day a 'mockery of religion'.[11]

Many tourists were treated well by Catholics, and noted this in the case of Catholic clergy. Cardinal Alessandro Albani (1692–1779) was particularly hospitable in Rome. Indeed, Albani warmly received Edward Thomas, who had a letter of introduction to him, and got Thomas a passport for Naples from the Neapolitan Ambassador, as well as writing a letter to the papal nuncio at Naples, who came to visit Thomas at his inn. As Protector of Germans, Albani took an interest in the Hanoverian dynasty. He helped arrange the visit to Rome of

Edward, Duke of York, George III's brother, in April 1763, the first visit to Italy of a member of the British royal family as a tourist. Pope Clement XIII (r. 1758–69) held a reception in his honour and gave him presents. The Jacobite Cardinal-Duke of York left Rome in protest at this important sign of a Papal determination to achieve reconciliation with Britain. The willingness of the Papal government thereafter to grant excavation licences to British searchers for antiquities was another important sign.

In the 1770s, it became relatively common for Protestant tourists to be received by the Pope. In 1767, Kildare found Clement XIII 'very agreable' and his toe, when he kissed it, 'very sweet'. Philip Francis was most impressed in 1772 by his reception by Clement XIV (r. 1769–74), who told him that he would have supported Henry VIII. Francis noted, 'he converses freely and amicably with heretics, and has no idea of converting them'. However, he also claimed that 'it is evidently against the interests and of course against the principles of the Roman Catholic Church to encourage polite learning or any inquiries after truth'.[12] In 1778, Philip Yorke was presented to Pius VI (r. 1775–99) with six other British tourists:

> he was civil and polite and thanked [Charles] Lord Lucan for the favours that had been lately shown to the Roman Catholics in Ireland. The only ceremony to which we were obliged to conform was that of taking off our swords and arms and hats and making a genuflexion to his holiness on entering and going out of the room.[13]

A decade later, Thomas Watkins (1761–1829), and another former Oxford student, George Pocock (1765–1840), later an MP, were received by the Pope in his dressing gown, although they found their conversation in Italian about hunting a strain. The presence of a large cosmopolitan community in Rome helped make the tourist experience of the city more secular than it would otherwise have been.

There are some signs that religious antagonism became less of a theme in the accounts of many tourists in the second half of the century. Jacobitism became a curiosity, rather than an issue, and religious tension became less significant after the Seven Years War. Other factors were also important. Eighteenth-century 'rationalism' emphasised the unity and, generally, the soundness of Christian tenets, while deriding the non-rational elements in both Catholic and Protestant observances. A stronger distinction began to be drawn between religious observance and the clergy. As more tourists met priests, monks and cardinals, they discovered that the Catholic clergy were human, and usually educated and sensible, not 'whores of Babylon'. Catholicism could be found amusing rather than threatening. Arriving in Turin in 1783, Thomas Brand was affected by his poor Italian:

> I was seized with a fit of despair on going into St. Christina where a monk of the fattest order was singing a sermon in recitative with most musical cadences in honour of Sta. Theresa.

37. *Sir Edward Gascoigne*, by Francesco Trevisani, 1725. Gascoigne (1697–1750), who had succeeded his father as baronet in 1723, left for Europe in August 1724, spending most of his Grand Tour in Italy. He took courses in architecture and antiquities in Rome, before pressing on to Naples. Gascoigne bought paintings, prints, marbles and Roman coins, commissioned architectural designs and returned to England in 1726, getting married that year. The Venetian Trevisani (1656–1746), who arrived in Rome in about 1682, succeeded Carlo Maratti, who died in 1713, as Rome's leading portraitist.

The Devil a syllable could I understand for above ten minutes. The foam of his eloquence, his extraordinary action, the inflections of his voice rising two successive thirds and sinking to the key appeared so ridiculous that nothing but vexation at not understanding him could have prevented my laughing outright. In about a ¼ of an hour, however, having got the tune pretty perfect, I began to pick up words enough to guess at a meaning and at last succeeded pretty well, which put me in better humour, and some music after the sermon though neither *very* well sung or accompanied, sent me away tolerably satisfied and very much amused.[14]

Many tourists, nevertheless, continued to stress the pernicious consequences of Catholicism. This was especially marked in southern Italy and Sicily. There, tourists, such as

Watkins and William Young, wrote of the dire consequences of ecclesiastical and feudal tyranny. In 1786, Thomas Whalley (1746–1828), the son of a cleric and himself ordained, criticised Catholic practice in Florence and praised Grand Duke Leopold's unpopular attempts at ecclesiastical reform.

The French Revolution led to an increased tolerance of Catholicism. Having visited Loreto with Lord Bruce in 1792, Brand wrote:

> Ld. B. has a sort of *awe* in seeing these kind of scenes which I never dare to touch upon but leave just as it is. I think it necessary only to drop a slight remark on the credulity of the Romish Church without exposing it too much ... in these times of turbulence and *Philosophy* everything that throws contempt even on the Catholic Church is as well avoided.

The following year, visiting Vallombrosa, Brand joined the monks in denouncing the Revolution.[15]

Some tourists also visited the large Jewish communities in Rome and Venice. Given the presence of a sizeable community in London, Jewish practices need not have been unfamiliar, but it is apparent that, for many, the Jewish ceremonies they saw were new. In Rome, Sacheverell Stevens visited a synagogue, while Richard Pococke saw a circumcision, 'a most terrible execution'. Discrimination to a degree unknown in Britain was also noted. Richard Creed reported that in Ancona the many Jews were 'all obliged to wear red silk over their hats to distinguish them'.[16]

In contrast, there were very few opportunities to take part in Protestant ceremonies. Visiting Italy in 1792–3, Sir William Forbes found only one, an Anglican service ironically in Rome. Some tourists, such as Sir John Perceval in 1707, commented on their pleasure in reaching Geneva and being able to worship publicly, but most made no such comment.

Some tourists were Catholics. For many, a visit to the Continent was linked to the education of children in schools and convents, although this was far more true of the Austrian Netherlands (Belgium) and northern France than Italy. Not all Catholics, however, travelled for educational reasons. Others pursued similar interests to Protestant tourists, although there was the added religious dimension. To be received by the Pope was a high point. Catholic nobles were allowed to wear a hat and sword when they did so. Thus, Thomas, 8th Duke of Norfolk (1683–1732) and Alexander, Marquess of Huntly (c. 1678–1728) were received by Clement XI in November 1703. At Loreto, Sir Carnaby Haggerston arranged the saying of Masses that his mother desired. William Constable (1721–91) visited Italy, where he had relations, in 1750, 1765 and 1770–1. Henry, 8th Lord Arundell (1740–1808) spent over a year at the Academy in Turin (1758–9) and then travelled in Italy with Charles Booth, a Jesuit bearleader, beginning a career of purchasing Italian paintings. Henry Swinburne (1743–1803) spent 1763–4 and 1776–80 in Italy, and published an account of his visit to southern Italy.

Increasingly, Catholics could rely on the hospitality of British envoys. Frequently educated abroad, many with relatives there, they tended to be less critical of Continental society. Aside from their religious devotions and their visits to foreign relatives, Catholic tourists did the same as their Protestant counterparts. Some indeed were critical of Catholic practices. Constable and his sister Winefred (*c.* 1733–74) were criticised in 1771 for a lack of respect and devotion. An anonymous Catholic defended the shrine at Loreto, but added that he could not 'give into all those spiritual fopperies and out of the way devotions that some of our own communion unthinkingly run into'.[17]

Not all tourists were struck by the Catholicism of Italy. Charles Abbot claimed in 1788 that 'crucifixes, which abound in Flanders, are much more rare in Italy – now and then a chapel by the way side'.[18] Nevertheless, whatever their comments on the extent of devotion, it was clear that Catholicism helped define the foreignness of Italy.

14.   The Arts

Is there a portal, colonnade, or dome,
The pride of Naples, or the boast of Rome.
We raise it here, in storms of wind and hail,
On the bleak bosom of a sunless vale;
Careless alike of climate, soil and place . . .
Hence all our stucco'd walls, mosaic floors,
Palladian windows, and Venetian doors.

Of Taste (1756) by James Cawthorn (1719–61), a humbly born
teacher who became headmaster of Tonbridge but never travelled abroad

Tourism greatly enriched the British élite culturally. The length of tours, the guidance available, from experienced bearleaders and local guides, and the interest of most tourists, helped to ensure that many acquired considerable experience in assessing operas, paintings and buildings. Acquiring knowledge of the arts was a reason advanced to justify tourism, although some tourists displayed scant interest. Hugh, Lord Warkworth (1742–1817), later an MP, 2nd Duke of Northumberland and a general, wrote of Florence, which he visited in 1762, 'There are a great many curiosities at this place in the Grand Duke's Gallery and also in several private houses', and nothing more. Of Rome, which he visited the following year, he added, 'During my stay here went to see the antiquities and palaces as *vide Roma antique and moderna*'.[1] However, judging from surviving letters and journals, many tourists were far more interested and were also critical appraisers and purchasers of Continental art. Whether the tours were in the interest of British culture was a question that aroused heated debate at the time.

Painting, sculpture and architecture were the arts appreciated by tourists that made the most impact on the development of British culture, but they were not the sole arts to excite the interest of tourists. Indeed, for many, the distinctive cultural goal of travel to Italy was none of the above but, instead, music. This was a product of interest in modern Italy, not a residue of the past.

There are far more references to opera than to other forms of music, but it was a sensitive political and cultural issue in Britain. The preference of aristocratic society for this expensive foreign art form led to widespread condemnation, particularly in the second quarter of the century. Opera was held to be an unnatural art, an attitude expressed most strongly in press criticism of the popularity of Italian castrati. Aristocratic preference for opera led to attacks on the supposed abandonment of British culture in favour of a pernicious, effeminate import. The difference between Italian opera and vernacular works, especially John Gay's *Beggar's Opera* (1728), was employed to contrast foreign and British culture. Little of this criticism was voiced by aristocratic British tourists, although the response of William, 2nd Earl Cowper (1709–64) to the opera in Rome in 1730 was that it was very disagreeable to see men 'drest in women's cloaths'.[2] The majority of the attacks made by tourists on opera, as opposed to criticism of specific performances, came from those who were not members of the British élite. The Anglican clergyman Robert Gray, while visiting Rome, criticised the idea of men dancing dressed as women. In 1787, Adam Walker launched savage attacks on opera as irrational, effeminate and likely to lead to subservience.[3]

Such sentiments were voiced by few, and Walker's attacks were made late in the century when new vernacular forms were rising at the expense of older ones. Most tourists sought to attend the opera in all the towns that they visited where there were performances, and many altered their itineraries to attend specific performances and to hear famous singers. The singers commanded attention, rather than performances of specific operas. In 1734, Richard Pococke attended the opera at Rome, was disappointed by the opera at Venice, and travelled to Vicenza, as did Thomas, 4th Duke of Leeds (1713–89), Sir Henry Liddell and Sir Hugh Smithson, 'to hear the opera of the famous Farinelli', the stage name of the celebrated castrato Carlo Broschi. Thomas Pelham visited the elderly Farinelli at Bologna in 1777, and Francis, Marquess of Carmarthen (1751–99) did so in 1769–70. In 1778, Philip Yorke 'heard the Gabrielli [Caterina Gabrielli] sing in the opera of Armida' at Lucca. In 1782, Thomas Brand went with Sir James Graham and Sir James Hall to 'Mantua on purpose to hear [Luigi] Marchesi in the opera of the Fair'. Eight years later, Brand went to Bologna, partly to hear the famous tenor Giacomo Davide perform, though, when he heard him in Florence in 1793, he thought him 'too French in his manner of passing from the extreme of sweetness to that coarse bellowing which he calls expression and force'.[4] John Parker, 2nd Lord Boringdon (1772–1840), however, was very impressed by Davide that year in Livorno.[5] Robert Gray heard the great castrato Girolamo Crescentini at Bologna, and had his pocket picked.[6]

Opera played a large role in tourism in Italy. It was one of the major attractions of the peninsula, and the leading glory of modern, as opposed to ancient, Italy. Bologna, Milan, Naples and Reggio (in Emilia not the Reggio in Calabria) attracted tourists as a result of their operas. In 1720, George Parker visited Reggio to attend the opera. Edmund Allen noted in 1729, 'a good many English gentlemen at Milan in order to take the diversion of the opera'.

38. *Senesino and Faustina together in Oriental Robes*, by Marco Ricci, *c.* 1729. Two of the leading Italian singers of the age possibly depicted in Geminiano Giacomelli's opera Gianguir, produced in Venice in 1729. Both of the singers were well known in London, indicating how much the operatic world spanned the Channel. Francesco Bernardi, a castrati from Siena, hence Senesino, performed in many operas in London between 1720 and 1735. Faustina Bordoni, a Venetian soprano, spent 1725–8 in London, where, like Bernardi, she appeared in Handel operas.

William, 3rd Earl of Essex went to Bologna in 1733 to hear 'the finest opera that ever was heard, and a vast deal of company, there was 32 English'. Earlier that year, Philip, 2nd Earl Stanhope (1714–86) wrote from Milan: 'The opera is the chief entertainment of all the strangers here.' He found the audience very noisy, the orchestra very good and the dancers poor. He also attended rehearsals at Milan. In 1735, Stanhope's brother George referred to British tourists travelling in order to hear Farinelli.[7]

Audience noise irritated other tourists. Orrery, who preferred British to Italian opera, complained in 1754 that the audience in Florence was too noisy for him to hear the opera. Joshua Pickersgill reported in 1761 that the tragic opera was only changed once during the Turin carnival, and he ascribed audience noise to their consequent boredom with the repetition; Pickersgill, however, was pleased by the low admission price.[8] David Garrick

(1717–79), the famous actor, who visited Italy with his wife in 1763–4, was astounded by the audience noise at the Turin opera in 1763. He was also surprised that the players engaged in conversation with members of the audience. Charles Abbot went to the Florence opera house in 1788. 'The decorations of scenery and dresses' were 'splendid', but 'the company paid very little attention to the performance except at particular airs – and the buzz of conversation actually prevented us very often from hearing the singer, though we were seated within three rows of the stage'.[9]

Individuals certainly appreciated the performances they heard. In 1709, Lord Charles Somerset (1689–1710), second son of the Marquess of Worcester, visited the opera in Bologna 'which appeared to me extraordinarily delicate and fine; but was esteemed by them but as one of the middle rank, so much does the excellent music of this country excel any that we can pretend to, that I am sure it would be the highest vanity for us in England to compare the best of any of our new operas to that which was counted but indifferent among the Italians'.[10] Eight years later, also in Bologna, George Carpenter (*c.* 1695–1749) saw 'a very fine opera. I went to it every night: the singing and music was incomparable'.[11] In 1760, Thomas Robinson (1738–86), later an MP, Lord Grantham and Ambassador to Madrid, visited the opera at Parma: 'The magnificence of the Italians and the taste of the French contribute unitedly to render it so agreable as it is.' Philip Francis attended several opera houses. At Naples he 'saw a miserable thing they called an opera buffa'. He was pleased by the opera house at Lucca; and at Turin 'he killed the evening at a comic opera', enjoying the same production when he saw it the following evening.[12] Thomas Pelham attended the opera at Florence in 1777:

> it is tolerable and by far the best I have heard in Italy for that at Naples the great school for music was abominable; the management of the theatre being in the hands of people whose only interest is to get money; and who consequently are satisfied provided that their house be full.[13]

British tourists were impressed by the scale and magnificence of opera in Italy. The grand opera house in Turin attracted particular comment. In 1750, Edward Thomas thought it

> the finest opera in Europe, both on account of the music and machinery . . . You might see cities taken by storm and elephants on the stage with their castles and as it were whole armies drawn up . . . sometimes above 40 dancers together with a chorus of above 200 persons in gorgeous apparel. I never saw anything come up to this show.

Brand was also impressed in 1783:

> The great Opera house is only open during Carnival. It is immense. In the ballets, in triumphal entries and other great shows, there are sometimes 70 horse manoeuvring upon the stage at a time, real horse of the Piedmontese cavalry: and there is room in the house for 3,200 seated spectators. The only amusement at present is the *Opera* buffa at the Prince

de Carignan's theatre, a *little* theatre about the size of the Opera house at London. We arrived here just at the change of the Opera and have therefore seen two. The first an exceedingly pretty one of Cimorosa's *Ginnina and Bernardone*. Laschi the woman has a most sweet voice and just intonation. Lipparini has a better voice and much more humour than Morigi. The tenors are tolerable and the orchestra good. Cimorosa's music is very pleasing though I cannot think there is much originality in it . . . The other Il Conte di Bel-Umore is by a Marcello da Capua . . . and is much inferior to Cimorosa.

Moving on to Alessandria, Brand found the opera still on, although the fair had finished:

The moment I entered, the hero, the awkwardest and worst made of all the species had squawked his air and Zelinda was left alone to sigh . . . It was a very fine opera and gave me the greatest pleasure. The woman was Pozzi whom you remember in England . . . the composer Gaetano Andreazzi a Neapolitan full of fire and genius.

Like other travellers, Brand commented on the performances he saw. In 1784, he fell asleep at Mantua: 'The heat was intense and we were fatigued beyond all conception.' Also like other travellers, Brand offered general comments on Italian opera. In 1791, he attacked the excessive flourishes of opera singing: 'This is the degenerate taste of Italy, where methinks everything else is equally degenerate.' Nevertheless, in 1792, Brand praised an oratorio he heard in Palermo and a burletta (musical farce) in Milan. The following year, at Milan, he 'feasted on a charming burletta of more sense as well as humour than the general run of those great products of whim and caprice'.[14]

After they had left their bags at their hotel, opera performances were often the first destination for tourists when they arrived in cities with opera houses. Arriving at Turin in 1788, Charles Abbot and Hugh Leycester 'went immediately to the opera at the Theatre Carignan. It was a buffo opera, few people there – the music very moderate. The principal woman La Ciaffei seemed to sing well and in good taste. The rest were execrable. The dances were extremely long. They resembled the humour of a pantomime.'[15]

The appeal of opera was widespread, although for a variety of reasons. In 1778, Philip Yorke found the opera at Venice 'the only place where one sees the society of the place'. An anonymous visitor to Turin in 1782 commented, 'the music is never attended to by the people of the country unless a new opera and the first representation perhaps – or a favorite air by a favorite singer – it appears to be rather a general conversazione, and that on a high key'.[16]

There was also a sexual dimension. Opera dancers and singers were pursued by tourists. The opera provided an opportunity for female display. Richard Garmston deplored the dancers jumping and showing their legs in Turin – it was 'by no means graceful' – and the 'very tiresome' five-hour-long performance of a serious opera in Naples, where the female dancers displayed their behinds. He did, however, applaud the scenery and the dancing at the Rome opera.[17]

39. *Kenneth Mackenzie, 1st Earl of Seaforth (as Viscount Fortrose) at Home in Naples: Concert Party with the Mozarts*, by Pietro Fabris, 1771. Seated at the piano are, possibly, Wolfgang Amadeus Mozart and his father. The musicians include Sir William Hamilton and Gaetano Pugnani. The artist is seated in the corner. Kenneth Viscount Fortrose (1744–81) was on his third visit to Italy. He had been in Naples in 1752 and 1763 and returned in 1768. Fortrose was interested in the arts, and also seeking the hand (unsuccessfully) of Harriot Walter.

Tourists expected a high standard of performance, and were a critical and appreciative audience. In no sense can they be described as provincial or as praising whatever they saw. This stemmed from the high level of musical culture in London and the well-developed awareness of operatic technique. In opera, as in much else, tourists were part of an international society with common cultural forms and interests. Opera was central to the cosmopolitanism of the period, and British tourists shared fully in this.

The musical experiences of tourists were dominated by opera, but many enjoyed other aspects of Italy's varied musical life. Italy, 'this country of music', as Sir Francis Head described it in 1724, offered many opportunities for the music lover. Sir Thomas Samwell Bt. (1687–1757), later an MP, and John Blathwayt (1690–1754) played trios with Robert Valentine (*c.* 1680–1747), a musician Blathwayt met in Rome in 1707 who dedicated a flute sonata to Samwell. Other musicmakers included Willoughby, 4th Earl of Abingdon (1740–99), who visited Italy in 1763–5.

Relatively few tourists made music, but many others were interested in what they heard. Richard, 3rd Earl of Burlington (1694–1753), who returned to Britain in 1715 from his first trip to Italy with 878 trunks, crates and other items of baggage, as well as the violinists Pietro and Prospero Castrucci and the cellist and composer Filippo Amadei (the sculptor Giovanni Battista Guelfi followed), had ordered harpsichords in Florence and Venice. Sir John Buckworth Bt. (1700–58), later an MP, accumulated a large collection of musical scores on his tour in 1728–30. Swinton was delighted by the musical lovers he heard in Livorno and found the voices of Genoese castrati 'exceeding sweet and melodious'.[18] In 1758, Batoni's portrait of John, Lord Brudenell depicted him with a lute and the score of a Corelli violin sonata. Peter Beckford gave an outdoor concert in Rome in 1766 and brought back to Dorset the harpsichordist Muzio Clementi. In 1775 in Rome, Wharton heard some apprentice barbers give a very vocal serenade for a few women. He also attended some small private concerts where Boccherini quintets were played. Nine years later, Brand complained from the same city: 'there is nothing to be heard but now and then an oratorio with a wretched band and worse voices', but, he added, three weeks later, 'The holy week is at last over that season of wonder and enjoyment for all that are not blind or deaf. The first verse of the Miserere frightened me it so far exceeded all ideas I formed of it.' Thomas, Lord Grey de Wilton (1749–1814) enjoyed hearing the violinist Nardini play in Florence in 1785.

Sacred music, particularly oratorios, impressed some tourists. In 1791, Brand rushed to Venice, travelling, against his custom, by night, to hear an oratorio, Anfossi's *Ninive Conversa*: 'I never expect so long as I live to hear such music and such execution. The accompanied recitatives especially were beyond all conception expressive. I assure you such a Jonas as Bianca Sacchetti might turn more to repentance than the preaching of ten metropolitans or twenty archdeacons.'[19] Four years earlier, James Robson (1733–1806), a London bookseller, had been pleased by the oratorio he heard performed by nuns at the 'Medicanti Church' in Venice.[20] Many tourists mentioned the rich and varied musical life of Italy. Most enjoyed the music that they heard, although, like so many of the tourist pastimes, it was confined largely to the major cities.

This was also true of the theatre. Tourists tended to be more critical of the theatre than the opera they encountered. The British believed the Garrick school of acting to be superior to Continental acting styles. This opinion was echoed by foreign visitors to London who were particularly impressed by the comedy acting they saw. Language was also an issue. Many British tourists could follow French, but not Italian, plays. In 1759, Thomas Robinson sent from Turin a critical commentary on Italian theatre:

> Their tragedies are execrable, no probability in the plot, no dignity in the diction . . . As to the action of the Italian actors, it is very bad, in high parts; and where any delicacy of sentiment or stroke of passion is required to be well expressed, they know nothing of the matter, but for the common scenes of life, I cannot help thinking they execute them more naturally and with less stiffness than we do.[21]

The plays were usually regarded as bawdy. In Genoa in 1717, Carpenter thought 'the plays abominable lewd and illacted', while, in Bologna, he complained about 'horrid senseless bawdy actions and expressions'. Brand commented: 'In general the Italian theatres have pleased me much though in some of them I have lost all patience with the absurdities of Arlecchino and the still worse attempts of the more serious characters.' Abbot thought the acting at the Italian theatre in Florence 'indifferent', while Charles James Fox was concerned about the looks of actresses and dancers. In Florence in 1775, Wharton was ready to see the comic side of what seemed to him to be bad acting:

> Grecian captains in great hoops, white gloves, bag wigs and little couteaux de chasse by their side shrugging their shoulders like French barbers! With such action and such accent! I never laughed more at a deep tragedy acted in a barn in England.[22]

Italian art made a far more powerful and positive impression. Renaissance and later Italian paintings were valued greatly in Britain, where they were regarded as the best examples of their kind. For many tourists, seeing these paintings was a major motive for their trip. Whereas French cooking and Italian opera could be sampled in London, it was necessary to visit Italy in order to appreciate Italian art and, even more, architecture to any degree. This was in spite of the increasing number of Italian paintings imported into Britain, the development of the art market there, and the extent to which images of paintings circulated in the form of prints. There was a lack of public galleries in Britain. In Italy, many tourists purchased paintings and were willing to buy pictures of most subjects, including religious ones. In addition, tourists were willing to commission paintings by Italian artists, such as Pompeo Batoni, or by British artists visiting or resident in Italy, for example Nathaniel Dance, Gavin Hamilton and Robert Fagan.

Most British artists who travelled in Europe visited Italy. The list included James Barry, Alexander Cozens and his son John Robert, Nathaniel Dance, Gavin Hamilton, William Hoare (Hoare of Bath), Thomas Jones, William Kent, William Marlow, John Parker, Allan Ramsay, Willey Reveley, Joshua Reynolds, George Romney, Jonathan Skelton, Francis Towne, Richard Wilson, Joseph Wright of Derby, and the sculptors Joseph Nollekens and Joseph Wilton. In addition, less successful artists visited Italy. For example, Edmund Garvey was there in about the mid-1760s and then again in 1792–3. It was symptomatic of the sway of Italy that Garvey's Royal Academy Diploma work was *A View of Rome* (1783), and he produced a number of versions of it. Some artists received financial support from institutions or patrons. Thomas Kerrich (1748–1828) used the Worts travelling scholarship from his university, Cambridge, to visit Italy in 1772–4. James Russel reported from Rome in April 1749, 'now here of English and Scotch, painters and sculptors, to the number of sixteen'.[23]

After the foundation in London of the Royal Academy in 1768, artists increasingly took on the role of Grand Tourists, but their motivations and approaches were different (and

40. *Samuel Savage*, by George Knapton, 1744. Savage visited Venice and Rome in 1733, returning to Venice in 1734 and leaving Italy for Vienna. In 1738, he was elected to the Society of Dilettanti, whose official painter was George Knapton, who had been in Rome in 1725–32.

varied). Picturesque tourism played a role for some. James Barry (1741–1806) went to Italy in 1766–71 to look at ancient sculpture, in order to equip himself to be a history painter, but John Robert Cozens (1752–97) went there in 1776–9, and again in 1782–3, to look for dramatic scenery. Market forces directed the actions of some artists and even required them to have spent a period in Italy. Joseph Wright of Derby (1734–97) went there in 1774–5 in the hope of fanning his reputation, and he abandoned his 'Flemish' style upon his return, in favour of the then popular classical manner of Joshua Reynolds. The Italian school of painting was considered superior to the Dutch school and Wright greatly admired the Italian old masters he saw, especially the Michelangelos.

Some painters who went to Italy stayed there, including Jacob More (1740–93), James Durno (*c.* 1745–95) and William Pars (1742–82), who worked in Rome from around 1771, 1774 and 1775 respectively, until their deaths. Thomas Patch (1725–82) lived in Rome from 1747 until 1755, and after being expelled by the Inquisition, probably for homosexual activity, at Florence until his death.[24] Like other artist-residents, Durno, a noted history painter, also engaged in art dealing for British patrons. Furthermore, engravings and the dispatch of paintings for exhibition at the Royal Academy ensured that painters who settled in Italy were not lost to British view. More sent five works to be exhibited at the Society of Artists in 1775–7 and eleven to the Royal Academy in 1783–9.

41. *Lieutenant-Colonel William Gordon of Fyvie*, by Pompeo Batoni, 1765. Gordon (1736–1816), the second surviving son of the 2nd Earl of Aberdeen, was depicted in the uniform of the Queen's Own Royal Highlanders wearing the Huntly Tartan as if it were a toga.

42. *Samuel Egerton*, by Bartolomeo Nazari, 1733. Egerton (1711–80) was in Venice in 1729–34, as apprentice to Consul Joseph Smith. It was unusual for tourists to sit for a full-length oil portrait in Venice, but Egerton does not appear to have travelled more widely in Italy.

Travel to Italy also provided the opportunity to meet British patrons, as did residence there. Studying painting in Rome, William Kent (1685–1748), who was sent to Italy in 1709 by a group of Yorkshire gentry, met Richard, 3rd Earl of Burlington in 1719, who brought Kent back to England to complete the painted decorations of Burlington House. William Hoare of Bath (1709–92) spent nine years (1729–*c.* 1738) in Rome, improving his technique, which was influenced by antique sculptures, and copying paintings for tourists. It was probably through Joseph Spence, whom he met in Rome in 1732, that Hoare made the contacts that were to lead to numerous commissions from the Pelham family. The impact of their travels on British artists varied greatly, which was not surprising as some went to Italy when young and in order to be educated, while others, such as Joseph Wright of Derby, travelled when already established.

Some tourists were themselves capable of painting or drawing. Sir Richard Colt Hoare (1758–1838), who visited Italy in 1785–7 and again in 1788–91, seeking diversion after the death of his wife in 1785, was taught to draw by John 'Warwick' Smith (1749–1831) and made 604 drawings on his travels. He was especially fond of landscapes. Hoare was particularly energetic, but his example of industry was matched by other tourists who liked to paint or draw. Their response to Italy was not a passive one. As painters and drawers they entered into and interpreted what they saw. Smith himself was sent to Italy in 1776–81 by George, 2nd Earl of Warwick, who had toured there in 1766–7, and those years provided the basis for much of his work after he returned to England.

British tourists employed painters for a variety of reasons. Many wanted their portraits painted, often in elevating poses in Classical surroundings. This was a way to leave a mark on history. In Pompeo Batoni's portrait of Colonel William Gordon of Fyvie (1736–1816), painted in 1766, the vigorous and martial Scot, wearing his tartan and holding his sword amidst the ruins of Rome, was awarded an orb of command and a victor's wreath by the statue of Roma. Batoni, Carriera, David, Nazari, Dupra, Maron, Masucci, Mengs and Trevisani were popular portraitists. Agostino Masucci (1692–1768) and Francesco Trevisani (1656–1746) were most popular earlier in the century, Batoni (1708–87) and Anton Raphael Mengs (1728–79) later. It is known that Batoni painted 154 British tourists. Some, however, found him too expensive. In 1773, Robert Harvey, a Norfolk merchant, decided that 200 sequins for a full-length portrait was too much. Instead, he chose Venceslao Verlin at 30 sequins. Batoni's high prices reflected the extent of the demand for his work, which principally came from British visitors. His zest for colour helped make his portraits striking and sensuous, while he showed his subjects at ease, rather than putting an emphasis on elaborate dress and rank as in court portraits. Instead, rank was suggested by the noble and refined actions shown, such as looking at antiquities.

Other portraitists were less expensive. Not all depictions were exalted. Thomas Patch produced caricatures of many tourists who passed through Florence, some of which can be

43. *John Talbot, later 1st Earl
Talbot*, by Pompeo Batoni, 1773.
Talbot (1750–93), educated at Eton
and Magdalen College, had
succeeded his father in 1756. In
1772–3, he travelled in Italy with Sir
John Rous, visiting Florence, Siena,
Capua, Naples, Venice and Rome.
Talbot subsequently became an MP
and Earl Talbot. Rous (1750–1827),
who had also been at Magdalen,
had succeeded his father as baronet
in 1771, and was later an MP and,
eventually, Earl of Stradbroke.

seen at Dunham Massey in Cheshire. Group portraits reflected the role of tourism in male
bonding and were a celebration of the Grand Tour as a social activity.[25]

Tourists also commissioned paintings of what they had seen. Many purchased views of
Venice. Canaletto painted several hundred, virtually all of which were sold to British buyers,
many of them while in Venice. The Canalettos now in Woburn were doubtless ordered by
Lord John Russell, later 4th Duke of Bedford (1710–71), when he was in Venice in 1731. There
were four Canalettos in the dining room at Farnborough Hall, which William Holbech (*c.*
1699–1771) remodelled in the late 1740s to display what he had collected in Italy in 1733–4. At
Felbrigg Hall from 1749, William Windham (1717–61) created the Cabinet, a room devoted to
the Grand Tour, which he had made in Italy in 1738–40. Its images hang on every wall,
creating an extraordinarily evocative interior. John, Lord Brudenell bought six views by
Francesco Guardi while in Venice in 1758–60. Francis, 10th Earl of Huntingdon commissioned pictures of the bridges on the Arno at Florence from Patch in 1756.[26]

Painters accompanied tourists to Italy or while there. Richard Wilson developed his Italianate and Classical style as a landscape painter while in Italy in 1750–6. He travelled in 1753 from Rome to Naples with William, 2nd Earl of Dartmouth (1731–1801), for whom he produced more than sixty drawings, including a set of twenty views of Rome's surroundings. Wilson also painted a pair of views of Rome for Dartmouth. His *St Peter's and the Vatican from the Janiculum*, painted in 1753–4, was a view of the city in repose. It has a sense of timeless calm, not of bustle, and the dome of St Peter's in the background is subordinated to a Classical landscape in which a well-known antique relief from the Medici collection takes a prominent, albeit shadowed, role in the foreground. Wilson also painted Roman views that were purchased by Stephen Beckingham (1730–1813), a Kent landed gentleman, and on behalf of Thomas, Earl of Leicester (1697–1759) who, as Thomas Coke, had toured Italy in 1713–17. Wilson's attempt to create the calm, golden stillness of a Claude Lorraine was another means of recreating the ideal Italy of the past.[27]

44. *The Water Entrance to the Arsenal at Venice*, by Canaletto, *c.* 1731. Painted for Lord John Russel (1710–71), who was in Venice in 1731 and became 4th Duke of Bedford in 1732, this shows not only the entrance above quiet waters but also the sixteenth-century Oratorio della Madonna, which was to be demolished by the French in 1809.

45. *Bacino di San Marco*, by Canaletto, *c.* 1734–40. A panoramic view, crowded in the foreground and cluttered along the water's edge, but beneath a majestic sky, this is a work presented by bringing together various high viewpoints. The buildings are depicted in detail, enabling the painting to be dated to after October 1738 when the bell tower of the church of Sant' Antonin was finished. By June 1740, there were Canaletto paintings at Castle Howard, thanks to the enthusiasm of Henry, 4th Earl of Carlisle, who visited Venice for the second time in late 1738, accompanied by his son Charles, Lord Morpeth. In Rome in 1739, Carlisle commissioned a series of six capricci by Panini.

Many other artists accompanied tourists. John Robert Cozens painted at least ninety-six watercolours for William Beckford, whom he accompanied to Italy in 1782 as his draughtsman. Henry Tresham (1751–1814) visited Sicily with Colonel John Campbell, MP (1755–1821) in 1783–4, painting views for him. Richard Colt Hoare travelled down part of the Appian Way in 1789 with Carlo Labruzzi and acquired sepia drawings made by the latter as a record. The following year, Hoare made excursions from Naples with the landscape painter Jakob Philipp Hackert and the engraver Georg Hackert.

Some tourists commissioned reproductions of paintings that they liked. Henry Hoare had copies of four Renis and one each of Veronese, Guercino, Bourdon and Van Dyck painted for Stourhead. Batoni, Mengs, Masucci and Costanzi collaborated on copies for Northumberland House, Batoni copied a Subleyras portrait for Burton Constable, and Reni's *Aurora* was copied for Buckland, Castletown, Fonthill, Hovingham, Northumberland House, Rievaulx, Shugborough, Wardour and West Wycombe. In 1758, John, Lord Brudenell purchased a copy of Raphael's *Self Portrait* in the Uffizi, painted by Thomas Jenkins (1722–98), who acted as a dealer, painter and antiquarian in Rome from 1751 until he left for home shortly before the French invasion in 1798. George Romney (1734–1802), who was in Rome in 1773–5, was allowed to have a scaffold erected in the Vatican *stanze* in order to make copies of the famous Raphaels there. George, 2nd Earl of Warwick had asked for the right of first refusal for the copies he painted in Italy. Richard Colt Hoare had copies made of many of the Raphael frescos in the Vatican in 1793, and Thomas Brand commissioned a copy of a 'head of Rossi in the gallery of Florence, an angel playing the guitar, the sweetest thing I ever beheld, more than Correggesque'. Franciszek Smuglewicz, a Polish artist in Rome between 1763 and 1784, painted large copies of Guercino's *Death of Dido* and Reni's *Rape of Helen* for Sir John Goodricke, who is not known to have visited Italy.[28] Much copying was on commission, but some was not. James Durno copied Raphael's *Transfiguration* in 1779, selling it to the Earl-Bishop of Bristol in 1783.

The purchase of paintings was mainly concentrated in Italy. Tourists preferred Italian to French art, and contemporary Italian art was less popular than the painters of the two previous centuries, although certain modern Italian painters, such as Canaletto, were viewed with favour. Coke, Burlington and William Windham built up particularly impressive collections. Thomas Coke, later 1st Earl of Leicester (1697–1759), was in Italy in 1713–17. He prided himself on becoming 'a perfect virtuoso', was acquainted with many contemporary painters, purchased many paintings, some of which he had specially commissioned, and had his portrait painted by Francesco Trevisani in 1717. Nevertheless, by December 1788, Sir Joshua Reynolds, the President of the Royal Academy and the Principal Painter to the King, in his *Fourteenth Discourse* to the Students of the Royal Academy, was drawing attention to what he claimed was the poor state of modern Italian painting:

> Pompeio Battoni and Raffaelle Mengs, however great their names may at present sound in our ears, will very soon fall into the rank of Imperiale, Sebastian Concha, Placido Constanza, Masuccio, and the rest of their immediate predecessors; whose names, though equally renowned in their lifetime, are now fallen into what is little short of total oblivion.

Already, in his *Essay on the Theory of Painting* (1715), Jonathan Richardson had argued that the English could equal Italian 'old masters'. Reynolds visited Italy in 1750–2 and was particularly impressed by Raphael, but he displayed little interest in contemporary Italian artists. Richardson (1694–1771) visited Italy in 1720–1 and in 1722 published a work that was to be very useful to many tourists: *An Account of some of the Statues, Bas-reliefs, Drawings and Pictures in Italy, etc. with Remarks*.

Later tourists tended to collect less in Italy, because of the increasingly active art market in London,[29] as well as export controls in Italy and the drying up of supply, which in itself created a more efficient agent network. In 1785, James Byres had to resort to subterfuge in order to purchase Poussin's *Seven Sacraments* from the Bonapaduli family in Rome. In order to evade strict export regulations, copies were secretly produced and hung in their place. Bought for £2,000, the paintings were sold to the Duke of Rutland, who had not visited Italy. Aside from purchases, foreign artists were brought to England by travellers to Italy and elsewhere.

Some tourists, such as Thomas, 1st Lord Camelford (1737–93), who toured Italy in 1787–8, admired but did not buy,[30] while others bought a lot. To give a few examples of the variety and intensity of collecting, the antiquarian and collector Sir Andrew Fountaine (1676–1753) visited Italy in 1702 and the mid-1710s, collecting coins, as well as much painting and statuary. A bronze portrait-medal of him was made at Florence in 1715 by Antonio Seli. In Padua, in 1720, George, Viscount Parker 'bought some pictures amongst which there is a very fine deluge of Giulio Romano which everybody here thinks cheap at the price I gave for it viz. a hundred pistoles'. Henry, 3rd Duke of Beaufort (1707–45), visiting Italy in 1726–7, purchased paintings by, or attributed to, Raphael, Veronese, Palma Vecchio, Caravaggio, Domenichino, Leonardo da Vinci, Guercino, Rosa and Reni. He also commissioned paintings by Pietro Berton, as well as the elaborately inlaid cabinet later known as the 'Badminton Cabinet'. When sold in 1990, it became the most expensive piece of furniture in the world. Ninety-six cases of works of art were shipped back for Beaufort in 1728.[31] Robert Jones (1706–42), a Welsh landowner, who visited Italy in 1730–1, spent £700 on paintings while abroad, including several pictures in Rome.[32] John Bouverie (*c.* 1722–50), who visited Italy in 1741–2, 1745–6 and 1749–50, brought back the first large collection of Guercino drawings to enter England. George, Viscount Mandeville, later 4th Duke of Manchester (1737–88), bought a Tintoretto in Italy in 1758; he also sat for a full-length portrait by Mengs.[33] It cost John, Lord Brudenell £50 to buy Giordano's *Truth finding Fortune in the Sea* in 1758. Charles Townley (1737–1805) purchased copies of three paintings, including a Titian, at Florence in 1786.

Paintings could be expensive and too much so for some tourists or those for whom they were purchasing. In 1716, the 1st Duke of Kent was unwilling to accept the fee of 700 Roman crowns (£180) agreed by his son, Anthony, Earl of Harrold (1696–1723), for Giuseppe Chiari to paint *The Meeting of Dido and Aeneas* and *The Death of Dido* for Wrest Park. In October 1778, Philip Yorke, later 3rd Earl of Hardwicke, who visited Italy in 1778–9, found Batoni asking £700 for his latest *Holy Family*, the colours of which he thought 'too glaring'.[34]

Many tourists purchased not only when abroad, but also after their return home. In Italy, Yorke sat for his portrait by Batoni and commissioned two large landscapes of scenes near Naples from Thomas Jones. He subsequently commissioned James Byres to obtain a set of busts for his library, as well as ordering two paintings from Jacob More.[35]

Agents, often *ciceroni* (guides), such as Mark Parker, John Parker, Colin Morison and James Byres in Rome and Owen Swiney in Venice, assisted in arranging purchases. John

46. *Thomas William Coke, later 1st Earl of Leicester*, by Pompeo Batoni, 1774. Coke (1754–1842), later an MP and, eventually, Earl of Leicester, left for Italy after finishing at Eton in 1771. He spent the winter of 1771–2 at the Academy in Turin and stayed in Italy until 1774. Batoni's portrait placed Coke before the Vatican *Ariadne*, whose features allegedly resembled Charles Edward Stuart's young wife, the Countess of Albany, whom he was fond of. Coke also visited Herculaneum, climbing Vesuvius, and had an audience with Pope Clement XIV. Renowned for his good looks, Coke collected gems and casts, and, at Rome in 1774, commissioned from Thomas Banks the marble relief of *The Death of Germanicus*.

Parker, a painter himself, in 1752 became Director of the British Academy at Rome, but this body proved short-lived. Swiney (1676–1754), who was also called among other things McSwiney, introduced Canaletto to the British, and really began his career as a popular view painter, although Joseph Smith (*c.* 1674–1770), consul in Venice from 1744 until 1760, took over his role from 1730. John Udny (1727–1800), consul there from 1761 until 1776, and John Strange (1732–99), Resident in Venice from 1774 until 1786 (he finally resigned in 1789), also helped arrange the purchase of paintings and drawings. In Florence, Ignazio Hugford (1703–78), a painter of British parentage who was Secretary of the Academy from 1762 until 1772, arranged art deals. There were frequently difficulties, and, in these, agents could be very helpful. Colonel John Campbell (1755–1821), an MP, who was in Italy in 1783–8, purchased the Lante Vase in 1788, but its export required careful negotiation by Thomas Jenkins and could not be achieved until 1790. British guides and agents were not alone in helping tourists. Alexander, 4th Duke of Gordon (1743–1827), who toured Italy with his younger brother Lord William Gordon (1744–1823) in 1762–3, was shown round the remains of Classical Rome by Johann Winckelmann, the Prefect of Papal Antiquities, although he did not respond to the latter's commentary.[36]

Some of the paintings, medals and supposedly antique statues that were purchased were fakes. They were manufactured in considerable quantities in Italy and purchased by gullible tourists misled by dishonest guides. In 1753, Northall wrote of young British aristocrats deceived in Rome by antiquarian guides into purchasing copies, rather than originals, of works by Michelangelo, Raphael and Titian. Smollett gave a similar warning in 1767. Jacob More warned the Earl-Bishop of Derry about the many forgeries of the work of Raphael, Reni and Titian.[37]

Few sculptures were outright 'fakes', although they were often heavily restored and, occasionally, so retouched as to make them unrecognisable. The restrictions placed upon export – papal and other ecclesiastical ownership in many cases and the entails affecting other collections – encouraged subterfuge, which lent itself to exploitation by tricksters. At the same time, it is important not to overlook contemporary conventions about restoration, which was a part of the process of acquisition and preparation expected by collectors. This could extend to joining parts of what had been different figures in order to produce a re-creation.

The purchase of fakes was seen as more than simply evidence of fraud. Contemporary critics argued that many tourists did not truly appreciate art, and that their pretensions to culture were superficial and dangerous, opening the way to their being tricked into purchasing fakes, as well as to neglecting British culture. *Cognoscente* and connoisseur became terms of abuse. Cultural pretentiousness and praise of foreignness for its own sake were mocked in the *Connoisseur*, a London weekly of 1754–6, as well as by William Hogarth and others.

These criticisms did not trouble tourists. Nor were they much affected by criticism of the prevalence of religious themes in Italian art. Some of those who complained were Anglican clergymen. Catholic art was believed by such commentators to represent a threat. Swinton condemned some pictures and statues that he found in Italian churches. Gray and Stevens were also critical.[38]

In contrast to such criticisms, it is striking how far tourists sought to counter prejudices and to respond to paintings as works of art. Judging from their correspondence and journals, many tourists were, or sought to be, discerning critics. George, Viscount Nuneham went repeatedly to the Uffizi in 1756. Thomas Pelham was impressed by the paintings in Genoa and Parma, and benefited from Mengs's advice in touring Rome. Philip Yorke spent over a week examining the paintings at Bologna.[39]

Tourists recorded their responses to individual works, and these offer valuable indications about taste and how it was expressed. Visiting Venice in 1755, George, Viscount Villiers commented on San Giorgio Maggiore:

47. *Venice: Campo di San Vidal and Santa Maria della Carità (The Stonemason's Yard)*, by Canaletto, 1727–8, showed stonecutters working in the Campo di San Vidal, and, on the other side of the Grand Canal, the bell tower of the church of Santa Maria della Carità, which fell down in 1741, and the buildings of the Scuola. The painting was the property of Sir George Beaumont (1753–1827), who visited Italy in 1782–3, and then became an active connoisseur and art collector.

> It is famous for a great picture by Paul Veronese of the Marriage in Cana. It is a prodigious work, but greatly confused. In the Sacristy is a Presentation to the Temple by old Palma: it is without the usual hardness of his manner, and is a striking picture . . . In the Church of La Carità is one single picture by Leonardo Bassano: the subject is the raising of Lazarus. The expression in the countenances of all the figures is excellent, and of all that I saw at Venice, this piece struck me the most.

Villiers went on a detour from Bologna to Cento specifically to see the Guercinos in the artist's birthplace. One of the best was 'The appearance of our Saviour to the Virgin after his

Resurrection: the colouring is good, but the countenances want the proper expressions, and the drapery is very indifferent.' In the Treasury at Loreto, Villiers noted,

> is a picture by Annibal Carracci of the Virgin with Elizabeth, and several women performing the offices of nurses to the Bambino. It has great force and spirit and yet at the same time softness and elegance; it is indeed altogether a most pleasant painting. There is also an Holy Family by Raphael, the figures seem really living, and the head of our saviour is particularly fine, but in the whole there is a great dryness and want of elegance.

Recollecting this tour when he returned home, Villiers advised Lady Spencer that it was at Bologna that she would find herself 'most struck with the force of' painting.[40]

As another example of taste, John Hinchliffe observed in Venice in 1762:

> It is true what Montesquieu says in his little essay on Taste, that Paul Veronese makes good what he promises at first sight, though he does not like Raphael do more. The great picture at the Convent,[41] of the miracle of changing the water into wine, is certainly a first-rate work.[42] The general objection to it that the figures are not at all concerned at the miracle has been repeated over and over like many others, without any other reason than that it has been said before. There is in the Pisani Palace a very capital picture of Paul's which excepting some few errors in the drawing unites all the excellencies of the art. The subject is the family of Darius supplicating Alexander.[43] The character of Alexander is very expressive, of a manly beauty touched with a generous compassion. The mother, wife and two daughters are on their knees before him, a family likeness is preserved through the whole, with such a just proportion of difference that age occasions . . . The colouring is excellent . . . The work of Titian's which pleased me most is a single figure, St. John in the Wilderness. He has not like Raphael represented him as a sleek lad of eighteen, with a stare of wildness in his eyes, but as a man of thirty, his hair neglected, and his countenance expressive of a state of mortification.[44]

In 1788, James Robson condemned Giulio Romano's *Fall of the Giants* in the Palazzo del Tè in Mantua:

> which though esteemed an inestimable composition amongst the connoisseurs, I think loses all its grandeur and majesty in so small a room, by bringing such monstrous figures of human form, down to a level with the eye, nay even to the floor you walk upon. For want of height and distance they lose much of their dignity of character, and so does the scenery that accompanys them.[45]

He thus missed the point of the frescos, which were designed to make the spectator feel involved in the giants' fate.

Most of the paintings that were seen and appreciated were by Italian painters, but there were also pieces by others. John Boringdon thought 'the Turin collection of pictures one of the most select in Italy' and praised two that were by non-Italians, one a Van Dyck. In Florence, he was more impressed by the paintings in the Pitti than those in the Uffizi: 'The number of good pictures in the gallery at Florence was not very considerable. It abounded however with the finest specimens of sculpture collected with unbounded trouble and expense by the Medici family . . . In the Palais Pitti . . . was perhaps the largest and finest collection of pictures in Italy', those by Raphael and Titian attracting particular praise.[46]

Tourists also discussed their response to famous sculptures. Interest in acquiring paintings declined in intensity after about 1750 (although it still remained strong), but the discovery of Pompeii and Gavin Hamilton's excavations around Rome (1769–94) stimulated great interest in Classical sculpture. This was increased by the greater access made possible by the foundation in Rome of the Capitoline Museum in 1734 and the Museo Pio-Clementino of 1771, a response to what was seen as the threat from tourist purchases to the Classical heritage. Through sculpture, unlike painting, it was possible to appreciate and to respond to Classical models. Hamilton (1723–98) was also a major dealer in Classical sculptures.

Some tourists took a personal interest in archaeological excavations. In 1793, Prince Augustus (1773–1843), George III's sixth son, obtained with the archaeologist, painter and dealer Robert Fagan (1761–1816) a licence to conduct excavations in Ostia, where the first mithraeum (mithraic temple) was discovered. The following year, both men and Sir Corbet Corbet Bt. (1752–1823) joined in excavations at Campo Iemini. Corbet had already sponsored excavations near S. Sebastiano on the Via Appia in 1792–3 which had led in 1793 to the discovery of the tomb of Claudia Semne.

British stately homes soon began to display increasing quantities of Classical statuary. In the vaulted entrance hall at Houghton, the seat built for Sir Robert Walpole, there was a statue of a gladiator given by the Earl of Pembroke and displayed on a large substructure. The statue was influential: in 1741, an anonymous visitor to Houghton wrote, 'This gladiator is the original from whence so many have since been taken, and are very common in grand gardens.'[47] A fine collection of Classical statuary built up by Charles Wyndham, 2nd Earl of Egremont (1710–63), who visited Italy in 1729–30, survives at Petworth. In 1749, the 1st Marquess of Rockingham instructed his eldest son, Charles, Lord Malton (1730–82), later 2nd Marquess and chief minister in 1765–6 and 1782, to obtain in Rome statues for his rebuilt seat at Wentworth Woodhouse. Malton purchased four copies of antique sculptures, and a marble group of Samson slaying the Philistines by Vincenzo Foggini. William Lock (1732–1810), who visited Italy in 1751–2, 1767 and 1774, assembled an important collection of antique sculptures for his seat at Norbury Park, as well as Claude's *St Ursula* from the Barberini Palace. William Weddell (1736–92), later an MP, sent nineteen cases of Classical

48. *Charles Frederick*, by Andrea Casali. Frederick (1709–85), son of Sir Thomas Frederick, Governor of Fort St David, educated at Westminster and New College, Oxford, travelled with his elder brother John (1708–83), visiting Italy in 1737–8. From Genoa, they travelled to Rome via Pavia, Milan, Parma and Bologna. Charles sat to Casali in Rome in 1738. The brothers sailed on to Constantinople. A prominent antiquarian, who bought marbles in Italy, Charles was Director of the Society of Antiquaries in 1736 and 1740, and an MP from 1741. John lacked his brother's serious tastes.

statuary back to Britain from his tour in 1764–5. The most famous work, bought for £1,000, was the Barberini Venus, found by Gavin Hamilton and 'restored' by Thomas Jenkins, a process that included the provision of another antique head by the sculptor Joseph Nollekens.

While Malton and his generation were satisfied with copies, Weddell, whose collection is still complete at his seat of Newby Hall in Yorkshire, was not. The sculpture gallery at Newby was built soon after his return, with Robert Adam working on the designs and pedestals. Another major collection was built up by Charles Townley (1737–1805), who visited Italy in 1767–8, 1771–4 and 1777. He also acquired a collection of Roman coins and terracotta reliefs. After his death, Townley's antiquities were acquired by the British Museum, where a new gallery was built to house the collection. Townley's fellow Lancastrian Catholic, Henry Blundell (1724–1810), who travelled as a middle-aged widower in Italy in 1777, 1782–3, 1786 and 1790, was another important collector of Classical sculpture. He bought heavily, including, in 1777, via Thomas Jenkins, eighty statues from the Villa Mattei, the collection of which had been dispersed from 1770, and in 1786 the *Athena* from the Palazzo Lante. In 1785, on his third trip to Italy, Richard Payne Knight bought *Diomede*, an antique head, from Jenkins, beginning what was to be a large collection of Classical sculpture.[48]

The response to statuary was not simply aesthetic. Some tourists were unwilling to set aside the practical. Philip Francis wrote in 1772:

> I cannot help thinking that some of the capital ancient statues stand in very awkward attitudes. Let any man try to put himself in the posture of the Gladiator, and he will find himself hardly able to stand much less to fight. The Hercules at Florence is evidently on the wrong side of the Centaur; in consequence of his position, he must strike across his own left arm. Even the Apollo, great and powerful as he is, ought in my opinion to rest upon his left leg, especially if we suppose him in the act of shooting an arrow.[49]

For a culture that sought to define quality, at least in part, in terms of truth and politeness, such criticism was not without weight, but, in general, the requirements from Classical art were different from those of post-Classical works. The latter could be found wanting in terms of truth, politeness and other aspects of quality, while Classical remains had an air of reborn integrity.

The scale of the import of sculptures was such as to be at least as significant as that of paintings. Some tourists explicitly compared the appeal of the two. In 1764, Henry, Viscount Palmerston wrote:

> Sculpture though not a more easy art than painting if one may judge by the very small number who have attained any great degree of merit in it yet is a more natural and simple one. For this reason the ancient sculpture at Rome generally has its turn of admiration sooner than the works of the great painters many of whose beauties are so obscured by time and others originally of such a nature as to be quite imperceptible to an unpractised eye . . . I had seen before I came to Italy pictures almost as good as those at Rome, but I never saw a statue worth looking at till I crossed the Alps or which gave me the least idea of the powers of the art.[50]

He created a sculpture hall at Broadlands, and bought statues through Gavin Hamilton.

In addition to the interest in Classical sculptures, Neo-classicism was of growing note, one tourist writing from Rome in the mid-1780s: 'Canova is one of the most excellent sculptors since the revival of the arts, his Theseus and the Minotaur is equal in my opinion to almost any antique'.[51] Antonio Canova (1757–1822) had arrived in Rome in 1779. He produced the *Amorino* for Colonel John Campbell, as well as *Cupid and Psyche*, although the second was impounded by Murat and sent to the Louvre. Henry Blundell paid about £300 for the *Psyche* he commissioned from Canova. British sculptors in Italy were less successful, although Christopher Hewetson (1737–98), who was in Rome from 1765 until his death, was very

49. *A View of Burlington House*, by Antonio Visentini and Francesco Zuccarelli, 1746. Richard, 3rd Earl of Burlington (1694–1753) played a major role in the British reception of Italian culture. He paid two visits to Italy – in 1714–15 and in 1719. An admirer of the work of Palladio, Burlington was an active builder. Aside from being responsible for Chiswick House, Burlington also altered Burlington House, and was an active patron of Italian musicians, bought paintings and porphyry vases and commissioned a history painting from Giuseppe Chiari.

successful, especially in the 1770s and early 1780s, largely for portrait busts. In contrast, Thomas Banks (1735–1805), who was in Rome from 1772 until 1779, initially thanks to support from the Royal Academy, produced relief sculptures, including *The Death of Germanicus* for Thomas Coke of Norfolk and *Caractacus* for George Grenville, the commissions reflecting familiarity with Roman history.

On a very different scale, architecture was another important cultural interest for tourists. A lively interest in architecture was one of the attributes of gentility in Britain, and many members of the élite were knowledgeable enough to play a role in the construction or alteration of stately houses. In the design both of houses and of interior layouts, British architecture was heavily influenced by Italian models, first those of Andrea Palladio (1508–80) and, subsequently, models from a wider variety of sources, including Classical Roman, and, eventually, in the 'Greek Revival', Classical Greek, which was known initially through Greek remains in Italy.

Tourists paid great attention to Palladian buildings, especially in the first half of the century. Travelling in Burlington's footsteps, William Lee (*c.* 1726–78), the only son of Sir William Lee, visited Vicenza in 1753: 'I saw the Rotunda from whence Lord Westmorland's house in Kent [Mereworth] is taken, and the hint of Lord Burlington's at Chiswick. The copies are different from the original and in external beauty exceed it.'[52] Palladianism could also be seen in Britain at Holkham Hall, Wanstead House, Stourhead, and in innumerable other country houses. It was considered a British style that drew on Italian roots, as much through the influence of architects having seen Palladio's buildings as of patrons wanting them, and was contrasted with the heavier Baroque of Sir Christopher Wren and, in particular, Sir John Vanbrugh. There was also a vogue for Palladianism in Ireland until about 1760. The architect Sir Edward Lovett Pearce, MP (*c.* 1699–1733), who visited Italy in 1723–4 and took a strong interest in Palladio's buildings, was responsible for Parliament House in Dublin and for Castletown, while the architect Francis Bindon (*c.* 1690–1765), who visited Italy in 1716, worked on Russborough House.

Interior decorating at the beginning of the eighteenth century was greatly influenced by Italian artists who came over to work at houses such as Burghley. Italian *stuccatori* were particularly influential, for example at Castle Howard, from where they went on to tackle the interiors of merchants' houses in Leeds. The light, elegant style introduced by Robert Adam (1728–92), who returned from Italy in 1757, subsequently made a major impact. This included ornamental motifs from Classical antiquity, especially after the discoveries at Pompeii.

Some tourists sought the advice of foreign architects. In 1716, Anthony, Earl of Harrold received the comments of Juvarra on the plans prepared by Leoni for remodelling Wrest Park, the seat of his father, the 1st Duke of Kent. Harrold himself had an architecture master in Rome. In 1718, Sir Carnaby Haggerston planned to discuss possible changes to his seat and gardens at Haggerston with Italian architects. In 1725, Sir Edward Gascoigne (1697–1750), a Catholic baronet, commissioned designs for a new house and a pavement for the family chapel, neither of which was in fact used, from the Florentine architect Alessandro Galilei, as well as a design for a monument to his parents erected in All Saints, Barwick-in-Elmet in 1729. In 1734, Andrew Mitchell described the lazaretto being built in Ancona, noting that 'the architect Luigi Vanvitelli is a civil sensible man, he shewed me the plan and elevation of it'.[53] The Earl-Bishop of Derry planned the rebuilding of Ickworth while in Italy, and the principal architect was Italian, Mario Asprucci the Younger. The Mussenden Temple, a domed rotunda built for Derry at his Irish estate at Downhill in 1783–5, was based on the Temple of Vesta at Tivoli.

Here, interest in architecture looked towards a more general engagement with the Classical world in the shape of an interest in ruins and surviving buildings. These were often described and illustrated. They seemed more impressive because they were in Italy. Furthermore, those who had entered Italy via Lyons and the Mont Cenis pass, or the Swiss Confederation, or the Holy Roman Empire – the vast majority of tourists – had not yet had a chance to see the major Roman sites in southern France. Thus the impact of the Classical remains in Italy was greater for these tourists. John Holroyd recorded that at Susa in 1764 'I first saw a triumphal arch. It

50. *Frederick Hervey, 4th Earl of Bristol and Bishop of Derry, and his grand-daughter, Lady Caroline Crichton*, by Hugh Hamilton, *c*. 1790–3. They are depicted in the English garden of the Villa Borghese designed by Jacob More. Bristol had considered buying the Altar of the Twelve Deities depicted in the picture. Hamilton (1740–1808) spent from 1782 to 1791 in Italy, mostly in Rome, being an active portraitist as well as painting Classical themes. Bristol (1730–1803) was a frequent visitor to Italy and lived there most of the time from 1794 until his death.

was erected in honour of Augustus which considering its antiquity is surprisingly perfect. I was delighted with its beauty and fine proportion. There is no mortar or cement used in the construction of it.'[54] The mixture of his reporting and his own response was characteristic of accounts in the second half of the century; earlier, there was more of a factual response.

Tivoli, in the Sabine hills east of Rome, with the ruins of the Villa of Maecenas, Hadrian's Villa (excavated from 1724), and the Temple of the Tiburtine Sibyl above the cascade on the Anio, was particularly important as a Classical setting that encouraged a 'pre-Romantic' response. The river provided a natural tumult to match the grandeur of the setting. Interacting with patrons, painters responded to the site, ensuring the continued popularity of a pictorial record that was not that of the city. Richard Wilson's *Tivoli: The Temple of the Sibyl and the Campagna* (1752) depicts the artist at work in the foreground, not Joseph Henry (1727–96), who was in Italy for much of the period 1750–61, the son of a Dublin banker, for whom the work was painted. Clouds, cliff, buildings, most prominently a Classical temple, and a tree in the foreground, all contribute to the dramatic scene. More generally, the close relation between artists and patrons played a major role in the pictorial record. Thus, in 1754, Wilson sketched in Tivoli with 'the Earls of Pembroke, Thanet and Essex and Lord Viscount Bolingbroke who dined and spent the day together on the spot under a large tree'.[55] Such proximity helped make many patrons more aware of the artistic process than if they had remained in Britain. Many tourists visited studios. Thomas, Lord Camelford, his wife and daughter, both Anne, all together in Rome for the second time, in 1792–3, visited the studios of Durno, Fagan, Canova, More and Head, in late 1792.

51. *The Falls at Tivoli*, by Jakob Philipp Hackert, 1770. Hackert (1737–1807), a German landscape painter, arrived in Rome in 1768. The Falls were depicted by many painters, providing a dramatic sense of energy.

52. *(below) Gavin Hamilton Leading a Party of Grand Tourists to the Archaeological Site at Gabii*, by Giuseppe Cades, 1793. Gabii was discovered in excavations carried out in 1792–4. Hamilton's prominent excavations served to produce more statues for sale. Cades's sketch was an unusual depiction of the charismatic nature of archaeological activity.

The role of the Antique was indicated by the extent to which Classical subjects dominated the presentation of Tivoli. In contrast, although many tourists visited the superb sixteenth-century gardens of the Villa d'Este there, these left a far slighter artistic record. They were noted for their fountains and hydraulic effects, but the symmetrical and ordered character of the gardens with the series of terraces lined with cypress and ilex did not match the appeal of the dramatic gorge outside the town, its sweep of cascading water juxtaposed with the Villa as shown in John 'Warwick' Smith's painting *The Villa of Maecenas, Tivoli* (*c.* 1776–81).

Tivoli was scarcely overrun by tourists, but its popularity was such as to undermine the notion of the tourist prospect as a private response to the magic of Italy. Most pictures and drawings communicated the idea of individual communion, but, as already indicated, the practice of tourism was more that of travel in company and, in cities and at sites, socialising and viewing in groups. This was seen particularly in the response to excavations, as captured in drawings such as Henry Tresham's of *Grand Tourists Purchasing Antiquities* of about 1790.[56] This illustrates the social dimension, with Italians digging for antiquities and carrying their finds while a group of tourists, four of whom are women, looks at the finds laid out for their examination. In Giuseppe Cades's sketch of *Gavin Hamilton Leading a Party of Grand Tourists to the Archaeological Site at Gabii* (1793), the party is considerable – at least twenty-three strong – and many again are women.

The Romantic period was to put far more of an emphasis on the individual response, but during the eighteenth-century Grand Tour there was no sense that this was incompatible with a collective appreciation. This was heavily shaped not only by the experience of others, including experts (which contrasted with the cult of untutored feeling seen in Romanticism), but also by the sense of a living artistic tradition. This response looked back to the Classical world and its remains, and was greatly affected by them, but this Classicism was not perceived as a dead weight, nor as the heavy hand of the past. Instead, the past was seen as a world that could be approached and reinterpreted; and much of the aesthetic of Italy, both of the landscape and of tourist activities, centred on living in and being part of this world where past and present met.

15. The Impact of Italy

I am in high spirits at the thought of seeing Italy in so short a time, ever since I can remember I have been wishing to go into a country where my fondness for painting and antiquities will be so indulged. I expect every day a letter from Mr. [George] Knapton with a catalogue of all the finest galleries and his remarks on them, for I intend not only to improve my taste, but my judgement, by the fine originals I expect to see there.

> George, Viscount Nuneham, 1755.[1] Knapton (1698–1778)
> was a painter who had spent from 1725 until 1732 in Italy

Travelling independently and in relatively small numbers, tourists found that, across most of Italy, the facilities that existed for them were limited and often inadequate, a situation that further encouraged their tendency to concentrate on the major cities. There, they had an opportunity to participate in local social life, a process facilitated by their small numbers, the widespread use of letters of introduction, and the belief that such socialising was an important aspect of the education that travel was believed to offer. Rather than seeking special facilities, as Victorian tourists to Alpine or coastal Europe were to do, their eighteenth-century predecessors sought entrée into local society. Furthermore, the general absence of special arrangements for them encouraged participation in such local life.

Exposure to Italian influences was lessened by the employment of bearleaders, the majority of whom were British, the preference for the company of other British tourists, and the tendency to visit cities where these were to be found. Nevertheless, a large number of tourists met and conversed with Italians as social equals and attended ceremonies or visited institutions which it was more difficult, or impossible, to attend and visit in Britain.

British tourists had sufficient self-confidence and national pride not to praise practices, institutions or events simply because they were foreign; the reverse, instead, was a greater danger among the exponents of a xenophobic public opinion and, alongside their interest in

53. *Capriccio: St Paul's and a Venetian Canal*, by William Marlow, *c.* 1795–7. A testimony to the imaginative grip of Venice, this painting intermixed scenes of Venice and London possibly prompted by the end of Venetian independence in 1797 and concerns that Britain might follow. Marlow (1740–1813) was in Italy in 1765–6, visiting Venice, Florence, Rome, the Campagna, Naples and Capri, making sketches that served as the basis of Grand Tour souvenir paintings.

Italy and Italian models, this affected tourists. Despite the claims of contemporary critics, there was relatively little unthinking assumption of Italian customs, manners and mores, although tastes acquired or refined in Italy were seen in much of polite society as defining culture and style. The impact of these tastes in particular localities could be striking, as with Robert Clayton (1695–1758), who travelled in Italy in the 1720s and amazed the inhabitants of Cork (where he became Bishop in 1735) with his taste and cultural activity.[2] The openness of British society at the highest ranks had limits, but there was a response to foreign influences in which tourism played a key role.

This openness, and, more generally, the response of tourists to Italy, varied greatly by individual. Some were both serious and keen to use their experience of Italy in order to comment on Britain. In April 1777, Thomas Pelham wrote to his mother from Rome: 'the great use I found is the obtaining clearer ideas of the Roman magnificence than history conveys, and the reflections that must necessarily arise on the comparing our situation with theirs, with the melancholy thoughts of the imperfection and instability of every work of man',[3] a reference to the War of American Independence (1775–83).

Thus shifting and contrasting views of Britain interacted with the complex presentation of Italy that drew on the strong influence of a Classical education and of a public ideology that was heavily based on Classical images and themes, alongside the pernicious consequences of Italy being the centre of Catholicism and an exemplar of Machiavellianism and autocracy. These contrasts were interpreted, even 'contested', not only in the debate about tourism, but also in terms of another cultural product for which eighteenth-century Britain was famous: landscape gardening. This represented an Anglicisation of Classical notions of rural harmony, retreat and beauty. Many landscapes were enhanced by buildings that referred directly to the Classical world, such as Henry Flitcroft's Pantheon at Stourhead, and the Column and Statue of Liberty at Gibside, a Roman Doric column topped by a statue dressed in Classical drapery.

The new landscape design derived in large part from artistic models, especially the presentation of the landscapes of Roman Italy in the paintings of Claude Lorraine which influenced Henry Hoare (1705–85) when he laid out the gardens at Stourhead after he inherited the estate. Hoare, an MP as well as a banker, was in Italy in about 1739–40. It is scarcely surprising that John Hinchliffe, who took up painting oils in Rome in 1761, sought to imitate Lorraine. Far from reflecting a lack of confidence in British products, landscapes such as Stourhead were part of the appropriation of the Classical past to contemporary purposes. A sense of Britain as the new Rome developed as imperial responsibilities accumulated and taste became more refined. Similarly, Classical ideas and designs came to inform British architecture, aspects of a redefinition of taste and style that reordered fashion and acceptability. This led to significant expenditure, as country houses were built or rebuilt, and new townscapes created.

Building and rebuilding reflected a taste and style moulded by cultural interests to which travel and the cult of Italy contributed greatly. Lyme Park, a stately home built in the 1590s, was transformed by the Venetian architect Giacomo Leoni in the 1720s. Born in 1686, Leoni arrived in England in 1713, and in 1716 published an English edition of the first book of Palladio's *Quattro Libri*. He also built Clandon Park to replace an earlier Elizabethan house. Other older houses were swept aside to mark the new taste. Osterley Park, remodelled by Robert Adam in 1761, was earlier a Tudor house. Other Tudor houses, including Dunham Massey, were also rebuilt. In the 1760s, Sir Nathaniel Curzon (1726–1804), an MP who had travelled in the late 1740s, had an early eighteenth-century house at Kedleston demolished and replaced by a mansion in which Robert Adam embellished the established Palladian plan with Roman motifs, making the Marble Hall seem like a Classical atrium. Ambrose Phillipps (1707–37), who visited Italy in 1731–2, making a particular study of Roman architecture, erected a temple, arch of triumph and obelisk at the family seat of Garendon.

Thomas Worsley (1710–78), who made numerous detailed architectural drawings in Italy in 1739–40, was responsible for the rebuilding of Hovingham Hall in the 1750s and was Surveyor-General at the Office of Works from 1760 until his death.

The environment in which the élite lived reflected the role of Italy in their collective imagination. The tradition of aesthetic creation and taste shaped in this period indeed retained a continuing influence that has since been central to English culture.

Alongside the large number of buildings influenced by the inspiration and perception of Italy, and her architecture, a few were specifically designed to show off Italian acquisitions. In the grounds of Ince Blundell Hall, Henry Blundell displayed his collection of nearly 600 pieces, including many sculptures, in a garden temple and a pantheon he had built. Thomas, 2nd Lord Berwick (1770–1832) had Attingham Hall rebuilt to display the paintings and statues he had acquired in Italy in 1792–4. The Outer Library, also called the Museum, housed part of his sculpture collection, and the giant pilasters struck a clear Classical theme. The Picture Gallery at Attingham, built in 1805–7, displayed works that served to recall the Tour, including Philipp Hackert's *The Ruins of Pompeii* and *The Lake of Avernus*. Both of these were commissioned from Hackert by Berwick. The Picture Gallery still contains other Classical landscapes, including some by J.F. van Bloemen, Jean-Pierre Pequignot and Ludwig Strack. Also in the house are the three Angelica Kauffmanns commissioned by Berwick, his portrait and two Classical scenes: *Euphrosyne Complaining to Venus of the Wound Caused by Cupid's Dart* and *Bacchus and Ariadne*.

The Italianate influence also affected those who did not go to Italy. Sir Robert Walpole, the leading minister in 1720–42 and later 1st Earl of Orford, had a palace built at Houghton that reflected contemporary ideas of grandeur, and the role of Italianate influence in contemporary fashionable style. Pillars, pilasters, capitals, friezes, marble overmantels, dramatic chimneypieces, brackets and impressive staircases contributed to a heady sense of opulence, and many of the paintings were by Italian masters, including Domenichino and Leonardo.[4] Walpole himself ensured that his sons travelled, the eldest, Robert, in 1722–3, the second, Edward, later an MP, in 1730–1, and the third, Horace, later the 4th Earl, in 1739–41. His nephew, Horatio, later an MP and 2nd Lord Walpole, followed in 1744–6.

The impact of Palladianism on urban architecture could be seen in new townscapes such as that of Bath. More generally, Classical ideas were transferred to houses, churches and public buildings. This was not easy as the prototypes were mostly temples, baths and other surviving Classical works, and it proved necessary to design a new architectural grammar for design and ornamentation. Classical details directly inspired by the Grand Tour included the wall monument in the church at Sleat on the Isle of Skye, for Sir James Macdonald (1742–55), who had died far from home at Rome. Piranesi designed the column erected above his grave there and James Byres, whom he had met in Italy, was responsible for the wall monument. Byres also designed chimneypieces for Badminton and Fyvie, the first commissioned by

Elizabeth, Duchess of Beaufort (1719–99), a widow who toured Italy in 1771–4. Fyvie was the seat of Lieutenant-Colonel William Gordon (1736–1816), later an MP and a general, who had visited Rome in 1765.[5]

The aesthetic response to Italy conditioned the re-presentation of Britain, as buildings were built, rebuilt and decorated, but it is also necessary not to lose sight of the more direct impact of Italy on tourists. At the most banal level – but one that should not be neglected, as it usually is, not least because it left scant record in paintings – this impact was greatly affected by the weather. Poor weather had an effect on visits to cities, but was even more important for trips in the country and for travelling between cities. The latter was generally accepted as an aspect of tourism that might not be of great interest, but there was a growing interest in trips into the countryside, in particular to see sites near Rome and Naples. The idea of visiting Classical ruins in a rural, and, in particular, a wild setting became much more attractive, especially in the second half of the century. This was a very different sensibility and response to Italy to that of the seventeenth century, a counterpointing of Classical and sublime in the mood of a *fête-champêtre*. There was an attempt to track down rural sites noted by Classical authors, such as Horace's Sabine Villa. The painter Allan Ramsay (1713–84), who had become increasingly interested in antiquarian pursuits, began his search for it on a visit to Tivoli in 1755 and identified the site in the Licenza valley in 1777 on his next trip.[6]

The mood of the *fête-champêtre* was replaced by a greater emphasis on the sublime in what has been termed the pre-Romantic period. Thus, *en route* for Rome in 1788, Abbot and Leycester took horses to make a detour to the Cascata della Marmore near Terni, an artificial waterfall created by the Romans. Abbot wrote that 'The scenery of rock and wood all round the waterfall is lofty and magnificent.'[7] In 1785, Brand noted a letter from Sir James Hall, which has not survived,

> on his return from Sicily an expedition which seems to have given him more pleasure than any he has had. He talks in raptures of the gigantic antiquities of Agrigentum and Selinimtum and laying very comfortably to sleep (like Ariel in a cowslip's bell) in the flute of a broken column.[8]

Rain, however, did not contribute to the enjoyment of rural trips and took away from the atmosphere. In April 1788, Nancy Flaxman noted of Frascati, 'the weather very unfavourable for some days being wet and windy, two great enemies to the pleasures of a country retirement'. In 1791, a diary entry for her visit to Tivoli noted that it was rainy 'all day'. In March 1790, the weather made Henry, Viscount Palmerston pleased that he had not wintered in Italy as he had intended. In March 1793, Mary, Lady Palmerston complained from Naples about 'bad weather which I fear will prevent our going to the islands'.[9] Arriving in Italy in September 1793 with George, Viscount Morpeth, John, Lord Boringdon recalled that by early 1794,

We had hitherto no great reason to be delighted with the climate of Italy. During the ten days we were at Milan [September 1793], there was a violent thunder storm every day, the sun never once appeared while we were at Florence, in Rome for several days the streets were filled with snow, and, during the first three weeks of our residence at Naples, it did not cease raining for two hours together.

Fortunately, 'the climate of February and March amply compensated for our former causes of complaint'.[10] February 1726 in Naples was less pleasant for Edward Southwell: 'there has not been known a sharper winter for twenty years past, and there is no lodging in the whole city that has a chimney or curtains to the beds'.[11] John, Lord Hervey found Naples very cold in early 1729, and not the 'reputed Eden, the garden of the world he had anticipated'. In February 1784, Naples also disappointed Thomas Brand, then in Italy with Sir James Graham (1761–1824), a young baronet who was to be an MP:

> We have had the most dreadful winter that the oldest Neapolitan . . . can remember . . . except one delicious day when I went to Pompeia with a large party male and female that we were forced to dine under shelter to avoid the sun's heat, we have had an entire month of wind, rain, hail and all sorts of electric confusion; and as you well know that there is not a single house in Italy whose doors and windows shut close, to say nothing of smoky chimneys and the affecting alcali of a wood fire, you will easily guess how little comfort we have had here.[12]

Tourists in Rome in June 1749 found themselves 'shivering with cold winds'. *En route* from Padua to Ferrara on 21 October 1792, Sarah Bentham found that 'till noon we had a fog as thick and damp as any I ever saw in London during a November month'.[13] Aside from poor weather, tourists also complained about its unpredictability. John, Earl of Cork criticised that of Tuscany on that head, while William Drake wrote in 1769, on the eve of his return home, that he would always prefer England 'to all the countries of the world. They may talk of its unsettled inconstant weather, but in good truth I have found great variableness even in fair Italy itself'.[14]

There was also the problem that travelling in the winter months meant shorter days. This could entail travelling in the dark, which was possibly hazardous and certainly curtailed the view. Villiers and Nuneham took the *burcello* (boat) from Venice to Padua on 19 November 1755, Villiers noting:

> This passage, I am told, is in summer when the weather is fine, extremely pleasant, but when I came it rained hard and was so late in the season that it was dark before I got into Padua and by that means lost the sight of a great many of the houses.[15]

This is a reminder of the extent to which the visual image of the Tour – blue skies and seas, landscapes bathed in light and lit with clarity – was less than a complete account and record. More generally, the weather played a relatively small role in the description of the Grand

Tour, particularly in the printed description. As far as manuscript accounts were concerned, it was probably a given that the weather would vary and sometimes be wet, although scattered through the surviving correspondence there are many comments on temperature and rainfall. Printed accounts express no real interest in the weather unless it was spectacular, and that was not expected of Italy.

The two exceptions were storms at sea and cold weather on the Alpine crossing. It was as if poor weather was expected for both episodes and this affected travel literature. As interest in the sublime and the response to it grew, so it was desirable if storms were more spectacular. Difficulties and drama in the Alps and at sea were important aspects of the rite of passage that entry into Italy presented. It seemed that challenge and suffering were necessary preludes to pleasure. This was captured in 1737 by George, Viscount Sunbury:

> If I am now in Paradise, as many call Italy, I am sure I have suffered a Purgatory in reaching it; and the six days journey from Geneva to this city [Turin] seems as if nature would not disclose her beauties at too cheap a rate and was resolved that some pains and labour should be undergone in order to deserve the view of so fine a country as this.[16]

Reference to Paradise was indeed a commonplace. It was related to a sense of Italy as the destination of tourism, and also to a magical appeal that it possessed. In 1726, Mills wrote of Genoa, 'it appears by its situation and the beauty of its buildings like an enchanted place such as may be described in the finest romances'.[17] A sense of wonder was also captured in Genoa by Thomas Pelham in March 1777: 'the villas abounding with groves of orange trees and close to the sea are to an Englishman wonderful sights'.[18]

Genoa had this impact not least because for many tourists it was their first sight of the Mediterranean and their first experience of its lush vegetation, both very different to what they were accustomed to in Britain. Accompanying Sir James Graham, Brand arrived in October 1783:

> Delicious coast! Superb city! and seen through that transparent atmosphere which I had so often heard and read of but which my imagination could never conceive. It was still summer – roses, carnations, jessamines and flowers of every hue were in vast abundance in every street. One would have thought it the Festival of Flora. We stayed there a week and most pleasantly did we spend it in visiting the splendid marble palaces with their noble collections of pictures and in sailing about the port and the shore in a handsome felucca. For the evening we had a charming Opera Buffa by Felice Alessandro a Roman. It was ill judged to visit Genoa first, it is so magnificent that Piacenza and Parma, Modena and Bologna appear shabby villages after it[19]

– the last an apt reference to the difficulty of recreating the sense of enchantment in northern Italy, and to the impact of the sequence in which places were seen. Only Venice

54. *Coast Scene*, by Francesco Guardi. For British patrons, Guardi (1712–93) did not have the appeal of Canaletto. They preferred the precision of the latter to Guardi's more atmospheric impact. Nevertheless, John Strange, British resident in Venice from 1774 to 1786, commissioned works by him, as did John Ingram who was in Venice in about 1790. Strange complained about Guardi's preference for 'spirit' over 'truth'.

seemed magical, but it did not have a site between mountains and sea; nor was it endowed with the fragrances of the Mediterranean. To recover these, tourists had to go to Naples. Nevertheless, for those tourists who travelled overland from Austria to Venice, the arrival in Venice could offer an opening into a pleasantly balmy world, and many tourists commented on the contrast. William Bentinck found this in March 1727: 'The difference of climate is very sensible, for we left very ugly cold weather, on one side of a mountain, and found the spring at t'other side.'[20]

The impact of Mediterranean plants was clearly much greater than for modern tourists who have benefited from the intervening import of plant species. The first camellia reached Britain in 1739, the first buddleia in 1774, the first fuchsia in 1788, the first geranium in 1796 and the first dahlia in 1798. William, 4th Earl of Rochford returned to Britain in 1755 from his diplomatic posting in Turin with a cutting of Lombardy poplar, the first that was planted in England. Some of these new plants came from outside Europe, mostly from North America or the Orient, but all contributed to an expansion in British plant life that lessened the surprise of visiting the Mediterranean. Nevertheless, the effect was still striking when Brand visited Palermo in April 1792:

> The situation and environs of Palermo are beyond expression beautiful at this season especially when the orange gardens are in their greatest glory. Every object is new and

55. *The Bay of Naples from Capodimonte*, by William Pars. A London-born painter who had already been to Greece, Turkey and Switzerland, Pars set off to Rome in 1775 with the wife of the painter Samuel Smart and with a three-year pension from the Dilettanti Society to study in Italy. He stayed there until his death in 1782, making visits to Naples in October 1780 and June–July 1781. The lush vegetation of the Bay appealed to him.

singular. The most beautiful plants of our greenhouses are the shrubs and flowers of Sicilian wastes and heaths.[21]

The plants enhanced the lushness of the pictorial impression of Italy. This image did not, however, capture the insects that troubled many tourists: 'the flies were extremely troublesome in the day time, and bit us severely,' complained Abbot in 1788, while Edward Thomas claimed, in 1750, that he was 'plagued with flies, fleas, and bugs' in Genoa.[22]

Similarly, there was the problem of 'the heat of summer, for Turin is insupportable in the dog days, there being hardly any flux of air or cooling breezes there at that season', as Edward Thomas complained in August 1750. Berkeley was forced in 1720 to travel in the evening or morning. Two years later, John Molesworth, the envoy, was 'driven' by 'the suffocating heats of Turin' in July into the countryside, in August 1772 Philip Francis found the heat in Ancona 'insupportable', while, in July and August 1793, Brand found the 'great heats' at Florence 'insufferable'. The heat affected itineraries, delaying the arrival of Lord Charles Somerset (1689–1710) in Rome in 1709. He was to die of smallpox in the city the following year.[23]

There was, however, a more mundane reality of sights and trips within Italy affected by the weather. In June 1734, Richard Pococke, Robert Bristow and John Delmé were forced to return from the citadel at Turin because of the rain. Fortunately, they had enough time to see it the next day.

The weather could contribute to a sense that, at least, parts of the Italian countryside were no more attractive than Britain. Leaving Turin in 1783, the reflective Brand offered a comparison with villages near Cambridge in a heavy clay area:

> Oh what glorious works have I seen since I left Turin. But lets have a little method or all will be incoherent rapture. First then in going from the said Turin I was in a great passion and fretted that I had left Ditton and Hornsey Feversham and Cherry Hinton to cross the Alps and see a heavy clay country on this side perfectly flat and disagreable with the fields divided by rows of willows or trained mulberries and with our wheels sinking up to the axle trees at every step. It required an unremitting attention in the postilions to keep out of deep holes sufficient to bury the Carriage Imperial and all. Add to this the rascally imposition of the innkeepers with whom it is absolutely necessary to make a bargain and who will cheat you after all.[24]

Travelling across much of northern Italy left little better an impression on many tourists. As mountains became an object of interest, indeed rapture, in the second half of the century, and the wilder they were the better, so the plains were felt to lack in appeal. That a very different attitude had prevailed earlier can be seen in the journal of Francis Drake who toured Italy in 1750–2:

France is certainly preferable to Italy. For though in the vast vale of Lombardy, the Campagna Felice, and the Val d'Arno, there is more scenery, and the passage is more picturesque, yet on the other hand, there are the Apennines. The whole country [France] is more regular and uniform.

In contrast, Dr Samuel Drew, a physician who accompanied the sickly Henrietta, Viscountess Duncannon into Lombardy in November 1792, noted:

the restless mind of man soon grows satiated with a constant view . . . the fertility of this extensive plain must at all times be interesting to its inhabitants but a continuance for so many miles of a level surface little varied or diversified in its productions wearies the sight of the uninterested traveller and makes him chearfully ascend the Apennines.

Similarly, Villiers, in 1756, grew jaded. Of his journey from Florence to Lucca via Pistoia, he wrote, 'the whole road is the finest and most pleasant that I ever went, being as it were through gardens, but at last it grew rather tedious'.[25]

The combination of flat terrain and reasonably good roads in northern Italy was such that it was possible to speed on to the next city, and they were more thickly distributed than further south. There the nature of the terrain pushed the landscape forward to the attention of tourists.

Mention of the weather serves, like the illnesses and accidents discussed in Chapter 10, as a reminder of the difficulties of travel. However, the century brought a much greater assertion and appreciation of the value of travel, as the need to see objects *in situ*, and not in some grand cabinet of curiosities, was asserted. John Boringdon claimed:

It is necessary to have been at Rome adequately to comprehend and feel the enormous difference of seeing the great works of antiquity in that city and out of it. In one case they form a whole equally interesting, improving, and imposing, demanding and seizing the entire of all our own sentiments and attention, all contributing to heighten the interest and to elucidate the history of those periods in which arts have most flourished.

The alternative was for the works to be 'insulated and disconnected and appear totally incapable of producing that elevation and that ardent enthusiasm'.[26]

The value of site was asserted by Brand when visiting Sicily in 1792:

I was more pleased with the antiquities of Taormina than those of Syracuse and Catania. The [Greek] Theatre is far superior to any still existing and the situation of it is I think the finest I have yet beheld. You see Etna from it in its richest point of view – the nearer mountains are wonderfully picturesque with towns and villages on their summits and skirts and the sea view with the sinuosities of the shore, the Faro of Messina and the opposite coast of Calabria harmonize in the completest manner and form the grandest picture imaginable . . . the *providence* of Ferdinand IV (as he calls it in some marble tablets which 'violate the Tophus' of the temples of Segesta and Agrigento) preserves the ruins from further caducity [decay] or what was more to be guarded against further depredations. How many fragments of fine granite columns have I seen stuck in the corners of Wales.[27]

Thus, the value of sights and sites combined, of sights *in situ*, was asserted. It contributed greatly to a view that seeing Italy was better than having Italy brought to Britain. John Holroyd wrote in 1764 of his 'fury for seeing the country of the ancient Romans and where the polite arts have been so highly cultivated'.[28]

Yet, to indicate the variety of what was appreciated, Holroyd was also enchanted by his crossing of the Alps into Italy, and saw that as in part more worthy of note for correspondents at home. *En route* for the Mont Cenis pass, Holroyd passed:

some villages very romantically situated and beautiful cascades rolling and spouting from the mountains . . . I have been very tedious in the description of my six days Alpine journey, apprehending that particulars of such an uncommon country might entertain you, great cities and polished, improved countries being much alike and in general well known do not encourage an attempt towards such exact accounts of them. I was much amused passing through a country so wild and more in a state of nature than any I had seen.[29]

The picturesque quality of the Alps was increasingly referred to in the latter decades of the century. The mountains were seen as of scientific interest and as an experience. In 1744, Peter Martel published *An Account of the Glaciers or Ice Alps in Savoy* and in 1763, Keate's *The Alps*, a poem by George Keate (1729–97), who had travelled in Italy in 1754–5, was published. Travelling from Cuneo to Turin in 1788, James Buller recorded:

the plain very broad terminated by the Alps which form a kind of triangular amphitheatre open only to the Italian side. Mount Viso towering above all the others and above the clouds particularly grand and picturesque and more perpendicular than the generality of the Alps.[30]

Within Italy, the nearest equivalent was Vesuvius, a potent demonstration of natural power, an impressive sight, and an inspiration for the descriptive power of tourists. In 1793, Mary, Lady Palmerston recorded:

The different tints and forms of the different lavas have a most picturesque appearance and looking into the mouths of these craters you see all the different colours which are formed by the sulphurous matter which first issues from the souterraine fires. In one we saw smoke issuing. During the time we were there the great crater emitted a most violent smoke and after a report like a cannon great stones were flung up to a great height.

She also saw Vesuvius in the dark:

the view was superb. The mountain continually throwing out red hot stones which resemble the stars of a number of rockets and the stream of lava which was considerably increased and fallen very low illuminated great part of the side of the mountain and made the valley quite luminous, and all dispersed over the mountain you saw lights, which looked like stars which were the torches of the different parties who were wandering about. The wind blew strong so much that in descending to Portici three torches blew out but fortunately a party coming up assisted us to relight them.[31]

Indeed, the volcano became such a sight that tourists had a chance of meeting compatriots on it. Sir James Hall and Thomas, Lord Grey de Wilton met on the summit in 1785. The attraction of Vesuvius reflected the extent to which modern Italy had a limited appeal. More significantly, Vesuvius offered a dramatic vista of the power of the natural world that could not be glimpsed in Britain. So also did Etna:

how grand and sublime is Etna and all its accessories! Lord Bruce scaled the very summit and stood on the edge of the crater whilst it projected showers of red hot scoria and ashes to a much greater height than we had seen from Vesuvius . . . Do not however expect description from me – it is far beyond it. It is not the first sight of Etna which is striking . . . but when you approach nearer, when you find the *little* excrescences on the surface to be all vast craters of old eruptions, when you travel a whole day without getting more than half round him and begin to measure by surer indices than sight, the conception swells with the progressive discoveries and you are lost exactly in the same manner as in meditations on infinity and eternity.[32]

The single other most distinctive sight was Venice, James Robson recording in 1787: 'The first prospect of the lagoons of Venice has a fine effect with the evening sun; It seems a noble city with lofty spires and cupolas rising out of the sea.' He left at 3 a.m.: 'our passage through the city up the Great Canal, at that early time, the moon shining bright, was grand and sublime'.[33] This aesthetic response, with its pictorial quality, was replicated in paintings that also sought to capture the sublime. As a recovered impression, it took precedence in British culture over the more detailed response to specific aspects of the city, and the same was true of other places and areas. Six weeks after Robson, Richard Garmston recorded:

Venice looks well at a distance, but I was very much disappointed when I came near it. The houses look indifferent and many of them have paper instead of glass for windows . . . I stopped at Venice only two days. The bugs, gnats, and fleas bit me so confoundedly, I was glad to leave it . . . I think Venice is certainly worth seeing. The oddity of the city built in the sea, and the water in every street, the number of gondolas, and other vessels continually passing, and repassing, in the canals are pleasant and a peculiarity that I believe cannot be seen in any other city in the world.[34]

The response to particular Italian sights contributed to the shaping of a notion of Italy, both as place and as people. This, in turn, provided a matrix of assumptions within which hitherto distinct places, such as Venice, could be experienced and understood.

The impact of travel was both accentuated and affected by the habit of travelling together, and, even more, spending time together at the places that were visited. The impression of being in a crowd was created by what today would seem small numbers. Brand wrote of his time in Genoa in October 1783, 'We were a terrible large party there and all dined together constantly', but he only mentioned eight other British tourists.[35] Mark Davis, who toured Italy in 1784–6, complained from Rome in December 1785, 'Italy though rich in arts and fine remains is poor indeed in courtesy. There being little easy intercourse with the natives; so that the recourse of foreigners is amongst one another.'[36] In Rome in 1787–94, Nancy Flaxman spent her time in high tempo socialising. A typical entry in her diary included: 'dined at Lady Spencer. Rode with Duke and Lady Bessborough to see Raphael's Tapestry'.[37] Aside from socialising, this provided an opportunity to develop assessments together. Similarly, back in Britain, the remembered experience of travel and the cultural response to Italy were shaped by collective assumptions. The social dimension of the tourist experience did not preclude individual responses to Italy, but it helped mediate the processes of appreciation and impact.

16.   Conclusions

The great uses of travelling may be comprehended in these few words, to raise in us new ideas, to enlarge the understanding, to cast off all national prejudices, to choose what is eligible in other countries, and to abandon what is bad, in our own, and lastly to learn to love our own happy island, by comparing the many benefits and blessings we enjoy, above any other country and climate in the world.

Francis Drake, who was in Italy 1750–2[1]

I suppose a little tour of Italy will be the next excursion; it furnishes rather an additional fund for elegant amusements in private life than anything useful.

James, 6th Earl Findlater (*c.* 1714–70), who, as Lord Deskford, visited Italy in 1739–40, to James Oswald about the latter's son, 1768[2]

You seem to be sensible of one advantage acquirable by travel, which I entirely neglected, and which perhaps is the most essential of any: I mean, the attending to the government and policy of the several states through which you pass. Switzerland, I believe, affords the best plans of a true republican constitution, and therefore what are mostly to the purpose of an Englishman for example; whilst other countries where arbitrary power is lodged in the hands of the King, only show us the inconveniencies of such a government and what we ought to avoid and abhor. It is very certain, that though a man reads of the different effects produced by free and despotic constitutions, attended with the truest reflections and reasonings of sensible writers; yet these by no means affect the mind of the reader or imprint the ideas so strongly in the imagination as the actual view of the consequences themselves. And without doubt these are the things most worthy the consideration of gentlemen, along with the knowledge of the several branches of trade and the reasons of their establishment, increase and decrease. For indeed no people, in my opinion, are happy without a good deal of action and the constant circulation of money; as the idle and indigent subjects of an absolute prince make the most despicable part of mankind. The being obliged to court, praise, and admire other people, instead of spending one's time in endeavouring to be independent and become respectable oneself – is very terrible to my apprehension. Unquestionably every gentleman should likewise acquaint himself with things of the virtuoso-kind, though not strictly reducible to any use in society, yet as the marks of gentility and a polite education: besides, some knowledge of buildings, printings, statues, and medals creates a very fine amusement, and communicates a wonderful air of elegance to the sensible connoisseur.

I repent of the manner in which I spent my own time abroad in some measure, though I was constantly active, and were I to travel again would certainly manage somewhat differently. In the first place I would endeavour to mix more with the inhabitants of a place, and make a longer residence in any one part; in order to find out the ways of thinking of each people, their notion of happiness and misery, and how they were superior or inferior to my own countrymen in wealth and content.

W. Graves to John Quicke, 1747[3]

Because tourism was viewed within Britain largely as a means of education and not as a leisure pursuit, the debate on its merits often appears remote from the actions of many tourists. Furthermore, the debate became increasingly irrelevant as the nature of tourism altered during the century and enjoyment and amusement came to the fore. In 1793, Phillipina, Lady Knight wrote from Rome: 'I am very apt to think that the present mode of travelling is turned rather to amusement than to improvement.'[4] There was a growing appreciation by tourists and their families that the purposes of travel were not primarily educational in any narrow sense. It was quite acceptable for William Drake (1747–95), later an MP, to inform his father (himself a former tourist), in 1769, that he stayed in Florence longer than anticipated 'in order to see a little the humours of a masque ball'.[5] Such actions had always been common, but, in the second half of the century, most tourists regarded them as appropriate activities that did not need defending.

At the same time, there was a self-conscious sense of the importance of the personal response to Italy in developing sensibility. One manifestation of this was the emphasis on a distinctive experience, for example of danger. In October 1783, Thomas Brand wrote,

We passed Mt. Cenis after bad weather and it was covered with snow 6 or 8 inches deep but even in that state we could not help shrugging our shoulders and shaking our heads at the

56. *Miss Cornelia Knight*, by Angelica Kauffmann, 1793. Cornelia (1757–1837) accompanied her widowed mother, Lady Phillipina, to Italy in 1778. Short of money, they lived there until 1799 when Lady Knight died at Palermo. Cornelia returned home in 1800. Lady Knight had known Angelica Kauffman in England; Cornelia's portrait was painted in Rome. A literary figure, Cornelia was also an accomplished drawer.

57. *A Sunset with a Distant View of Rome*, by Jacob More, *c.* 1780–90. Proclaimed the English Claude, More (1740–93) lived in Italy from 1773 until his death, mostly at Rome, although, in 1778, he went to Naples to see an eruption of Vesuvius. A specialist in landscape painting, More was agent for Frederick, 4th Earl of Bristol (also Bishop of Derry), and, increasingly, a prominent art dealer. He was regarded as a specialist in the depiction of light and air.

extravagant exaggerations of danger which most travellers indulge themselves in in describing that famous passage.[6]

This indulgence was very much part of the tourist record. Self-centred dramatisation was linked to a wish to cultivate and express a particular note. In recording responses to Italy, there was also an ongoing engagement with the available travel literature. John Boringdon wrote years after his tour:

> Of the different journies stated in the course of these memoirs to have been performed, I have with the exception of my passage through the Lithuanian forests from Moscow to Warsaw purposely omitted all detail or description, the far greater part of them being nearly as well known as the road from London to Bath; I can not however entirely pass over all allusion to my feelings as I approached the capital of the ancient world, and about twelve o'clock on Sunday, 3rd November at a considerable distance from the city first discerned the dome of St. Peters.[7]

The memory resonated across the years. Visiting Rome also encouraged tourists to contemplate their relationship, and that of Britain, to the past in a manner that was not provoked by living and travelling in Britain. The debate of ancients versus moderns – whether civilisation was more advanced in the past or in the present – was reawakened and reconceptualised by the experience of tourism. Henry, Viscount Palmerston concluded in 1764:

> in the real comfort and conveniences of life we surpass the ancients and we have many admirable inventions of which they were wholly ignorant, but certainly in the arts which they practised and in all the magnificence of luxury we have nothing to do but wonder and submit. The greatest painters that have been since the revival of the arts have formed themselves by studying the ancient artists and have borrowed from them their happiest ideas of simplicity, elegance and beauty. Every stroke of Raphael's pencil shows the great regard he had for them and in the Galleries of the Vatican he has taken every ornament from the sepulchral monuments etc. he met with about Rome.[8]

In other words, the wonder of Italian culture was that it echoed that of the Classics. To British tourists, this validated Italian art, and also made it worthy of attention. Taste, nevertheless, was largely about the appreciation of antiquities. By developing taste, tourists, it was believed, became better able to make moral decisions.

Many, but by no means all, tourists sought to keep their memories of Italy alive, particularly by purchasing views and also portraits of themselves in Classical settings. Some tourists took this process further. John Miller (d. 1798) and his wife Anne (1741–81), who visited Italy in 1770–1, established a literary society at their seat of Bath Easton in Somerset. This centred on an attempt to honour the Classical world by recreating elements of it.

58. *English Landscape Capriccio with a Palace*, by Canaletto, *c.* 1754. The remaking of the English landscape was an eighteenth-century goal to which Italianate influences contributed greatly. Parks were embellished with grottoes, follies, shell houses, columns and Classical statues. The new fashion in landscaping was less rigid and formal than its predecessor, and this permitted a more personal response by visitors to the tamed natural environment, and to nature which was to be such a major theme in Romanticism.

Guests were asked to write poems which they put in an antique urn the Millers had bought in Frascati in 1771. Wreaths of myrtle were used to crown the best three competitors. The Millers' response testified to the Tour as dynamic and developing through the century. Although there were certain fixed points, particularly Rome and Venice, around which it continued to revolve, there was also a shift, with greater interest in Naples, Paestum, Pompeii, Herculaneum, Sicily, the Greek revival, landscape, the early Renaissance and individual sensibility.

Throughout, the stress in this book has been on the variety of tourists' experiences. This was deliberately sought when there was an emphasis on personal response, as there was increasingly in the second half of the century. At a more mundane level, variety resulted from the ability of tourists to select their route and from the differences offered by the seasons and the events of the human calendar. This variety was constrained by the wish to see a series of established sights, but the role of choice can still be glimpsed in tourists' accounts. In February 1725, Alan Brodrick wrote to his father from Venice:

I am now in readiness to set out for Rome and Naples in a very few days, and shall take the road of Ravenna, Rimini, Pesaro, Fano, Senigaglia, Ancona, Loreto, Terni, Narni, Spoleto etc.; and at my return intend to come by Siena, Florence, Leghorn, Genoa, Milan etc; by which means I shall not omit seeing any one place of note in Italy. I do not think of making any stay at Rome in my way to Naples; Lent being the fittest time to spend at Naples, and the Holy Week to be at Rome. This will order my time in such a manner as to put me in a condition to come home in what time your Lordship shall command, without my losing the sight of anything worth notice; as I have never received any orders from your Lordship with respect to the route which I was to take, I have always endeavoured to inform myself which would be the most convenient both with respect to the season and also to avoid going and coming the same way.[9]

His correspondence from Italy showed how Brodrick responded to art and sought to understand and appreciate what he saw. It would be a condescension to such efforts to dismiss them in terms of contemporary criticisms of tourism. Alongside naïveté, and a self-indulgence that was sometimes far from naïve, there was frequently a diligent attempt to appreciate sights as well as a response to the wonders of Italy. The latter retained their hold. In 1763, George, Lord Lyttelton (1709–73), who had toured Italy in 1729–30, offered a friend advice on the route she should follow, urging her to look at the map 'and let your imagination travel there over the ground I have marked'.[10]

17. Epilogue

The French Revolutionary War broke out in 1792, with fighting spreading that autumn to include a successful French invasion of Savoy and the threat of French naval action against Rome and Naples. Britain entered the conflict in early 1793. Tourists had been affected by war or the threat of conflict for years, but this war was dramatically different. The bloodier acts of the Revolution aroused a sense of horror that meant that most tourists not only did not wish to visit France, or cross it *en route* to Italy, but did not consider it safe to do so. Those already in Italy were forced to take an interest in the developing conflict. Thomas, 2nd Lord Berwick (1770–1832) left Turin in October 1792 because of its proximity to the French. John, Lord Boringdon, who travelled there via the United Provinces and Germany in 1793, met Nancy, Lady Maynard in Turin that September: 'She had made herself perfectly mistress of all the passes of the Alps, and the various military positions occupied by the French and Sardinian troops.' Travelling on to Genoa, he was angry that a British warship had fired on and seized a French warship in the harbour, violating Genoese neutrality. Concerned that if he left, as he had intended, by land, he would be in danger of attack by Jacobins, and warned that this might indeed be the case, Boringdon chose to sail from Genoa.[1] The following year, Thomas Brand was anxious about his route home from Florence, but reassured himself by choosing a new servant:

> I have now got a very good natural clever lad by birth a Hanoverian who possesses all the tongues between this and the North Pole if the cursed Jacobins make it necessary for the *planet* to make so great a deviation from the *old orbit*.[2]

As French armies spread across the Continent, defeating Britain's allies and remodelling states, Italy became far distant. Contacts were executed or forced to flee, British diplomatic representation withdrawn, artistic treasures were seized by the French, and old activities, such as visiting nunneries, attending academies, being presented at court, and watching the ceremonies of court and religious society, ceased. The body of experience that was common to most eighteenth-century British tourists was shattered, and this was to distinguish them from their nineteenth-century successors. Italy became less accessible and the Grand Tour was a victim of this change.

In 1797, Anna, Lady Berwick was made frantic by fears about the French, while, in the wake of French success, in 1798, on his return from the Middle East and Greece, Randle Wilbraham (1773–1861) found it necessary to obtain from the French chargé d'affaires a passport from Naples to Florence. He deemed it prudent not to stay long in Rome and found Venice sadly diminished as a result of harsh plundering by the French. The same year, Mariana Starke had to get a French, a Cisalpine and an Imperial (Austrian) passport in order to travel from Florence into Germany.

Milan was captured by the French in 1796, while, that year, the British in Florence were advised to retire into the countryside. Venice lost its independence under the Treaty of Campoformio (1797), becoming first Austrian and then, in 1805, part of the French kingdom of Italy. For many, the fall of Venice was as powerful a symbol as that of Constantinople to the Turks in 1453. The Roman Republic was founded in 1798 when the French occupied the city, and Pope Pius VI was exiled to France the following year. Naples was conquered in the winter of 1798–9, but this was followed by a vicious counter-revolutionary war. Under Napoleon, the French annexed the Ligurian Republic (formerly Genoa) in 1805, Etruria (formerly Tuscany) in 1807, and the Papal States in 1809, while Napoleon himself became King of Italy in 1805 and, as such, ruler of Lombardy and Venetia, and his brother-in-law Murat became King of Naples in 1806.

The artists' colony in Rome disintegrated, and those who had eased the path of tourists departed. Byres, Jenkins and Sir William Hamilton managed to return home, although Jenkins lost most of his property and died soon after his return. Gavin Hamilton died in Rome in 1798. As artistic links with Italy were severed, taste swung in favour of Greece. Other longstanding British tourists and residents who had provided help or interest for compatriots suffered from the French. The Earl-Bishop of Derry, arrested by the French near Ferrara in 1798, was confined in Milan until his release the following year. Cardinal Henry fled from Rome in 1798 as the French invaded. The following year, Peter Beckford fled from Florence to Palermo.

The French pillaged the artistic riches of Italy, including those of British residents and works that had been accumulated for dispatch to British collections. Derry's valuable collection of antiquities was seized in 1798. Such confiscations were to help make Paris the art capital of the world and, in terms of the art theory of the time, the moral capital. It was not only the tourist link between Britain and the Mediterranean that was broken in the 1790s. The Italy that eighteenth-century tourists had known was transformed. Tourism would revive after the abdication of Napoleon in 1814, but it could not be the same.

Notes

Add	Additional Manuscripts
AO	Archive Office
Beinecke	New Haven, Beinecke Library
BL	London, British Library
Bod.	Oxford, Bodleian Library
Broadlands	Southampton, University Library, Broadlands collection
CRO	County Record Office
CUL	Cambridge University Library
Eg.	Egerton manuscripts
Gateshead	Gateshead Public Library
GLRO	Greater London Record Office
HL	San Marino, California, Huntington Library
HMC	Reports of the Historical Manuscripts Commission
HW	Farmington, Connecticut, Lewis Walpole Library, Hanbury Williams papers

NAS	Edinburgh, National Archives of Scotland
Orrery	John, Earl of Cork and Orrery, *Letters from Italy, in the Years 1754 and 1755* (1773)
PRO	London, Public Record Office
RA	Windsor Castle, Royal Archive
RO	Record Office
SP	State Papers
Swinton	Journal of John Swinton in Wadham College, Oxford
UL	University Library
WHA	Durham, University Library, Archives and Special Collections, Wharton papers

Unless otherwise stated, all works are published in London.

Preface

1. Lady Spencer, journal, 1763, BL, Add. 75744 fol. 20.
2. Broadlands 11/3.
3. Villiers to Lady Spencer, 17 Oct. 1763, BL, Add. 75670.
4. Lady Palmerston to her brother, Benjamin Mee, 27 June 1793, Broadlands 11/19/11.

1.   Introduction

1. On the earlier situation see, in particular, J. Paterson, '"The Very Paradise, and Canaan of Christendome": English Travellers in Late Renaissance Italy' (University of Sydney Ph.D., 2001); J. Stoye, *English Travellers Abroad, 1604–1667* (2nd edn., New Haven, 1989) and 'The Grand Tour in the

Seventeenth Century', *Journal of Anglo-Italian Studies*, 1 (1991), pp. 62–73; E. Chaney, *The Grand Tour and the Great Rebellion: Richard Lassells and 'The Voyage of Italy'* (Geneva, 1985); and *The Evolution of the Grand Tour. Anglo-Italian Cultural Relations since the Renaissance* (1998).

2. H.J. Müllenbrock, 'The Political Implications of the Grand Tour: Aspects of a Specifically English Contribution to the European Travel Literature of the Age of Enlightenment', *Trema*, 9 (1984), pp. 7–21.

3. J. Andrews, *Letters to a Young Gentleman* (1784), pp. 477–8. On travel literature, J.M. Black, 'Tourism and Cultural Challenge: The Changing Scene of the Eighteenth Century', in J. McVeagh (ed.), *English Literature and the Wider World. Volume I 1660–1780. All Before Them* (1990), and M. Cohen, 'The Grand Tour: Constructing the English Gentleman in Eighteenth-Century France', *History of Education*, 21 (1992).

4. Bod. Ms. Eng. Misc. d. 213; Truro CRO, J3/34/1.

5. C. Thompson, *The Travels of the Late Charles Thompson* (3 vols, Reading, 1744), I, 67.

6. E. Craven, *Memoirs of the Margravine of Anspach* (2 vols, 1826) I, 306–7.

7. B. Redford, *Venice and the Grand Tour* (New Haven, 1996); J. Eglin, *Venice Transfigured. The Myth of Venice in British Culture, 1660–1797* (Basingstoke, 2001).

8. BL, Add. 33127 fol. 216.

9. M. Sherlock, *New Letters from an English Traveller* (1781), pp. 147–9.

10. Broadlands 11/3.

11. Ibid.

12. Elizabeth, Lady Craven, *A Journey through the Crimea to Constantinople* (Dublin, 1789), I, 151–2.

13. Broadlands 11/3.

14. E. Chaney, 'Architectural Taste and the Grand Tour: George Berkeley's Evolving Canon', *Journal of Anglo-Italian Studies*, 1 (1991), pp. 74–91, 87.

15. BL, Add. 58319 fol. 7, cf. Add. 35538 fols 170–1.

16. Bute to Symonds – 1770, CUL, Add. 8826.

17. S. Stevens, *Miscellaneous Remarks Made on the Spot in a Late Seven Years Tour through France, Italy, Germany and Holland* [no date, 1756?], pp. 82–91.

2.   Sources

1. Magdalen College Oxford, Ms 246, p. 1.

2. P. Brydone, *A Tour through Sicily and Malta* (2nd edn, 1774), I, v–vii.

3. J. Ingamells, *A Dictionary of British and Irish Travellers in Italy 1701–1800* (New Haven, 1997), p. 150.

4. BL, Add. 47031 fol. 39.

5. Alnwick, Northumberland papers, vol. 113 p. 55.

6. BL, Add. 41169 fols 5, 10, 16, 53–4, 19–20; Exeter CRO, Quick papers 64/12/29/1/135.

7. Bute to John Symonds, from 1771 Professor of Modern History at Cambridge, – 1770, CUL, Add. vol. 8826.

8. BL, Add. 35516 fol. 296.

9. P. Smiths, *The Life of Joseph Addison* (2nd edn, Oxford, 1968), pp. 105, 101; C.L. Batten, *Pleasurable Instruction* (Berkeley, 1978).

10. P.M. Spacks, 'Splendid Falsehoods: English Accounts of Rome, 1760–1798', *Prose Studies*, 3 (1980), p. 206.

11. J. Black, 'Ideology, History, Xenophobia and the World of Print in Eighteenth-century England', in J. Black and J. Gregory (eds), *Culture, Politics and Society in Britain 1660–1800* (Manchester, 1991), pp. 184–216.

12. Beinecke, Osborn Ms C. 366 vol. 1, p. 95; Atwell to Lady Sarah Cowper, 13 May 1730, Hertford CRO, D/EP F 234; Beinecke, Osborn Ms. 52 Box 3, 26 April 1753, Osborn Ms. C. 200, pp. 68, 99.
13. BL, Add. 34887 fol. 155.
14. GLRO, Acc. 510/254, p. 124.
15. B. Connell, *Portrait of a Whig Peer* (1957), pp. 50–1.
16. [Villiers], *A Tour through Part of France* (1789), p. 7.

3. Into Italy

1. BL, Add. 61449 fol. 120; Hamilton, Broadlands 11/3.
2. Lady Craven, *Journey*, pp. 77–8; Molesworth to Lord Carteret, Secretary of State, 10 Feb., Molesworth to Robert Walpole, 18 Aug. 1723, PRO 92/31; Guildford CRO, Brodrick Mss 1248/6 fol. 302.
3. BL, Add. 58319 fols 61–7.
4. Beinecke, Osborn Ms. C. 200, pp. 72–89; Shelburne diary, BL, Bowood Mss, vol. 104 fol. 5.
5. Gloucester CRO, D2002 F1, pp. 86–7.
6. E. Elliott-Drake (ed.), *Lady Knight's Letters from France and Italy 1776–1795* (1905), p. 47; Craven, *Journey*, p. 91.
7. Head–Wake correspondence, Christ Church Oxford, Wake papers, vol. 264, p. 9.
8. BL, Add. 53790 fols 7–8.
9. BL, Add. 22978 fol. 90.
10. BL, Add. 34887 fol. 155.
11. BL, Add. 33127 fol. 171.
12. BL, Add. 19941 fols 1, 9–10.
13. BL, Add. 12130 fols 122–3.
14. Exeter CRO, 2065 M/CI/1.
15. London, Guildhall Library Ms. 10823/5b; Lady Eastlake (ed.), *Dr Rigby's Letters from France etc. in 1789* (1880), pp. 153–68.
16. Hotham to father, Sir Charles, 25 Oct. 1711, Hull UL, DDHo/13/4.
17. Huntingdon CRO, DDM 49/7.
18. GLRO, Acc. 510/254, pp. 70–3.
19. Gloucester CRO, D1245 FF38 D9.
20. PRO 30/9/43, pp. 96, 99.
21. BL, Add. 23828 fol. 148.
22. BL, Add. 35536 fol. 122.
23. Moore to William Mure of Caldwell, 31 Oct. 1775, William Mure (ed.), *Selections from the Family Papers preserved at Caldwell* (2 parts, 2nd part in 2 vols, Glasgow, 1854), II, ii, 262.

4. From the Alps to the Arno

1. BL, Add. 34887 fol. 156.
2. St Clair to Windham, 26 Oct. (os) 1738, Norfolk, Norwich CRO, WKC 6/24 401X; W. Anson (ed.), *Autobiography . . . of . . . Duke of Grafton* (1898), p. 17; BL, Add. 35509 fol. 203; Arthur Villettes, envoy in Turin, to Couraud, 4 Sept. 1737, PRO SP. 92/41.
3. BL, Add. 36249 fol. 140; Bod. North Ms. d 4 fols 144–5.

4. BL, Add. 75744 fol. 19.
5. BL, Add. 27732 fol. 76.
6. Bod. Ms. DD Dashwood (Bucks) B 11/7/14a; PRO SP 92/89 fol. 293.
7. BL, Add. 19941 fol. 19.
8. HL Montagu papers no. 1316.
9. BL, Add. 47031 fols 27–8, 35532 fol. 33, 35517 fol. 20, 32415 fol. 43.
10. Leeds AO, NH. 2826 no. 49; Chester CRO, DLT/C9/22.
11. Wharton to Brand, 19 June 1775, WHA 133; Head to Wake, 21 Nov. 1724, Christ Church Oxford, Wake papers, vol. 264.
12. BL, Add. 75744; PRO 30/9/40, p. 127.
13. Gloucester CRO, D2002 F1.
14. Creed journal, private collection, 1 Dec. 1699; Broadlands 11/3.
15. PRO 30/9/43, p. 102.
16. BL, Add. 36249 fol. 143, 47031 fol. 191.
17. Petworth Archives, Ms. 6320.
18. Beinecke, Osborn Ms. C. 366 vol. 1, p. 337.
19. BL, Add. 47031 fol. 169; Broadlands 11/3.
20. Brand to sister, 14 April 1787, CUL, Add. Ms. 8670/21; Craven, *Memoirs*, I, 128.
21. PRO 30/9/43, p. 113.
22. Ibid., p. 120.
23. Gloucester CRO, D2663 Z8.
24. Broadlands 11/3.
25. BL, Add. 36249 fol. 141; Nottingham UL, NeC 2401.
26. PRO 30/9/40, pp. 134, 150–1.
27. Beinecke, Osborn Ms. C. 366 vol. 1, pp. 20–1, C. 332; Magdalen College Oxford, Ms. 246, p. 13.
28. BL, Add. 36249 fol. 141.
29. Magdalen College Oxford, Ms. 246, pp. 17–18.
30. Leeds AO, Vyner 6005.
31. Beinecke, Ms. 52 Box 3, 15 Oct.
32. On 24, 27, 30 Sept. 1778, Beinecke, Osborn Ms. C. 332.
33. 3 Oct. 1778, ibid.
34. Broadlands 11/3.

5. Rome and the South

1. BL, Add. 19941 fol. 21.
2. PRO 30/9/40, pp. 211, 214, 220–1; E.W. Harcourt (ed.), *The Harcourt Papers* (14 vols, 1880–1905), III, 25–6; Lady Anna Miller, *Letters from Italy* (1776), II, 182; Francis, BL, Add. 40759 fol. 19.
3. Vyse to Harris, 6 Feb. 1770, Winchester CRO, Malmesbury papers vol. 169.
4. Chester CRO, DLT/C9/19; Truro CRO, J3/2/120.
5. BL, Add. 40759 fol. 30.
6. House of Lords RO, CAD/4/4, 23.
7. H. Gross, *Rome in the Age of Enlightenment* (Cambridge, 1990), p. 94.
8. BL, Add. 33127 fol. 216.
9. Gloucester CRO, D2002 F1, p. 87.

10. Extract of a letter from Venice, dated 22 June 1764, Broadlands 11/3, pp. 1–2.
11. G.A. Bonnard (ed.), *Edward Gibbon: Memoirs of My Life* (New York, 1969), pp. 136–270. More generally, J.G.A. Pocock, *Barbarism and Religion. I. The Enlightenments of Edward Gibbon, 1737–1764* (Cambridge, 1999), pp. 275–91.
12. Broadlands 11/3.
13. BL, Add. 48244 fols 247–8.
14. Hall to Wharton, 2 Aug. 1785, WHA 603; BL, Add. 33127 fol. 292; PRO 30/9/43, pp. 130–3.
15. BL, Add. 36249 fol. 143.
16. BL, Add. 41169 fol. 15.
17. Truro CRO, J3/34/1, p. 19; BL, Add. 36249 fol. 142.
18. BL, Add. 19941 fol. 23.
19. PRO SP 93/12 fol. 75.
20. Broadlands 11/3.
21. BL, Add. 75743, 34196 fol. 157.
22. William to Edward Blackett, 8 Jan. 1785, Newcastle, Northumberland CRO, ZBL 239; Magdalen College Oxford, Ms. 247 II, 48–9; Truro CRO, J3/34/1, p. 11.
23. J. Northall, *Travels through Italy* (1776), p. 124; Beinecke, Osborn Ms. C. 467 vol. 2, no. 28; BL, Add. 40759 fol. 15; Bod. Ms. Add. A 366 fol. 63.
24. BL. Eg. 1711 fol. 464.
25. Broadlands 11/3.
26. Broadlands 11/19/5.
27. Broadlands 11/3.
28. Huntingdon CRO, DD. M36/20 fol. 20.
29. Beinecke, Osborn Mss C. 455 64/66, 21/66.
30. House of Lords RO, CAD/4/4.
31. BL, Add. 40759 fol. 11.
32. Chaney, 'Architectural Taste and the Grand Tour: George Berkeley's Evolving Canon', pp. 86–90.
33. Sandwich's journal, London, National Maritime Museum, Sandwich papers F/50; published by John Cooke, *A Voyage Performed by the Late Earl of Sandwich round the Mediterranean* (1799).
34. BL, Add. 35540 fol. 93.
35. House of Lords RO, CAD/4/6.
36. Brand to Wharton, 13 July 1785, WHA 602.
37. Brand to Wharton, 3, 22 April 1792, WHA 698–9.
38. Broadlands 11/3.
39. PRO 30/9/43, p. 96.

6. Accommodation

1. BL, Add. 75744 fol. 19.
2. Pomfret to Countess of Hertford, 15 March 1741, Leicester CRO, D67 Finch D5. Cosimo ruled, as Duke of Florence and then Grand Duke of Tuscany, from 1537 until 1574.
3. BL, Add. 22978 fol. 90; Exeter CRO, 2065 M/CI/1.
4. BL, Add. 58320 fol. 16.
5. Stevens, *Miscellaneous Remarks,* pp. 277, 325; Gloucester CRO, D2002 F1.
6. GLRO, Acc. 510/254, p. 121.

7. Broadlands 11/3.
8. CUL, Add. 3551; P. Beckford, *Familiar Letters from Italy, to a Friend in England* (Salisbury, 1805), II, 406.
9. Brand to Wharton, 21 July 1791, WHA 690.
10. A. Walker, *Ideas Suggested on the Spot in a Late Excursion through Flanders, Germany, France and Italy* (1790), p. 330.
11. Part of a journal, 11 June 1793, Broadlands 11/19/11.
12. BL, Sloane 1522 fol. 9, Add. 22978 fol. 82; Pomfret to Countess of Hertford, 13 March 1741, Leicester CRO, DG7 Finch D5; Stevens, *Miscellaneous Remarks*, pp. 281–2.
13. BL, Add. 30271 fol. 25.
14. BL, Add. 53790 fol. 4.
15. PRO 30/9/43, pp. 96, 99–102, 104–5, 114–15, 121–3, 128–30; Truro, Hawkins papers, J3/34/1.
16. PRO, 30/9/40, pp. 93–4, 111, 129, 133, 159, 162, 207, 210.
17. Walker, *Ideas Suggested on the Spot*, p. 381.
18. Beinecke, Osborn Ms. C. 289.
19. Harcourt (ed.), *Harcourt Papers* III, 161; BL, Add. 35535 fol. 192.
20. Bod. Ms. Add. A 366.
21. Beinecke, Osborn Ms. C. 467.

7. *Food and Drink*

1. Miller, *Letters*, II, 66–70.
2. Broadlands 11/3.
3. Gloucester CRO, D2002 F1.
4. Leicester CRO, D67 Finch D5, pp. 99, 118, 100; Miller, *Letters*, II, 189; *Memoirs of Thomas Jones* (1951), p. 49.
5. PRO 30/9/40, p. 208.
6. Bod. Ms. Douce 67, pp. 142–3.
7. Beckford, *Familiar Letters*, II, 405.
8. Miller, *Letters*, II, 72, 92, 189–90.
9. Beckford, *Familiar Letters*, I, 246–7.
10. Leeds AO, NH. 2911.
11. BL, Add. 22978 fol. 90; T. Watkins, *Travels through Swisserland, Italy, Sicily, the Greek Islands, to Constantinople* (2 vols, 1792), II, 7, 56.
12. BL, Add. 58320 fol. 60; Beinecke, Osborn Ms. C. 467 vol. 2, no. 26; Swinton, 30 Jan., 4 Feb. 1731.
13. PRO 30/9/40, p. 133; Chester CRO, DLT/CP/7, 23; Lee, 9 May 1753, Beinecke Ms. 52 Box 3.
14. Magdalen College Oxford, Ms. 246, p. 5.
15. PRO 30/9/40, pp. 162–3.
16. GLRO, Acc. 510/254, p. 122; Watkins, *Travels*, II, 7, 41; Beckford, *Familiar Letters*, I, 52; Bod. Ms. Douce 67, p. 195; BL, Add. 30271 fol. 29; R. Gray, *Letters during the Course of a Tour through Germany, Switzerland and Italy* (1794), pp. 349, 453; Stevens, *Miscellaneous Remarks*, p. 363; Walker, *Ideas Suggested on the Spot*, p. 327; Swinton journal, Wadham College Oxford.
17. Magdalen College Oxford, Ms. 247 II, p. 49.
18. BL, Add. 22978 fol. 89; PRO 30/9/40, p. 213.
19. BL, Add. 41169 fol. 51.
20. PRO 30/9/40, p. 114.

8. *Transport*

1. Brand to Wharton, 24 Sept. 1793, WHA 721.
2. BL, Add. 34887 fol. 154.
3. Gloucester CRO, D2002 F1.
4. GLRO, Acc. 510/254, pp. 73–4, 79, 81–4.
5. Brand to Wharton, 5 Oct. 1792, WHA 707.
6. Stevens, *Miscellaneous Remarks*, p. 331; BL, Add. 58316 fol. 16.
7. Beinecke, Osborn Ms. C. 467 vol. 2, no. 48, C. 289.
8. BL, Add. 22978 fol. 86, 58319 fol. 48; Thompson, *Travels*, I, 92.
9. Stevens, *Miscellaneous Remarks*, pp. 324–5; Orrery, p. 71.
10. Pomfret, 15, 16 March 1741, Leics. CRO, D67, Finch D5.
11. Stevens, *Miscellaneous Remarks*, p. 156.
12. 19 Oct. 1778, Beinecke, Osborn Ms. C. 332.
13. BL, Add. 22978 fol. 89, 58319 fols 47–8, 51; Joseph Spence to his mother, 8 Dec. 1760, BL; Eg. 2234 fol. 227; Beinecke, Osborn Ms. C. 200, p. 147, C 289; BL, Add. 36249 fol. 140, 35538 fol. 170.
14. GLRO, Acc. 510/254, pp. 73–4; Walker, *Ideas Suggested on the Spot*, pp. 381–3; CUL, Add. 3551 pt. 1 fol. 1.
15. PRO 30/9/40, pp. 155–6.
16. Gloucester CRO, D2002 F1, p. 52; PRO 30/9/40, p. 128.
17. BL, Add. 36249 fols 142–3.
18. Beinecke, Osborn Ms. C. 332, 4 Feb.
19. Hamilton to Marquess of Carmarthen, Foreign Secretary, 20 Nov. 1786, PRO Foreign Office 70/3.
20. Swinton, 8 June 1731; Walker, *Ideas Suggested on the Spot*, pp. 186, 339, 341, 366, 369, 373.
21. Lee, 26 April 1753, Beinecke, Ms. 52 Box 3; BL, Add. 38837 fol. 28; Stevens, *Miscellaneous Remarks*, p. 342.
22. GLRO, Acc. 510/254, p. 74.
23. BL Stowe 750; Holroyd to Mrs Baker, 4 Sept. 1764, BL, Add. 345887 fol. 156.
24. BL, Add. 40759 fol. 10.
25. Brand to Wharton, 3 April 1792, WHA 698.
26. BL, Add. 19441 fol. 19.
27. BL, Add. 38837 fol. 23.
28. Beinecke, Osborn Ms. C. 332; BL, Add. 50261 fol. 20; PRO 30/9/40, pp. 207–8; CUL, Add. 3545 fols 3–4.
29. BL, Add. 19941 fol. 19.
30. GLRO Acc. 510/254, p. 74.
31. Brand to Wharton, 6 Dec. 1790, WHA 678.
32. Swinton, 8 June (os) 1731; BL, Add. 22978 fol. 86.
33. BL, Add. 30271 fol. 28.
34. Walker, *Ideas Suggested on the Spot*, pp. 334–5.
35. Watkins, *Travels*, II, 12.
36. Brand to Wharton, 21 July 1791, WHA 690.
37. BL, Add. 40759 fol. 15.
38. PRO 30/9/40, pp. 111–12.
39. Brand to Wharton, 24 Sept. 1793, WHA 721.
40. BL, Add. 30172 fol. 27, 38837 fol. 27.
41. BL, Add. 30271 fols 22, 29.
42. Nottingham UL, NeC. 2407.

9.   *Cost and Finance*

1.   Drake to father, 10 April 1769, Aylesbury CRO, D/Dr./8/2.
2.   Riddell (?) journal, 20 Nov. 1770, Northumberland CRO, ZRW 62.
3.   Brand to Wharton, 23 Nov. 1793, WHA 723.
4.   BL, Add. 19941 fol. 17, 40759 fol. 18.
5.   Walker, *Ideas Suggested on the Spot*, p. 381.
6.   BL, Add. 22978 fols 77–8, 82, 87; T. Martyn, *The Gentleman's Guide in his Tour through Italy* (1787), p. xx; BL, Add. 40759 fol. 13.
7.   Walker, *Ideas Suggested on the Spot*, p. 145.
8.   BL, Add. 22978 fol. 82, 19941 fols 20, 24, 40759 fol. 13; Beinecke, Osborn Ms. C. 289; Martyn, *Gentleman's Guide*, p. xx.
9.   Beinecke, Osborn Ms. C. 467, vol. 2, no. 3.
10.   Walker, *Ideas Suggested on the Spot*, p. 391; CUL, Add. Mss 3545 fol. 1; PRO 30/9/43, p. 112.
11.   BL, Add. 40759 fol. 13.
12.   PRO 30/9/40, pp. 152–4.
13.   Pickersgill to sister, April [1761], Aylesbury CRO, Saunders deposit.
14.   BL, Add. 19941 fols 1, 19.
15.   Holroyd to Mrs Baker, 4 Sept. 1764, BL, Add. 34887 fol. 157; BL, Add. 40759 fol. 20.
16.   PRO 30/9/43, p. 126.
17.   BL, Add. 47031 fol. 140; L.M. Wiggin, *The Faction of Cousins* (New Haven, 1958), p. 4; Nuneham to Lady Elizabeth Harcourt, undated, Aylesbury CRO, D/LE E2/20; Beinecke, Osborn Ms. C. 467, vol. 2, no. 15.
18.   P. McKay, 'The Grand Tour of the Hon. Charles Compton', *Northamptonshire Past and Present*, 7 (1986), pp. 246–7; John Thornton, Haggerston's tutor, to Francis Anderton, 18 Sept. 1718, Northumberland CRO, ZH6 VIII; Ingamells, *Dictionary*, pp. 311, 149.
19.   North to Hallam, 21 Feb. 1753, BL, Add. 61980; Bennett, Bod. Ms. Eng. Misc. f. 54 fol. 196.
20.   Magdalen College Oxford, Ms. 246, p. 14; Beinecke, Osborn Ms. C. 467, vol. 2, nos 19, 26.
21.   Aylesbury CRO, D/DR/8/3/3.
22.   Head, 21 March 1725, Christ Church Oxford, Head–Wake correspondence.
23.   F.A. Pottle (ed.), *Boswell in Holland 1763–1764* (1952), p. 222; F. Brady and F. A. Pottle (eds), *Boswell on the Grand Tour: Italy, Corsica, and France 1765–1766* (New York, 1955).
24.   BL, Add. 38507 fol. 33; Fenwick to Lady Haggerston, 8 April (os) 1718, Northumberland CRO, Haggerston papers; Carteret to Wetstein, 27 June (os) 1728, Stephen to Henry Fox, 24 June 1729, BL, Add. 32415, 51417 fol. 21; GLRO, Acc. 510/245.
25.   Wharton to Thomas Lloyd, 20 May, 23 Oct. 1775, WHA 167–8; BL, Add. 33127 fols 41, 43, 61, 266, 288; Drake to father, 25 Nov. 1768, Townson to William Drake senior, 28 Jan. 1769, Aylesbury CRO, D/DR/8/24, 3/4.
26.   Blackett to Sir Edward Blackett, 4 Jan. 1785, Northumberland CRO, ZBL. 188/289.
27.   Beinecke, Osborn Ms. C. 467, vol. 2, nos 28, 43, 48; BL, Add. 33127 fol. 266; Wharton to Thomas Lloyd, 18 April 1776, WHA 169; PRO 30/9/40, p. 100.
28.   Beinecke, Osborn Ms. C. 467, vol. 1, no. 124.
29.   BL, Add. 38507 fol. 41.
30.   Martyn, *Gentleman's Guide*, pp. vii–viii; Hoare, CUL, Add. Mss 3545 fol. 1.

10.   *Hazards*

1. Newcastle to Lincoln, 16 March (os) 1741, BL, Add. 33065 fol. 398.
2. Truro CRO, J3/34/1; Northall, *Travels through Italy,* p. 177; BL, Add. 30271 fol. 31.
3. Bagshaw to the Duke of Newcastle, 18 Dec. 1741, PRO SP 79/16.
4. BL, Add. 35540 fol. 93.
5. Metcalfe to Sir William Robinson, 30 Aug., 8 Oct. 1705, Leeds AO, Vyner Ms. 6005.
6. BL, Add. 36249 fol. 140.
7. Winchester CRO, 15M50/1303.
8. *St James Evening Post,* 28 Nov. (os) 1734; Pococke, BL, Add. 22978 fols 87–9; Mitchell, BL, Add. 58319 fols 39–43; Milles, Gloucester CRO, D 2663 Z8.
9. Alnwick vol. 113, p. 233.
10. Ibid., p. 147.
11. Ibid., pp. 328–9.
12. Ibid., p. 293.
13. BL, Add. 23822 fols 324–5, 19941 fols 10, 15.
14. BL, Add. 6830 fol. 24.
15. Stuart Mackenzie to Bute, 30 Jan., 22 Feb., 2 April, 18 June, 20 Sept. 1760, 14 March 1761, Mount Stuart, papers from Cardiff Public Library, 4/5–17. See also Mackenzie to Sir John Rushout, 14 April 1759, Worcester CRO, 750: 66BA 4221/26.
16. BL, Add. 36801 fols 43, 122, 162, 204, 208.
17. Belfast, Public Record Office of Northern Ireland, D/2433/D/5/21.
18. M.D. Sánchez-Jáuregui, 'Two Portraits of Francis Basset by Pompeo Batoni in Madrid', *Burlington Magazine,* 143 (2001), pp. 420–5; *El Westmorland. Recuerdos del Grand Tour* (Madrid, 2002).
19. Walker, *Ideas Suggested on the Spot,* p. 390.
20. Ibid., pp. 157, 203, 266–7, 307.
21. Northall, *Travels through Italy,* p. 127.
22. PRO 30/9/40, p. 109, 30/9/43, p. 107.
23. R. Wodrow, *Analecta, or Materials for a History of Remarkable Providences Mostly relating to Scotch Ministers and Christians*, III (Edinburgh, 1842), 305–6.
24. BL, Add. 19941 fol. 17.
25. BL, Add. 40759 fol. 18.
26. BL, Add. 35516 fol. 126, 30271 fol. 24; Truro CRO J3/34/1, pp. 20, 9.
27. Hall to Wharton, June 1784, WHA 590.
28. Beinecke, Osborn Ms. 52.
29. Magdalen College Oxford, Ms. 247 III, 76; GLRO, Acc. 510/254, p. 122; Hertford CRO, D/E Na F57.
30. BL, Add. 23829 fol. 194; Stevens, *Miscellaneous Remarks,* p. 160; Brand to Wharton, 13 Nov. 1792, WHA.
31. Walker, *Ideas Suggested on the Spot,* p. 414.
32. Brand to Wharton, 21 July 1791, WHA 690.
33. Brand to Wharton, 13 Nov. 1792, WHA 708.
34. BL, Add. 30271 fol. 26.
35. Stevens, *Miscellaneous Remarks,* p. 162.
36. Beinecke, Osborn Ms. C. 200, p. 142.
37. BL, Add. 41169 fols 58–9, 36495 fol. 335.
38. Colman to Duke of Newcastle, 29 Jan. 1725, PRO SP 98/25; PRO 30/9/40, pp. 115–16.
39. BL, Add. 27732 fol. 233.
40. Brand to Wharton, 18 Feb. 1784, WHA 586.
41. BL, Add. 35535 fol. 192. For a criticism of medical knowledge at Venice, BL, Add. 35540 fol. 159.

42. M. Starke, *Letters from Italy* (1800), II, 92, 193, 203; P. Beckford, *Familiar Letters*, II, 428, 451.
43. Garmston, BL, Add. 30271, fol. 32.
44. BL, Add. 61444 fol. 130.
45. Hollings to Atwell, 23 Jan. (os) 1730, Hertford CRO, D/EP F55 fols 31–4; Stephen to Henry Fox, 18, 31 March, 21 May 1729, BL, Add. 51417 fols 9, 11, 14–15; Thomas Winnington to Stephen Fox, 9 April (os) 1729, Dorchester CRO, D124/box 240.
46. Walker, *Ideas Suggested on the Spot*, p. 310; BL, Add. 30271 fols 27–8.
47. Stevens, *Miscellaneous Remarks*, p. 294.
48. BL, Add. 38471 fol. 199; Brand to Wharton, 23 Nov. 1793, WHA 723.

11. Activities

1. BL, Add. 23822 fol. 324.
2. BL, Add. 40759 fol. 20.
3. W.B. Stanford and E.J. Finopoulos (eds), *The Travels of Lord Charlemont in Greece and Turkey 1749* (1984), p. 5.
4. Tavistock to Upper Ossory, 29 July 1764, London, Bedford Estate Office, Russell letters.
5. Journal, possibly by Marmaduke William Constable, Hull UL, DDEV61/1.
6. Beinecke, Osborn Ms. C. 200.
7. BL, Add. 35505 fol. 335.
8. Hotham to Dear Cousin, 14 Sept. 1754, Hull UL, DDHo/4/5.
9. Beinecke, Osborn Ms. C. 366 vol. 1, p. 91.
10 HW, vol. 67 fols 203–9; Ingamells, *Dictionary*, p. 892.
11. BL, Add. 40759 fol. 20.
12. Stevens, *Miscellaneous Remarks*, p. 360; Pococke, BL, Add. 22978 fol. 84; HMC *Denbigh* V, 221; HW, Horace Walpole, *Commonplace Book*, p. 293; Tavistock to Upper Ossory, 12 Sept. 1763, Russell letters.
13. R. Warner (ed.), *Episotalary Curiosities; Series the Second* (1818), pp. 158–9.
14. P. Jenkins, *The Making of a Ruling Class. The Glamorgan Gentry 1640–1790* (Cambridge, 1983), pp. 227–8.
15. Mount Stuart, Cardiff papers 4/7; Farmington, HW, vol. 52 fol. 115; Truro CRO, PD/459.
16. *H. Walpole Correspondence*, ed. W.S. Lewis et al. (New Haven, 1937–82), vol. 30, p. 6.
17. J.B. Shipley, 'James Ralph: Pretender to Genius' (Columbia, Ph.D., 1963), p. 380; Brand to Wharton, 3 Jan. 1791, WHA 679.
18. R. Halsband (ed.), *Complete Letters of Lady Mary Wortley Montagu* (3 vols, Oxford, 1965–7), II, 342.
19. BL, Add. 33065 fol. 406.
20. *Walpole Corresp.*, vol. 30, pp. 43–6, 74, 1.
21. HW., vol. 69 fols 80–1.
22. M. Wyndham, *Chronicles of the Eighteenth Century: Founded on the Correspondence of Sir Thomas Lyttelton and his Family* (1924), I, 21.
23. Tavistock to Robinson, 10 April, 22 Dec. 1762, Russell letters, vols 45–6.
24. BL, Add. 35535 fols 302–3.
25. Brand to Wharton [March 1791], WHA 95.
26. BL, Add. 33126 fol. 163.
27. *Walpole Corresp.*, vol. 21, p. 460; J. Fleming, *Robert Adam and his Circle in Edinburgh and Rome* (1962), p. 130; HMC *Hastings*, III, 92.
28. Miller, *Letters*, I, 61, II, 179–80.

29. Magdalen College Oxford, Ms. 246, p. 25.
30. Bod. Mss Douce 67, p. 257; Creed journal, private collection.
31. PRO 30/9/40, p. 168; BL, Add. 40759 fol. 32.
32. Brand to Wharton, 22 April 1792, WHA 699.
33. HMC *Bath*, III, 432.
34. Lady Phillipina Knight, in E.F. Elliott-Drake (ed.), *Letters from France and Italy 1776–1795* (1905), p. 211.
35. Villiers to Spencer, 3 Nov. 1763, BL, Add. 75670.
36. B. Fothergill, *Sir William Hamilton* (1969), pp. 163–6; BL, Add. 48244 fol. 229.
37. Walker, *Ideas Suggested on the Spot*, p. 141; Davenant to Stair, 8 Dec. 1716, NAS, GD 135/141/6.
38. Brand to Wharton, 26 March 1793, WHA 713; A. Morrison, *The Collection of Autograph Letters and Historical Documents formed by Alfred Morrison: The Hamilton and Nelson Papers*, I (1893), pp. 45–8.
39. BL, Add. 36495 fol. 364.
40. Harcourt (ed.), *Harcourt Papers*, III, 13.
41. BL, Add. 47576 fol. 1; Tavistock to Robinson, 22 Dec. 1762, Russell letters, vol. 46.
42. Thornton to Anderton, 31 Sept. 1718, Newcastle CRO, Haggerston.
43. *Walpole Corresp.* vol. 18, p. 211.
44. Walker, *Ideas Suggested on the Spot*, p. 381.
45. A.W. Purdue, 'John and Harriet Carr: A Brother and Sister from the North-East on the Grand Tour', *Northern History*, 30 (1994), p. 134.
46. Exeter CRO, 2065 M/CI/1.
47. BL, Add. 36249 fol. 144.
48. Bod. North Ms. d 4 fols 144–5.
49. BL, Add. 34887 fols 156–7.
50. Ibid. 155.
51. BL, Add. 36249.
52. BL, Add. 22978 fols 89–90; Ingamells, *Dictionary*, p. 1034.
53. Bod. Ms. Add. A. 366 fol. 60.
54. BL, Add. 47031 fol. 102.
55. C. Rogers, *Boswelliana* (1874), p. 239.

12.   *Social and Political Reflections*

1. Bagshaw to Thomas, Duke of Newcastle, Secretary of State for the Southern Department, 18 Dec. 1731, PRO SP 79/16; William Mildmay, journal, Winchester, Hampshire CRO, 15 M50/1302; Mills to Thomas Robinson, 25 Nov. 1726, Leeds AO, Vyner Ms. 13591.
2. Ingamells, *Dictionary*, p. 659; Creed journal, private collection, 4 Dec. 1699, 2 June 1700, 1 Dec. 1699; Mills to Robinson, Vyner Ms. 13591.
3. BL, Add. 47031 fol. 100.
4. PRO 30/9/40, pp. 164–5; Shelburne diary, BL, Bowood Mss vol. 104 fol. 9.
5. Broadlands 11/3.
6. GLRO, Acc. 510/254, p. 75; Hinchliffe to Grafton, 5 May 1762, Bury St Edmunds CRO, Grafton papers 423/338.
7. BL, Add. 19941 fol. 17; Shelburne diary, BL, Bowood Mss vol. 104 fols 7–8.
8. Mildmay, Chelmsford Essex CRO, 15M50/1303, pp. 15, 32; Broadlands 11/3.
9. Magdalen College Oxford, Mss 246, pp. 1–12.

10. BL, Add. 19941 fol. 11.

11. GLRO, Acc. 510/254, pp. 127, 136–7.

12. BL, Add. 38837 fol. 27.

13. PRO 30/9/40, p. 117.

14. BL, Add. 36429 fol. 144.

15. GLRO, Acc. 510/255, pp. 53, 60, 48–9; Shelburne diary, BL, Bowood Mss vol. 104 fol. 14.

16. PRO 30/9/40, pp. 220–1.

17. S. Parissien, *Palladian Style* (1994), p. 79; D. Cosgrove, *The Palladian Landscape* (Leicester, 1993).

18. BL, Add. 51345 fols 18–19.

19. Guildford CRO, Brodrick Mss 1248/6.

20. Metcalfe to Sir William Robinson, 15 Dec. 1705, Leeds AO, Vyner Ms. 6005.

21. Truro CRO, J3/34/1, p. 6; BL, Add. 47031 fol. 139.

22. E. Gibbon, *The History of the Decline and Fall of the Roman Empire*, ed. J.B. Bury (1900), VII, 301.

23. Creed journal, private collection; BL Add. 19941 fol. 15 [Thomas], Holroyd to Mrs Baker, 13 Aug. 1764, BL, Add. 34887 fol. 154; BL, Add. 19941 fol. 15; Exeter CRO, 2065 M/CI/1.

24. BL, Add. 22978 fol. 89.

25. BL, Add. 48244 fol. 249.

26. PRO 30/9/40, p. 169; GLRO, Acc. 510/255, p. 47.

27. S. Daniels, *Fields of Vision* (1993).

28. N. Leask, *British Romantic Writers and the East. Anxieties of Empire* (Cambridge, 1993).

29. Brand to Wharton, 3 April 1792, WHA 698.

30. O. Millar, *Zoffany and his Tribuna* (1967).

31. Broadlands 11/3.

32. PRO 30/9/40, p. 149.

33. BL, Add. 58316 fol. 36; GLRO, Acc. 510/254, p. 77; Truro CRO, PD/460.

34. BL, Add. 40759 fol. 32.

35. Gloucester CRO, D2002 F1, pp. 93–6; BL, Add. 36249 fol. 141; PRO 30/9/40, p. 157.

36. T.J. Dandelet, *Spanish Rome 1500–1700* (New Haven, 2001); Gateshead, Ellison papers A28 no. 63.

37. For a recent introduction, P. Langford, *Englishness Identified. Manners and Character 1650–1850* (Oxford, 2000).

38. A. Wilton, 'Dreaming of Italy', in Wilton and I. Bignamini (eds), *Grand Tour. The Lure of Italy in the Eighteenth Century* (1996), p. 43.

39. GLRO, Acc. 510/254, pp. 90–1, 97.

40. Gibbon, *Decline and Fall*, VII, 324–5.

41. J. Buzzard, *The Beaten Track. European Tourism, Literature, and the Ways to 'Culture', 1800–1918* (Oxford, 1993).

42. J. Pemble, *The Mediterranean Passion: Victorians and Edwardians in the South* (Oxford, 1987); A. Corbin, *The Lure of the Sea. The Discovery of the Seaside in the Western World, 1750–1840* (Oxford, 1994); F. Kaplan (ed.), *Travelling in Italy with Henry James* (1994).

43. T. Tanner, *Venice Desired: Writing the City* (Cambridge, Mass., 1992).

44. A.G. Hill, 'Wordsworth and Italy', *Journal of Anglo-Italian Studies*, 1 (1991), pp. 111–25.

45. M. Hollington, 'Dickens and Italy', *Journal of Anglo-Italian Studies*, 1 (1991), pp. 126–36; K. Churchill, *Italy and English Literature 1764–1930* (1980); H. Fraser, *The Victorians and Renaissance Italy* (Oxford, 1992).

46. P. Usherwood, 'William Bell Scott's *Iron and Coal*: Northern Readings', in *Pre-Raphaelites: Painters and Patrons in the North East* (Laing Gallery exhibition catalogue, Newcastle, 1989), pp. 46–7, 55.

13. *Religion*

1. Hotham to father, Sir Charles, 2 April 1712, Hull UL, DDHo/13/4.
2. A. Schnapp, 'Antiquarian Studies in Naples at the End of the Eighteenth Century. From Comparative Archaeology to Comparative Religion', in G. Imbruglia (ed.), *Naples in the Eighteenth Century. The Birth and Death of a Nation State* (Cambridge, 2000), pp. 154–62.
3. Creed journal, private collection.
4. Broadlands 11/3.
5. BL, Add. 39787 fol. 64; Shelburne diary, BL, Bowood Mss vol. 104 fol. 13.
6. BL, Add. 58316.
7. Swinton, 5 Feb. (os) 1731.
8. Brand to Wharton, 16 May 1784, WHA 589.
9. Swinton, 23 Jan. (os), 18 Jan. (os), 5 Feb. (os) 1731.
10. Harcourt (ed.), *Harcourt Papers*, III, 82–3.
11. BL, Add. 19941 fols 12, 14, 53790 fol. 8.
12. BL, Add. 40759 fols 16–17, 25–7, 32.
13. BL, Add. 35515 fol. 139.
14. Brand to Wharton, 24 Oct. 1783, WHA 584.
15. Brand to Wharton, 20 May 1792, 3 Aug. 1793, WHA 700, 719.
16. Stevens, *Miscellaneous Remarks*, pp. 192–3; BL, Add. 22978 fol. 75; Creed journal, private collection, 16 Dec. 1699.
17. Beinecke, Osborn Ms. C. 366, vol. 2, p. 293.
18. PRO 30/9/40, p. 211.

14. *The Arts*

1. Alnwick, Alnwick Castle Ms. 146.
2. Cowper to sister, 10 March 1730, Hertford CRO, D/EP 234.
3. Gray, *Letters*, p. 424; Walker, *Ideas Suggested on the Spot*, pp. 178–9.
4. BL, Add. 35515 fol. 44; T. McGeary, 'Farinelli and the Duke of Leeds', *Early Music* (2002), p. 204; Brand to Wharton, 6 Dec. 1790, 25 May 1793, WHA 678, 716.
5. BL, Add. 48244 fols 237–8.
6. Gray, *Letters*, pp. 298–9.
7. Allen to Newcastle, 3 Sept. 1729, PRO SP 92/33; BL, Add. 60387 fol. 62, 27732 fol. 76; Stanhope to Earl Stanhope, 25 Oct. 1734, Maidstone, Kent AO, U1590 C708/2.
8. Orrery, pp. 11, 57, 140; Pickersgill to sister, April 1761, Oct. 1768, Aylesbury, Buckinghamshire CRO, Saunders papers.
9. PRO 30/9/40, pp. 170–1.
10. Somerset to Lady Coventry, 21 July 1709, Badminton House, Gloucestershire, Badminton Mss.
11. Bod. Ms. Douce 67, p. 145.
12. Leeds AO, Vyner Ms. 6032, no. 12328; BL, Add. 40759 fols 15, 19, 21.
13. BL, Add. 33127 fol. 310.
14. BL, Add. 19941 fol. 11; Brand to Wharton, 24 Oct., 17 Nov. 1783, 16 May–June 1784, 26 Aug. 1791, 3 April, 5 Oct. 1792, 24 Sept. 1793, WHA 584–5, 589–90, 691, 698, 707, 721.
15. PRO 30/9/40, p. 112.
16. BL, Add. 35514 fol. 72; Beinecke, Osborn Ms. C. 289.

17. BL, Add. 30271 fols 20, 33.
18. Swinton, 10 March (os), 9 May (os) 1731.
19. Wharton to Brand, 15 Nov. 1775, Brand to Wharton, 26 March, 17 April 1784, 14 Oct. 1791, WHA 155, 587–8, 693.
20. BL, Add. 38837 fol. 28.
21. Leeds AO, Vyner Ms. 6032 no. 12304.
22. Bod. Ms. Douce 67, pp. 150, 245; Brand to Wharton, 17 Nov. 1783, Wharton to his mother, 27 Oct. 1775, WHA 585, 168; PRO 30/9/40, p. 168; BL, Add. 47576 fol. 1.
23. BL, Add. 41169 fol. 19.
24. F. Watson, 'Thomas Patch (1725–1782): Notes on his Life together with a Catalogue of his Known Works', *Walpole Society*, 28 (1939–40), pp. 15–50.
25. A.M. Clark, *Pompeo Batoni. A Complete Catalogue of his Works with an Introductory Text* (Oxford, 1985); *The Swagger Portrait – Grand Manner Portraiture in Britain from Van Dyck to Augustus John 1630–1930* (Tate Gallery, 1992); F. Russell, 'Notes on Grand Tour Portraiture', *Burlington Magazine*, 136 (July 1994), pp. 438–43.
26. W.G. Constable, *Canaletto. Giovanni Antonio Canal 1697–1728*, 2nd edn revised by J.G. Links (Oxford, 1989); Russell, 'Guardi and the English Tourist', *Burlington Magazine*, 138 (Jan. 1996), pp. 4–11; F. Pedrocco, *Visions of Venice. Paintings of the 18th Century* (2002).
27. *Richard Wilson*, catalogue of Tate Gallery exhibition, 1982.
28. F. Russell, 'The Stourhead Batoni and Other Copies after Reni', in *National Trust Year Book 1975–76* (1976), pp. 109–11; Brand to Wharton, 23 Nov. 1793, WHA 723.
29. L. Lippincott, *Selling Art in Georgian London: The Rise of Arthur Pond* (New Haven, 1983); I. Pears, *The Discovery of Painting: The Growth of Interest in the Arts in England, 1680–1768* (New Haven, 1988).
30. Camelford to William Pitt, 10 Feb. 1788, PRO 30/8/120, p. 5.
31. O. Sitwell, *Sing High! Sing Low!* (1944).
32. Inventory of paintings at Fonmon Castle, 1743, Cardiff, Glamorgan CRO, D/DF F/190.
33. Huntingdon CRO, DDM 49/7, 30 May 1758.
34. Beinecke, Osborn Ms. C. 332.
35. Belfast, Public Record Office of Northern Ireland, Caledon papers D 2433/D/5/21, 7.
36. Swiney Correspondence with 2nd Duke of Richmond, Goodwood Mss 105 vol. 1; J. Fleming, 'The Hugfords of Florence', *Connoisseur*, 36 (1955), pp. 197–206.
37. Northall, *Travels through Italy*, p. 127; P.R. Andrew, 'Jacob More and the Earl-Bishop of Derry', *Apollo*, 124, no. 294 (Aug. 1980), p. 92; Francis, BL, Add. 40759 fol. 30.
38. Swinton, 1 June (os) 1731; Stevens, *Miscellaneous Remarks*, pp. 111–12; Gray, *Letters*, p. 402.
39. Aylesbury CRO, D/LE E2/20; BL, Add. 33127 fols 202, 216, 35516 fol. 212.
40. GLRO, Acc. 510/254 pp. 76, 88, 94–5; Villiers to Lady Spencer, 15 Sept. 1763, BL, Add. 75670.
41. The refectory of San Giorgio Maggiore.
42. Now in the Louvre, having been taken there during the French Revolutionary Wars.
43. Now in the National Gallery in London, having been sold.
44. Bury St Edmunds CRO, Grafton papers 423/338.
45. BL, Add. 38837 fol. 26.
46. BL, Add. 48244 fols 230, 238.
47. R.G. Wilson, 'Journal of a Tour through Suffolk, Norfolk, Lincolnshire and Yorkshire in the Summer of 1741', in C. Harper-Bill, C. Rawcliffe and R.G. Wilson (eds.), *East Anglia's History. Studies in Honour of Norman Scarfe* (Woodbridge, 2002), p. 273.
48. R. Guilding, *Marble Mania. Sculpture Galleries in England 1640–1840* (2001).
49. BL, Add. 40759 fol. 32.
50. Broadlands 11/3.

51. Hull UL, DDEV/61/1.
52. Lee, 26 April 1743, Beinecke, Ms. 52, Box 3.
53. BL, Add. 58319 fol. 23.
54. BL, Add. 34887 fol. 156.
55. W.G. Constable, *Richard Wilson* (1953), pp. 34–5.
56. Reproduced in Wilton and Bignamini (eds), *Grand Tour*, p. 218.

15.   *The Impact of Italy*

1. Aylesbury CRO, D/LE E2/16.
2. Countess of Cork and Orrery (ed.), *Orrery Papers* (1903), I, 206–7.
3. BL, Add. 33127.
4. A. Moore (ed.), *Houghton Hall, the Prime Minister, the Empress and the Heritage* (Norwich, 1996); J.M. Black, *Walpole in Power* (Stroud, 2001), pp. 70–3.
5. F. Salmon, *Building on Ruins: The Rediscovery of Rome and English Architecture* (2001).
6. B.D. Frischer and I.G. Brown (eds), *Allan Ramsay and the Search for Horace's Villa* (Aldershot, 2001).
7. PRO 30/9/40, p. 218.
8. Brand to Wharton, no date [Aug. or Sept. 1785], WHA 604.
9. BL, Add. 39787 fol. 93, 39792 A fol. 34; Broadlands 11/19/5.
10. BL, Add. 48244 fols 247, 249.
11. BL, Add. 47031 fol. 102, 41169 fol. 26.
12. Brand to Wharton, 18 Feb. 1784, WHA 586.
13. PRO 30/9/43, p. 114.
14. Cork, *Letters from Italy* (1773), p. 167; Aylesbury CRO, D/DR/8/2/20.
15. GLRO, Acc. 510/254, p. 78.
16. Bod. North Ms. d 4 fols 144–5.
17. Leeds AO, Vyner Ms. 13591.
18. BL, Add. 33127 fol. 202.
19. Brand to Wharton, 17 Nov. 1783, WHA 585.
20. BL, Eg. 1711 fol. 445.
21. Brand to Wharton, 3 April 1792, WHA 698.
22. PRO 30/9/40, p. 161; BL, Add. 19941 fol. 17.
23. BL, Add. 19941 fol. 11; PRO SP 92/31 fol. 113; BL, Add. 40759 fol. 11; Brand to Wharton, 1 July, 20 Aug. 1793, WHA 718, 720; Badminton House, papers of Lord Charles Somerset, pp. 30, 34.
24. Brand to Wharton, 17 Nov. 1783, WHA 585.
25. Magdalen College Oxford Ms. 246, p. 5; BL, Add. 75743; GLRO, Acc. 510/254, p. 127.
26. BL, Add. 48244 fol. 241.
27. Brand to Wharton, 22 April 1792, WHA 698. Ferdinand IV was King of Naples from 1759 until 1815.
28. BL, Add. 34887 fol. 154.
29. Ibid. fols 154–5.
30. Exeter CRO, 2065 M/CI/1.
31. Broadlands 11/19/5.
32. Brand to Wharton, 22 April 1792, WHA 699. For background, R. Hamblyn, 'Private Cabinets and Popular Geology: The British Audiences for Volcanoes in the Eighteenth Century', in C. Chard and H. Langdon (eds), *Transports: Travel, Pleasure, and Imaginative Geography 1600–1830* (New Haven, 1996), pp. 179–205.

33.   BL, Add. 38837 fols 28, 30–1.
34.   BL, Add. 30271 fols 24–6.
35.   Brand to Wharton, 17 Nov. 1783, WHA 585.
36.   BL, Add. 35535 fol. 331.
37.   BL, Add. 29792 A fol. 35.

16. *Conclusions*

1.   Magdalen College, Oxford, Mss 247 III, 89.
2.   *Memorials of . . . James Oswald* (Edinburgh, 1825), p. 206.
3.   Exeter, Devon CRO, Quicke papers, 64/12/29/1/124.
4.   E.F. Elliott-Drake (ed.), *Letters from France and Italy 1776–1795* (1905), p. 179.
5.   Aylesbury, Buckinghamshire CRO, D/DR/8/2/6.
6.   Brand to Wharton, 24 Oct. 1783, WHA 584.
7.   BL, Add. 48244 fol. 238.
8.   Broadlands 11/3.
9.   Guildford, Surrey CRO, Brodrick, Ms. 1248/6 fol. 137.
10.   HL MO. 1316.

17. *Epilogue*

1.   BL, Add. 48244 fols 229–36.
2.   Brand to Wharton, 16 Sept. 1794, WHA 731.

Bibliography

For reasons of space, only some of the primary and secondary material used has been mentioned. In addition, there are no references to newspaper, pamphlet, parliamentary and theatrical material. Unless otherwise stated, the place of publication is London.

Manuscript Sources

Alnwick, Alnwick Castle, vols 113 (Beauchamp), 146 (Warkworth).
Aylesbury, Buckinghamshire Record Office: Drake, Nuneham, Saunders papers.
Badminton, Badminton House: Beaufort papers.
Bedford, Bedfordshire Record Office: Lucas papers.
Bury St Edmunds, West Suffolk Record Office: Grafton papers.
Cambridge, University Library: Bute, Hoare papers.
Cardiff, Glamorgan Record Office: Fonmon papers.
Chelmsford, Essex Record Office: Mildmay papers.
Chester, Cheshire Record Office, Wilbraham papers.
Dorchester, Dorset Record Office: Ilchester papers.
Durham, University Library: Wharton papers.
Edinburgh, Scottish Record Office: Stair papers.
Exeter, Devon Record Office: Buller, Quicke papers.
Farmington, Connecticut, Lewis Walpole Library: Hanbury Williams papers.
Gateshead, Public Library: Ellison papers.
Guildford, Surrey Record Office: Brodrick papers.
Hatfield, Hatfield House: Cecil papers.
Hertford, Hertfordshire Record Office: Panshanger papers.
Hull, University Library: Constable-Maxwell, Hotham papers.
Huntingdon, Huntingdonshire Record Office: Manchester papers.
Leeds, Archive Office: Vyner papers.

Leicester, Leicestershire Record Office: Finch papers.
London,
  Bedford Estate Office: Russell letters.
  British Library:
  – Additional manuscripts: Althorp, Blenheim, Carteret, Compton, Cumberland, Egmont, Essex, Flaxman, Fox, Francis, Garmston, Grantham, Hardwicke, Holland House, Keith, Macclesfield, Milles, Mitchell, Molesworth, Morley, Newcastle, North, Pelham, Pococke, Robinson, Russel, Sheffield, Swinburne, Theed, Thomas papers.
  – Egerton manuscripts: Bentinck papers.
  – Sloane manuscripts: Compton papers.
  – Stowe manuscripts: Young papers.
  Guildhall Library: Boddington papers.
  House of Lords Record Office: Cadogan papers.
  London Metropolitan Archives: Villiers papers.
  Public Record Office: State Papers Foreign, Foreign Office papers, Colchester, Pitt papers.
Maidstone, Kent Archive Office: Stanhope papers.
Mount Stuart: papers of the 3rd Earl of Bute.
Newcastle, Northumberland Record Office: Blackett papers.
New Haven, Beinecke Library: Osborn Collection, Shelves c 200, 289, 332, 467; Lee correspondence.
Nottingham, University Library: Clumber papers.
Oxford, Bodleian Library: Bennett, Carpenter, Dashwood, Dewes, Milles, Tracy papers.
  Christ Church Library: Wake papers.
  County Record Office: Dillon papers.
  Magdalen College Library: Drake papers.
  Wadham College Library: Swinton papers.
Petworth: papers of Charles Wyndham.
San Marino, California, Huntington Library: Montagu papers.
Sheffield, City Archives: Wentworth Woodhouse papers.
Southampton, University Library: Broadlands collection.
Truro, Cornwall Record Office: Hawkins, Pendarves papers.
Winchester, Hampshire Record Office, Malmesbury papers.

Private collection: Creed journal.

Guidebooks, Published Travel Accounts and Correspondence

Addison, J., *Letters from Italy to the Right Hon. Charles Lord Halifax, in the Year 1701* (1703).
——*Remarks on Several Parts of Italy, 1701–1703* (1705).

Armstrong, J. ('Lancelot Temple'), *A Short Ramble through Some Parts of France and Italy* (1771).

Ayscough, G.L., *Letters from an Officer in the Guards to a Friend in England, containing Some Accounts of France and Italy* (1778).

Baretti, G., *An Account of the Manners and Customs of Italy* (1768).

Beckford, P., *Letters and Observations written in a short Tour through France and Italy* (1786).

——*Familiar Letters from Italy, to a Friend in England* (2 vols, Salisbury, 1805).

Beckford, W., *Italy, with Sketches of Spain and Portugal* (1834).

Berkeley, G., *The Works*, ed. A.A. Luce and T.E. Jessop (1955–6).

——*Viaggio in Italia*, ed. T.E. Jessop and F. Fimiani (Naples, 1979).

Boswell on the Grand Tour: Italy, Corsica, and France; 1765–1766, ed. F. Brady and F.A. Pottle (New York, 1955).

Breval, J., *Remarks on Several Parts of Europe* (1726).

Brydone, P., *A Tour through Sicily and Malta* (2nd edn, 1774).

Burney, C., *The Present State of Music in France and Italy* (1771).

Butler, A., *Travels through France and Italy* (1803).

Connell, B., *Portrait of a Whig Peer. Compiled from the Papers of the Second Viscount Palmerston 1739–1802* (1957).

Drummond, A., *Travels through Different Cities of Germany, Italy, Greece* (1754).

Dryden, J., *A Voyage to Sicily and Malta* (1776).

Garrick, D., in G.W. Stone (ed.), *The Journal of David Garrick describing his Visit to France and Italy in 1763* (New York, 1939).

Gibbon, E., in G.A. Bonnard (ed.), *Gibbon's Journey from Geneva to Rome* (1961).

Gray, R., *Letters during the Course of a Tour through Germany, Switzerland and Italy* (1794).

Hervey, C., *Letters from Portugal, Spain, Italy and Germany in the Years 1759–61* (1785).

Hill, B., *Observations and Remarks in a Journey through Sicily and Calabria in the Year 1791* (1792).

Hoare, R., *Recollections Abroad: Journals of Tours on the Continent between 1785 and 1691* (Bath, 1817).

——*A Classical Tour through Italy and Sicily* (1819).

Hobhouse, B., *Remarks on Several Parts of France, Italy, etc. in the years 1783, 1784, and 1785* (Bath, 1796).

Hurd, E., *Dialogues on the Uses of Foreign Travel* (1764).

Jefferys, David, *A Journal from London to Rome* (2nd edn, 1755).

Knight, Lady Philippa, in E.F. Elliott-Drake (ed.), *Letters from France and Italy 1776–1795* (1905).

Knight, Richard Payne, *Expedition into Sicily*, ed. C. Stumpf (1986).

Martyn, T., *The Gentleman's Guide in his Tour through Italy* (1787).

Miller, Lady Anna, *Letters from Italy* (1776).

Moore, J., *A View of Society and Manners in Italy* (1781).

Morritt, *The Letters of John B.S. Morritt of Rokeby*, ed. G.E. Marindin (1914).

Muirhead, L., *Journals of Travels in Parts of the late Austrian Low Countries, France, the Pays de Vaud and Tuscany, in 1787 and 1789* (1803).

Northall, J., *Travels through Italy* (1766).

Orrery, John, Earl of Cork and Orrery, *Letters from Italy* (1773).

Orrery, Countess of Cork and Orrery (ed.), *Orrery Papers* (2 vols, 1903).

Owen, John, *Travels into Different Parts of Europe* (1796).

Pembroke Papers ed. Lord Herbert (2 vols, 1942–50).

Piozzi, H.L., *Observations and Reflections Made in the Course of a Journey through France, Italy and Germany* (1789).

Pomfret, W. Bingley (ed.), *Correspondence between Frances, Countess of Hartford and Henrietta Louisa, Countess of Pomfret* (1805).

[Russel, J.], *Letters from a Young Painter Abroad to his Friends in England* (2 vols, 1748-50).

Sharp, S., *Letters from Italy* (1766).

Smith, J.E., *A Sketch of a Tour on the Continent* (1793).

Smollett, T., *Travels through France and Italy* (1766).

Spence, J., *Letters from the Grand Tour*, ed. S. Klima (Montreal, 1975).

Starke, M., *Letters from Italy* (2 vols, 1800).

Sterne, L., *A Sentimental Journey through France and Italy* (1768).

——*Letters*, ed. L.P. Curtis (Oxford, 1935).

Stevens, S., *Miscellaneous Remarks Made on the Spot in a Late Seven Years Tour through France, Italy, Germany and Holland* [no date, 1756?].

Swinburne, H., *Travels in the Two Sicilies, 1777–1780* (1783–5).

Taylor, J., *Travels from England to India by Way of the Tyrol, Venice …* (1799).

Thompson, C., *The Travels of the Late Charles Thompson* (3 vols, Reading, 1744).

Walker, A., *Ideas Suggested on the Spot in a Late Excursion through Flanders, Germany, France, and Italy* (1790).

Walpole, H., *Correspondence*, ed. W.S. Lewis et al. (New Haven, 1937–82).

Watkins, T., *Travels through Swisserland, Italy, Sicily, the Greek Islands, to Constantinople* (2 vols, 1792).

Whately, S., *A Short Account of a Late Journey to Tuscany, Rome, and other Parts of Italy* (1746).

Wright, E., *Some Observations Made in Travelling through France, Italy etc.* (1730).

Young, A., *Travels, During the Years 1787, 1788 and 1789* (1929).

Young, W., *A Journal of a Summer's Excursion by the Road of Montecasino to Naples, and from thence over all the Southern Parts of Italy, Sicily and Malta in the Year 1772* (?1773).

Secondary Literature

For reasons of space, this is restricted to works published since 1990. Earlier works can be traced through the bibliographies and footnotes of these works.

Ackerman, J., *The Villa: Form and Ideology of Country Houses* (1990).

Barnard, T. and Clark, J. (eds), *Lord Burlington: Architecture, Art, and Life* (1995).

Bermingham, A. and Brewer, J. (eds), *The Consumption of Culture 1600–1800: Image, Object, Text* (1995).

Black, J.M., *The British Abroad. The Grand Tour in the Eighteenth Century* (Stroud, 1992).

Buttery, D., *Canaletto and Warwick Castle* (Chichester, 1992).

Chaney, E., *The Evolution of the Grand Tour: Anglo-Italian Cultural Relations since the Renaissance* (1996).

Chard, C., *Pleasure and Guilt on the Grand Tour. Travel Writing and Imaginative Geography, 1600–1830* (Manchester, 1999).

Chard, C. and Langdon, H. (eds), *Transports: Travel, Pleasure, and Imaginative Geography, 1600–1830* (New Haven, 1996).

Colley, L., *Britons: Forging the Nation 1707–1837* (New Haven, 1992).

Dolan, B., *Ladies of the Grand Tour* (2001).

Eglin, J., *Venice Transfigured. The Myth of Venice in British Culture, 1660–1797* (Basingstoke, 2001).

Everett, N., *The Tory View of Landscape* (New Haven, 1994).

Harris, J., *The Palladian Revival: Lord Burlington, His Villa and Garden at Chiswick* (New Haven, 1994).

Hulme, P. and Youngs, T. (eds), *The Cambridge Companion to Travel Writing* (Cambridge, 2002).

Ingamells, J., *A Dictionary of British and Irish Travellers in Italy 1701–1800* (New Haven, 1997).

Jenkins, I. and Sloane, K., *Vases and Volcanoes. Sir William Hamilton and his Collection* (1996).

Links, J.G., *Canaletto* (2nd edn, 1994).

Lloyd Williams, J., *Gavin Hamilton 1723–1798* (Edinburgh, 1994).

MacDonald, W.L. and Pinto, J.A., *Hadrian's Villa and Its Legacy* (New Haven, 1995).

Marciari, J., *Grand Tour Diaries and Other Travel Manuscripts in the James Marshall and Marie-Louise Osborn Collection* (New Haven, 1999).

Martineau, J. and Robinson, A. (eds), *The Glory of Venice. Art in the Eighteenth Century* (1994).

Pemble, J., *Venice Rediscovered* (Oxford, 1995).

Pointon, M., *Hanging the Head: Portraiture and Social Formation in Eighteenth-Century England* (New Haven, 1993).

Potts, A., *Flesh and the Ideal: Winckelmann and the Origins of Art History* (New Haven, 1994).

Redford, B., *Venice and the Grand Tour* (New Haven, 1996).

Russell, F., 'Notes on Grand Tour Portraiture', *Burlington Magazine*, 136 (July 1994), pp. 438–43.

——'Guardi and the English Tourist', *Burlington Magazine*, 138 (Jan. 1996), pp. 4–11.

Tanner, T., *Venice Desired: Writing the City* (Cambridge, Mass., 1992).

Tinniswood, A., *The Polite Tourist. Four Centuries of Country House Visiting* (1998).

Wilton, A. and Bignamini, I. (eds), *Grand Tour. The Lure of Italy in the Eighteenth Century* (1996).

Worsley, G., *Classical Architecture in Britain: The Heroic Age* (New Haven, 1995).

Index